W9-BRX-747

Books by Dennis T. Jaffe, Ph.D.,
and Cynthia D. Scott, Ph.D., M.P.H.
From Burnout to Balance:
A workbook for peak performance and self-renewal
StressMap (coauthors with Esther Orioli)

By Dennis T. Jaffe, Ph.D
Healing from Within
TM (coauthor with Harold Bloomfield, M.D.)

By Cynthia D. Scott, Ph.D., M.P.H.
Heal Thyself (coeditor with Joanne Hawk)

How to Change Your Work Without Changing Your Job

DENNIS T. JAFFE, Ph.D.

CYNTHIA D. SCOTT, Ph.D., M.P.H.

A FIRESIDE BOOK • PUBLISHED BY SIMON & SCHUSTER INC.
NEW YORK   LONDON   TORONTO   SYDNEY   TOKYO

TAKE THIS JOB AND LOVE IT

Copyright © 1988 by Dennis T. Jaffe, Ph.D.,
and Cynthia D. Scott, Ph.D., M.P.H.

A FIRESIDE BOOK
Published by Simon & Schuster Inc.
Simon & Schuster Building
Rockefeller Center
1230 Avenue of the Americas
New York, New York 10020
FIRESIDE and colophon are registered trademarks of Simon & Schuster Inc.

Designed by Barbara Marks
Manufactured in the United States of America

10 9 8 7 6 5 4

Library of Congress Cataloging in Publication Data
Jaffe, Dennis T.
   Take this job and love it.

   "A Fireside book."
   Bibliography: p.
   1. Job satisfaction.   2. Career development.   3. Job stress—Prevention.
4. Burn out (Psychology)—Prevention.   5. Work—Psychological aspects.
I. Scott, Cynthia D.   II. Title.
HF5549.5.J63J33   1988   650.1   87-32343
ISBN 0-671-63854-8

ACKNOWLEDGMENTS

Many people helped and inspired us. They include Karé Anderson, Bob Beard, Warren Bennis, Lynn Berberich, Les Berkes, Juanita Brown, Hyla Cass, Sherrie Connely, Paul duBois, Andy Elkind, Marilyn Ferguson, Dan Flora, Rick Gilbert, Willis Goldbeck, Carol Goodman, Roger Harrison, Jack Jones, Kate Ludeman, Rollo May, Emmett Miller, William C. Miller, Jan Nilsen, Jay Ogilvy, Esther Orioli, Harrison Owen, Jordan Paul, Margaret Paul, Howard Rheingold, Rachel Naomi Remen, Bob Rosen, Tom Ucko, Kerry Weiner, and Elaine Willis.

Business and Health, Corporate Commentary, Vision/Action, and *New Age* magazines, and *Transforming Leadership,* edited by John Adams, printed earlier versions of some chapters. The Organization Development Network, American Society for Training and Development, and Association for Humanistic Psychology gave us opportunities to present our work in progress.

............................*To our fathers,*
Adrian M. Scott
and Sidney Jaffe,
who helped make us
who we are
in ways
they never dreamed.

CONTENTS

....
....

Work is Love made visible.
And if you can't work with love but only with distaste,
It is better that you should leave your work
and sit at the gate of the temple and
take alms of the people who work with joy.

KAHLIL GIBRAN, *THE PROPHET*

. . . .

This is an exciting time to be a part of American business. Companies are going through tremendous changes to create environments where everyone can contribute their creativity and good work—"Heart Work." Some people work in companies where this "Heart Work" environment is a reality; if this is true for you, read this book as a confirmation of the great work you and your company have done. However, for most, it's going to take time to reach this optimum performance level where employees and organizations share responsibility for creating a vision of meaningful work.

Take This Job and Love It provides individuals and organizations with the steps necessary to move forward and create exciting and rewarding work, now! Because of your emerging desire to give and get the most from the work you do, *Take This Job and Love It* will give you the information to help yourself and your company achieve this goal.

WARNING:

In reality this book might put you slightly ahead of your company. Remember that to inspire your company you need to be standing on higher ground. Take This Job and Love It is the first step for you to join resources with others to lift your company to the next level of improved organizational environment and productivity.

INTRODUCTION

. . . .

This book is about rekindling your spark of excitement about work and keeping it alive, even in tough, trying work settings. You spend one-third of your waking life at work. What you do there and how you think about it are very consequential to your well-being. Working only so that you can enjoy your time off is perhaps the greatest threat to your health and well-being. Allowing the spark of intensity, commitment, and creativity to die in your work life is like killing half of yourself.

What makes the difference between people who are fired-up about their work and those who burn out? How can companies, work teams, and individual managers create workplaces where all employees get the most for themselves from their work and give the most to the company? When people work up to their potential and contribute their incredible resources of energy and creativity to their work, incredible things happen.

This book grows out of our twenty years of combined experience working with employees to improve personal productivity in many public and corporate settings. Organizations call us to deal with stress and burnout—problems reflected in low morale, productivity decline, and high conflict. We help people to gain greater control over their work and personal life, increasing their value to the organization and to themselves.

When a work team, department, or whole company is "running on empty," one of us is likely to be consulted. After a needs assessment, including interviews with employees at all levels, we design a workshop and follow-up. The major principle of our work is: *Change can begin anywhere in the organization, with anyone.* In the workshop people redesign their own jobs and often their workplace.

In all settings, we find a few people who are creating positive work experiences for themselves, despite adverse conditions. They do not wait for the company to change. They decide for their own well-being to take action to redesign their work. By adopting specific attitudes and styles of approaching their work, they become what we call Independent Business Units, initi-ating change for themselves and their workplace. They become beacons of light and inspiration to the people around them. We have studied how they do it, and we want to make their wisdom available to everyone.

This book expands upon our Heart Work seminar program, which has been offered within many of America's most successful companies. In these seminars, we show people how to re-create their jobs from the inside out. People learn how to reconnect with their individual mission and vision, how to turn their mission and vision into creative involvement in their jobs, and how to work caringly with others.

We have helped people—in all types of jobs at all levels of the organiza-tion—rekindle their spark when it dims and keep it burning. Your job does not have to be just a job—it can be an opportunity for you to learn, to grow, and to do something important and meaningful. We have helped people on an auto assembly line take more control over their workplace, improving the quality of its cars and their own positive motivation. Hospital nursing staffs, airline ticket agents, hotel staffs, and bank branch staffs have all learned to take more responsibility for customer service and have found their frustrating work more rewarding.

Your work can offer you the opportunity to stretch boundaries, connect deeply with people, discover yourself, and feel excitement. You probably know people who see their jobs as burdens, as energy drains, and as dead ends. It is not the job, the company, or the salary, but the way they approach their job, the basic skills and habits of mind they bring to work, that creates this depressing outcome.

This book contains the skill training and exercises from our Heart Work seminar. It addresses the primary struggle many people face today: how to bring *all* of themselves to work, while maintaining their health and well-being. We call it Heart Work for two reasons. First, we envision work as promoting greater physical and emotional health. Second, these new skills foster greater connection to the inner self and to other people. The heart is a symbol of both health and connection.

This is our contribution to the management revolution documented in the recent "excellence" books, starting with William Ouchi's *Theory Z* and Richard Pascale and Anthony Athos's *The Art of Japanese Management*, and including the mega-seller *The One Minute Manager*. These books offer examples of a new spirit and new vision of human nature taking root in the workplace. The best news in these books is that the new workstyle is not just good for people, it is also good for business. Companies that care are companies that make money.

But we see a down-side to the excellence revolution. Many people become frustrated and burned out after being promised a "commitment to excellence." Corporate shakeups, buyout threats, and strategic shifts left many employees waiting for the corporate culture to change.

Take This Job and Love It is for the people who are still working, while waiting for the company to change. In these pages you can find out what you can do to change your job, and perhaps your company, from the inside. It is not necessary to work in one of the "excellence" companies to create a job that is inspiring, to find work that is personally rewarding, or to overcome burnout. You can set your own workstyle and act as an "excellence agent" on your own.

The going will be tough in some companies. You may find that you have to go somewhere else. But we have seen hundreds of people in small and large companies create their own niche, where they work according to their new values. Amazingly, some of them send powerful waves through the company or work team that challenge their supervisors, division leaders, and coworkers, to act differently. They create a quiet revolution, a shift in consciousness, and then in action, within their companies. *Our fundamental purpose in writing this book is to mobilize people everywhere to change their own ways of working, to redesign their own jobs, so that their work supports the values and assumptions of the new management.*

OUR PROGRAM FOR REDESIGNING WORK

Each chapter in this book presents one key area in which to redefine your connection to your work. Each one contains personal visioning and self-exploration exercises to develop these skills in your own work situation. Chapter 1 explores the pressures that lead to burnout and introduces the possibility of creating skills to become an optimal performer under pressure. Chapter 2 explores, first, the new workstyle that is reshaping the workplace and, second, ways that you can build your own internal motivation and re-create your job. It examines how learning and growing now have a place in the workplace and how you can create new workstyles to make your work a fuller, richer experience.

Chapter 3 shows you how to formulate your personal mission and vision. You will look at your values and what is important to you about your work. Knowing what you stand for and what vision you are moving toward can inspire you with boundless energy. Looking at your own values, personal mission, and vision of what you want to achieve at work helps you discover a core interest that will guide you beyond what you do well, toward accomplishing something extraordinary.

Chapter 4 is about managing change and transition. Declining energy at work may be a signal that you have begun, or need to begin, a personal transition. All life involves change and growth. You must learn the skills for living with change. You may be burning out because you are not allowing yourself to go through the natural period of transition that follows a change. You will learn how to learn and become a lifelong learner.

Chapter 5 looks at inner limiting beliefs, expectations, and patterns that keep you from realizing your vision at work. We teach how to take charge of your inner voice and substitute positive affirmations for negative self-criticism. The chapter also looks at your inner communication system. The first signals of distress often take the form of vague feelings or physical symptoms that many people ignore. But discomfort is not something to ignore—it must be faced. People who burn out have not asked themselves what they want or what they really feel; you will learn how to do a better job of tuning-in to yourself.

Chapter 6 shows how to expand your own personal power, the power to get what you need. Burned-out people feel they cannot get what they want or need. They put out vast amounts of energy, depleting themselves, without making any improvement. Developing personal power includes looking at where you are "spending" energy and seeing if it fits your personal priorities and goals. It is possible to increase the personal power of *everyone* in an organization, reducing the sources that burn out individuals.

Chapter 7 looks at the skills for making connections to other people, and using these connections as resources to help get your job done. People need people. When a person begins to burn out, the best thing to do is to talk with others and begin to share the burdens. Just talking to another person is helpful; the other person does not have to resolve the problem. People at work need an environment where they can ask for help and feel that their needs are heard and taken into account. When workers strike or when managers quit, the most cited reason is that they did not feel respected.

RESOURCES

....

For further information about *Heart Work, Visionary Management,* and *Mastering Change* seminars, keynotes, and corporate consultations related to *Take This Job and Love It* contact Dennis T. Jaffe, Ph.D. (415) 665-8699, or Cynthia D. Scott, Ph.D., M.P.H. (415) 664-7661, at 764 Ashbury St., San Francisco, California, 94117.

INTRAPRENEUR OR ENTREPRENEUR? THE CHOICE IS YOURS

CHAPTER 1

ESCAPE BURNOUT— TRY HEART WORK

Caring about our work, liking it, even loving it, seems strange when we see work only as a way to make a living. But when we see work as the way to deepen and enrich all our experience, each one of us can find this caring within our hearts, and waken it in those around us, using every aspect of work to learn and grow.

—TARTHANG TULKU, TIBETAN BUDDHIST TEACHER

Growing up, we were told that excitement was for play and games. Work was supposed to be dull and boring. We learned to be "realistic" and not expect anything more. Our parents taught us that people worked because they had to: to earn money so they and their family could have a good time outside of work. Work time was down time; it was just something to get through. People often spent their whole lives working for a dream of retirement.

Sadly, many people still see their work this way. They do not know how to make their work come alive; they do not even believe this is possible. Often this attitude is a reaction to having once felt excitement at work, an excitement that was ground down by daily routine. The pattern is so common it almost seems inevitable. You begin a job, a career, or a relationship with the fire of passion. Filled with excitement, you charge in with intensity, deep dedication, caring, creativity, and boundless energy. "I will make a difference," you say, "because what I am doing matters, and I matter to myself." But, a few years later, you are bored, distracted, just going through the motions. The fire has dampened, and in its place are the ashes of your enthusiasm and a feeling that nothing matters, nothing is important. You have burned out. This is a dangerous situation that needs attention. It is not irreversible.

CAN YOU FIX A BROKEN JOB?

Even the best job can get stale, and the worst jobs can become deadly. This book is about redesigning your job to make it fit you better. When your car, your house, or your body breaks down, you want to repair it. You go to mechanics, roofers, or healers, who fix things. But that is not enough for maximum performance. You have to practice *preventive medicine,* to watch for early warnings of difficulty. Like your car, house, or body, your job needs maintainence, as well. If you find yourself dreading work or feeling that you have come up against a brick wall, if you find pleasure giving way to resentment, it is time to act. Do not let things deteriorate to the point where you need major surgery.

This is a handbook of preventive medicine on the job. Workplaces are changing, and many are in turmoil. The nature of work and the content of each job are also in flux. What is a sensible person to do? Sit still and wait it out, or get active in re-creating work to respond to the changes? Each time something outside changes—your company or the work environment—you need to make a corresponding change in your job. Some of the possible changes are consciously imposed by your company: reorganizations, job redesigns, procedural shifts. But others are often unseen by the company. A new supervisor, a new product, or simply some new feelings inside you—all change your work situation. Every day you need to respond to new realities.

At work you sometimes need to make tough choices. This is not the only job you could have. Is it right for you? If it was right for you yesterday, will it still be right tomorrow? When is the time to leave? These questions are faced frequently today, and there is no formula for when to change jobs. But before you leave, you should take time to see if the job you have can be changed. Is there a way that you can redesign your job or change it, so that you can get what you want without leaving? Many times people leave a job, or a relationship, and then find that the problem lay within themselves. The exercises in this book will help you explore the possibilities for changing your job, so you will be sure when a move is right for you.

Few jobs are given to you "whole." Usually you are given an outline of expectations, rules, and guidelines. Then you contribute yourself. The way you "inhabit" your job is up to your own personal style and creativity. Even a job as routine as driving a bus can be a creative adventure. Some drivers scowl and take your money. A few energized souls approach the job quite differently. Ernie says hello to everyone and keeps a running conversation with his passengers. He brings people together and he shares the frustrations of delays and difficulties, explaining clearly what is going on and what people can expect. People feel good on his bus, because his attitude is "This is your home until you get where you are going." Passengers often learn helpful things about the city. Ernie feels much better about his job, and is much healthier, than the scowling driver, who is likely to leave work with a disability or chronic back pain. What makes the difference? It is a combination, as we will see, of attitudes and skills that can be applied to the basic framework of any type of work.

Think of your job as an empty house. You move in and look at its form and structure. Then your own creativity takes root. You design your space, decorate, and make the house into your home. You personalize it by putting your stamp on it. Just doing what is expected at work is like living in a bare house—there is no "you" there. It becomes fertile ground for job burnout.

Imagine your own job or your professional work in this way. What was the framework you were given when you started work? How did you inter-pret it and build on it? How did you "decorate" your job? What are your most creative contributions to it? What things make you feel best about your job, and which drain your energy the most? Write a list of things about your job you would like changed. Then write a second list of things about your work that you possibly could change. By the time you finish this book, you will see many more possibilities for changes you could make—more ways to redesign your work.

LEADING YOURSELF THROUGH TURBULENT TIMES

John Gavin was a public relations manager. After his company was acquired by another firm and eighteen months before he was qualified for his pension—after a fifteen-year career with the same organization—he was let go. "I was always taught loyalty," he has said, "to school, to the marine corps, to my employer. In the end, though, it was a one-way street. . . . They said they wanted to be represented by somebody identified with the new company, rather than a holdover from a company they considered a loser." We found a reaction similar to Gavin's when we worked with a division of AT&T after its massive downsizing; many people were aghast at discovering that Bell would depart from a no-layoff policy that had been in effect even through the Depression.

Gavin joined the 11 million U.S. workers who were dislocated between 1979 and 1984 by mergers, deregulation, "downsizing," acquisitions, and business failures. As companies flatten their management teams, many people fall through the cracks.

Many people have followed the pattern of the Organization Man. They moved with the company, conformed to the company image and values, and devoted themselves to whatever direction the business took. Mastering a job took precedence over building a career. "It was considered close to treason to leave a company back then," said Bob Beck, executive vice president of human resources at Bank of America, who has presided over one of the largest corporate downsizings in America, 6,000 people in 1985–1986. "There was an almost blind corporate loyalty—you did everything for the company—no matter what."

Today, many workers at all levels of the organization know better. They are evolving a new philosophy. After a layoff or a company merger, their code of survival becomes, "I don't want to depend on anybody." For example, Kevin Dobbs, a thirty-three-year-old store manager, has learned after several job shifts that he has to create his work for himself. He sees himself not as a company dependent but as someone who makes an agreement with a company, an agreement that has benefits for both sides. Employees like Dobbs mystify employers that are still trying to recruit resourceful workers with "company loyalty." Dobbs and people like him are evolving what Kate Ludeman, Vice President of KLA Instruments, called the "New *Worth* Ethic."

When upheaval in organizations speeds up, the entire work force begins to act more like Dobbs than like the pre-layoff Gavin. They become leery of loyalty and instead learn, as University of Chicago management professor Paul Hisch writes, to "pack [their] own parachute." He adds, "Managers might like to be loyal, but a lot of companies won't let them. Companies want long termers, but they can't live up to their ideals."

Some workers opt to go it alone and become independent contractors. Many others, however, prefer to remain in their jobs and try to make the most of them. We have found many people in organizations creating work for themselves that they can love. An example is Peter Klein, a toll collector on the Golden Gate Bridge. His job might seem monotonous to many people, but he says, "Working for this place is like working for a national monument. . . . You have to realize that people come out to see you. I have the idea that if you make them laugh they'll always come back for more."

In contrast, there is Ben, a riveter on an auto assembly line. Ben says, "I've learned a new approach to job monotony. . . . The key is to grind your job down into a series of empty, vacant gestures. Aspire to vegetation and dance that trance around. . . . Working on the rivet line is like being paid to flunk high school the rest of your life."

Now, both have similar pressures (rapid transactions) demanding performance criteria (on the bridge, no shortages more than $1 per $1,000 collected), and often-frustrating personal interactions. But the important difference is in the ways these people approach their jobs. Klein observes about the monotony of the job, "It can be a hard job for those that make it hard. But if you make it easy, you can really have a lot of fun."

How does someone who works under high pressure and continual monotony keep from becoming bored and deadened? How do some people take their not-very-spectacular jobs and fill them with meaning, challenge, and beauty? These are the questions we will answer.

CAN PEOPLE LOVE THEIR WORK?

During his trip to America, Sigmund Freud put his ideas about the difference between a healthy person and a neurotic in layman's terms. "A healthy person," he said, "must be able to work and love." In the nearly a century since Freud started his inquiry, psychologists have written thousands of books about the struggles to create loving personal relationships. Surprisingly few books have been written about the skills needed to establish healthy work relationships.

We see a lot of confusion and suffering as people struggle to develop a vital and satisfying relationship to their work. Your relationship to work is one of the deepest, most important relationships in your life. Work is often where you try to make a difference in the world, to do something of significance. You give a large share of your energy, your intelligence, your creativity, and your time to work. You want to do it wisely and profitably. Or, as cellist Pablo Casals said on reaching an active age 90, "You ask what my legacy to the world is. It is always the same—the lesson of never underestimating life, of never losing touch with it. To respect and love life in every sense, one's own and that of others. To resist doing things that have no meaning for life."

"That's very nice," you may feel, "but it certainly doesn't apply to *my* job. There's nothing I could do to improve that mess!" People everywhere seem to want more from their work than just a salary. They often see their job as *preventing* them from achieving their personal goals. Their job does not want what they have to give.

This negative notion has a long history. The ancient Greeks saw work as a curse and the enemy of the independent spirit. Their word for work, *ponos,* also means *sorrow.* The early Hebrews saw work as the punishment for sin, the result of being cast out of Paradise.

The United States was formed with a somewhat more positive attitude toward work. The country was to be the "land of opportunity," welcoming people who believed that they could make a new start for themselves, that working hard would eventually bring rewards. Successive waves of immigrants believed that hard work would create opportunities for their children to get ahead. The Horatio Alger stories became classic Americana: tales of the opportunistic entrepreneur who used his skills to achieve success. Significantly, though, the immigrants' beliefs and the Alger stories suggest that hard work creates success *external* to the work itself. There was no regard for how work felt. If people did their jobs well, whatever those jobs were, and looked for opportunity, they would improve themselves.

Since the 1960s there has been a backlash developing against the idea that diligent work brings rewards. People have begun to question whether work pays off. Popular music chronicles these shifts in attitude. In the early '60's, a top hit mocked parents who told their teenagers to "Get a Job." A few years later, disenchantment with traditional work was evident as Bob Dylan sang about how he wasn't going to work on Maggie's farm no more. In the '80's, Johnny Paycheck recorded the blue-collar anthem, "Take This Job and Shove It!"

Recently a highly significant shift away from these defeatist attitudes has emerged. This is the vision of work as a means of attaining personal fulfillment. Work helps us achieve our potential to be creative and to do something meaningful. Some people take the view that work should combine personal fulfillment with service to the community and the preservation of the earth. This *right livelihood* notion connects individual fulfillment with global needs. If you sense this connection in what you are doing, even the most routine and mundane daily activities can feel meaningful and important.

Good work is essential to a complete life. Albert Camus said, "Without work all life goes rotten. But when work is soulless, life stifles and dies." Sounds just like burnout. Today, more and more people notice the deadening effects of some work experience. People have always had these experiences. What has changed today is that we have begun to question what work can be. The more we are able to see the possibilities, the more closely we can move toward building new structures and relationships at work.

THE NEW WORK ENVIRONMENT

What is new today? Several unique factors about today's working environment seem to lead more people to burn out, while other people initiate powerful personal experiments in new work.

Social prophet John Naisbitt, in *Megatrends,* suggests we are in between two social eras: leaving the industrial age and entering of information. In this in-between period, individuals, and tions and communities, experience the stress of having to

The old ways do not work and the new ones are not formed yet. Much of what you experience as upheaval and burnout in work and career can be traced to living in the time of this great societal transition.

Two sources of pressure combine today to create work distress. First, there are outside pressures. In the industrial era, you would learn a trade or a profession and expect to practice it in roughly the same way for the rest of your life. You might get bored, but life would be somewhat predictable, as would the rewards and your increasing competence. Today, however, your work is most likely a job that did not exist in its present form a decade ago. Few people can learn a set of skills and expect to stick with them for long. Even trades like printing and electronics shift so drastically that a skilled craftsperson must continually learn new ways.

Paternalism and job security are out these days. Taking responsibility for your own career is in. The New Employment Contract is quickly taking shape. More and more employees are assuming full responsibility for their own careers. They keep their qualifications in tidy order, salt away their own retirement funds, and work out their own path to satisfaction. They operate more often out of an open-eyed sense of self-regard.

The company, while making no promises, gives employees more opportunity to do their jobs differently, with more participation and flexibility. The company's part of the bargain is to provide a work environment that is stimulating and economically rewarding, for the time the employee is there.

Employees will act like good career custodians, finding out what their inventory of skills and experience can bring them on the open market. This will potentially have some effect on management style, shifting it once and for all to a more participatory mode, because the new worker will no longer listen to I-am-the-boss-and-I'll-tell-you-how-to-do-it.

Old notions of job security and company loyalty are shifting, as people need to fend for themselves. One thirty-five-year-old worker who exemplifies this new direction is Keith Kusky, who typifies how some people adapt. He sees himself as a free agent, moving from job to job, playing the job market as capitalists play the stock market. He mixes full-time and part-time work with a small business he is starting. He has his own retirement system, in part because his father, after retiring from thirty-five years as a steelworker, found his own retirement funds held up by a company bankruptcy. Kusky wants to depend on himself alone, so that he can manage the changes. Many people today have to become improvisational about their workstyles, because they cannot find solid ground.

The only constant is continual change. Companies merge, are spun off, and people switch jobs, even careers and professions, frequently. You have probably had a number of jobs and possibly one or two major career shifts. What can you expect tomorrow? The pressures of future uncertainty and the difficulty in remaining competent are immense.

THE INNER-DIRECTED SEARCH FOR FULFILLMENT

It is not just the external work environment that is changing. The second source of increased pressure comes from inside you, your inner expectations and what you want from work. In the industrial age, people expected only the external rewards of income, status, and sometimes service from their work. Today, people are also demanding inner satisfaction, meaning, self-fulfillment and challenge from their work.

The Values and Life Styles (VALS) Program at SRI International, one of the nation's most prestigious think tanks, monitors this change in work attitudes. For nearly a decade, SRI polled a random national sample of people concerning their values and how they live their lives. The pollsters found a deep and profound change in values for many people about their work. The traditional view of work is what they call *outer-directed*. For people with outer-directed values, the external trappings of success—cars, houses, perks, money, prestige—are the major rewards expected from work.

Over the past fifteen years, the VALS survey has located a new orientation involving *inner-directed* values. The ranks of inner-directed people have grown to include nearly a quarter of the workforce. *Inner-directed people look to work to provide them not just with income, but with an opportunity to learn, to grow, to develop skills, to be part of a community, and to do something personally meaningful.* For example, such a person might take a lower-paying job with a smaller company where he or she could be part of a creative team rather than work on a narrower task in a more prestigious company for more money. Or the individual may strike out on his or her own. Pete Hanson did just that when he left a civil service job to go into the restaurant business.

> I quit my job. I threw over eighteen years toward retirement in Federal Civil Service. If I fall on my face out here, so what? I've fallen by the wayside many times, but I always get back to it. Nobody wants

to take the risks—they're afraid to take a chance. They say, "I'll starve, I'll lose my house, lose my car, lose my boat." So what? People put up with all this stuff because of the comforts, and I want more than that. I realized that none of these people employing me had my best interests at heart. I want more than the system will give me and the only way to get it is to go out and get it for myself.

One consequence of this shift toward inner-directed values is that, with people's higher expectations of the workplace and greater inner demands, the realities of work may lead even more quickly to burnout or frustration. Inner-directed people want more than work that is challenging, creative, and interesting. Their work represents a choice of how they will spend their life energy. It becomes a primary vehicle for expressing their life purpose. In addition, many inner-directed people are what the VALS group calls *societally conscious,* feeling their work must make a contribution to the broader community. Take John, Nancy, and Marty, for example. They wanted work that served the community and their families. Their belief that "work performed in the right spirit is half praying" guides their company, DEVA Natural Clothes, in Burkittsville, MD. They make everything at home, where they can "sew the care right in." Their concept of cottage industry extends to everything they "produce," including all the good feelings and the smiles the customers get from dealing with their company.

Social theorist Michael Phillips and others note several key dimensions of this inner-directed sense of good work:

1. Work should be a focus of great passion. You should have the same excitement for going to work that you feel for vacation.
2. Work is something you can spend your life doing. Your work is where you make your mark. It should have room for "your constant curiosity, to keep learning, to grow in compassion, and offer you challenges that will try you and yet appeal to you time and again. All work has this potential, whether it is garbage collecting or systems programming, because the range of subtle and delicate refinements is always present."
3. Work should serve the community. "Nearly every livelihood has the potential to serve people, and you will be serving people best when you are using your unique skills most effectively."
4. Work should be totally appropriate to you. Your work says something about who you are; it is more than just what you do. Consider it with respect, and do it with care.

Inner-directed people have discovered some keys to preventing burnout in their work and personal lives. The values of the inner-directed group are beginning to influence a wider segment of our society.

Physician/entrepreneur Larry Brilliant is an example of this new orientation. Brilliant's values were formed in the turbulent '60's. He was involved in many of the communal experiments of that time, and he sees his medical career as expanding, not rejecting, those values. When his company, Network Technologies, went public in 1986 he fulfilled a personal vow: to raise $1 million for the Seva Foundation, which sponsors projects to combat blindness in developing countries. He turned over 5 percent of the new company's stock to the foundation he started that did the work closest to his heart. He is also a creative inventor, and his company markets some of his personally designed communication software. He creates his work as a blend of his social involvement and personal creativity.

John Kao, a physician who is now a professor at the Harvard Business School, has gone on a similar journey. Kao was involved in many areas, ranging from the arts to social change. In college, he spent a summer touring with a rock group. In medical school, he studied Chinese medicine, following in the footsteps of his father, who brought acupuncture to the U.S. Then, during a psychiatric residency, John Kao grew interested in the new generation of business leaders and opted to pursue an M.B.A. at Harvard. Kao found that many of the new entrepreneurs had been involved in the activism of the '60's. They see their business work as continuing the service activities and also as reflecting the new social values that grew during this time.

Inner-directed work values are not just for highly educated people like Brilliant and Kao. In all types of businesses and trades, the fastest-growing sector is made up of independent workers who offer special skills and services. Don, the carpenter who renovated our office, is a good example. He believes in doing work well, and he loves the special workmanship of the many Victorian houses in the San Francisco Bay area. After working for several large contractors, like thousands of his peers he chose to work on his own and to maintain the special quality of his work.

We have observed evidence of an inner-directed orientation in our own friends. Many of those who prospered in business careers have, at mid-life, sold their companies or left executive careers to go into social service. One friend has become a foundation director, and another has moved from a corporate vice presidency to head a church social service project. And people like us with public service and community development careers are now finding that important work can be done in corporations. The phenomenon is not restricted to our acquaintances, though. Even former President Jimmy Carter can be found fixing up houses in poor urban communities working for Habitat. It has a lot to do with finding balance in life and with seeking new challenges, both of which are marks of inner-directedness.

Daniel Yankelovich, another social researcher documenting this shift in values, in *New Rules* tells how a group of people today are experimenting with activities to increase their self-fulfillment. They seek meaning, growth, personal challenge, and intimate relationships in work and personal experiments. He notes a shift in what he calls "the giving/getting contract" that a person assumes with his or her community. Instead of an ethic of self-denial, where people make sacrifices themselves to invest in a future, he sees a new ethic of commitment, where people seek fulfillment through personal development and doing work they see as important.

Companies are learning to appreciate the inner-directed employee for a number of reasons. Most important, for the baby boom generation, now at the mid-point of their careers, the old-fashioned career ladder has flattened into a large plateau. Many talented and dedicated people have risen as high as they will go. The outer-directed careerist worked for the prestige of a fancy title, raise, and promotion. But there aren't enough to go around. Inflation, loss of industrial productivity, and other economic pressures have eroded the possibility of continually expanding financial rewards. Not everyone can get to the top of the heap, and the possibility to move up or even to move out is diminishing. A management consultant estimates that every company needs to cut its employee ranks by 20 percent in the next years, just to remain at its current level of productivity. That means far fewer possibilities of career development through mobility. No longer is it expected that you will leave your company if you are passed over for a promotion.

Burnout and demoralization once greeted those who were no longer moving up. Now, people, led by inner-directed values, are creating other possibilities. They can discover ways to make their jobs offer more creative challenge; they can move laterally into other areas of their company; or they can develop more skills. Each of these options makes them more valuable to their company and increases their own personal and professional satisfaction. Previously people who made these kinds of decisions were often seen as lacking ambition or drive. Now they are viewed as people who know how to take care of themselves, who have vital, varied, and interesting careers, and who are in the core of an adaptive company.

Today we see an increase in burnout as well as experimentation, as people try to find the best way to ride the wave of inner and outer change that engulfs them. The creative experiments in new workstyles and new career paths are the best antidote to the threat of burnout. Change is not just an option—it is our only choice.

THE NEW COMPETENCIES

Burnout is increasing from the weight of the external pressures on us today and the new internal demands we are making from our work. It is not enough just to sit by and hope burnout will go away. It won't. It will continue to sap your creative juices unless you take action. Certain skills can help head off its effects. For years, we have been designing programs to help individuals and companies renew themselves.

In his classic book *Medical Nemesis,* Ivan Illich notes that in modern technological society people depend on others for so many services, such as health care, that they forget how to do many simple things for themselves. For a long time we, the authors of this book, worked within the health care and social service system, devising ways that people could learn to help themselves. We found that when people become more self-aware, make more conscious choices about what they want, and become more active partners in getting what they want, their health and their general well-being increase. The same is true in relation to your work: You can no longer expect your work to be given to you. You need to practice self-management, care for yourself, and continually renew your way of working, or you risk burnout. Many of the suggestions in this book come from our work with people moving through the crisis of personal illness to health.

Our Heart Work Seminar is based on research about how people actually learn new ways of working. Since you cannot any longer prepare for a specific career or job, you can instead learn the skills of living with change and uncertainty. In *On Learning to Plan and Planning to Learn,* management theorist Donald Michael calls these the *new competencies,* which involve *learning how to learn.* People who can grasp new situations and meet new challenges in an environment of uncertainty can be effective at any work.

BURNED-OUT ORGANIZATIONS

Because organizations are made up of people, the same growing pains and uncertainty individuals go through affect organizations as a whole. Whole companies can lose their spark and energy. As with individuals, this climate of energy exhaustion does not just go away. It calls for a renewal process that energizes the employees as well. The same things that make it hard for individuals to change—fear, denial, inertia, and lack of ideas—also make it hard for organizations to change. The more a company is set in its ways, the more difficult the change process.

We have found many approaches that work with individuals also help organizations as a whole regain their balance and spark. Organizations that develop a climate that values learning and creativity build in a burnout buffer. It is not enough for individual employees to enhance their skills; the workplace must grow to accommodate and support these people. Our Heart Work Program, presented here, provides a strategy for individuals and organizations to complete their own self-renewal successfully.

THE BURNOUT CRISIS

Everyone has seen it happen. Colleagues who had been excited, involved, and productive slowly begin to pull back, lose energy and interest. Someone who had been a beacon of vision and idealism retreats into despair or cynicism. What happened? How does someone energized, capable, and committed begin to function minimally, not seeming to care for the job or the people at work? An organization's most valuable resource—the dedication of its employees—is often squandered by a climate that frustrates the available energy.

Burned-out workers experience little satisfaction, feel uninvolved, detached, and uncommitted to their work and coworkers. While they may be adequately effective, they work far below their own potential. The people around them are deenergized by their attitude, and the whole work community begins to suffer. Burned-out managers report that the meaning has gone out of their work, that they do not feel valued or supported in their job, that they cannot get things done or do not know what is expected of them, and that they do not feel that they can use their skills in their work.

Burnout is a crisis of the spirit. It is especially consequential because it strikes some of the most talented—the best and the brightest. If they cannot maintain their fire, others ask, who can? Are these people lost forever, or can the inner flame be rekindled? People often feel helpless in the face of burnout. Actually, the evidence shows that individuals can safeguard and renew their spirit, and, more important, organizations can change the conditions that lead to burnout.

Organizational consequences of burnout include absenteeism, turnover, poor performance, and dissatisfaction. Burnout, therefore, is everyone's concern. It becomes an organizational challenge.

Burnout is less due to defective people than to difficult and demanding work environments. University of Georgia researcher Robert Golembiewski found that if one member of a work group is burned out, chances are high that the rest of the group is as well. Certain qualities and norms within work environments promote burnout or high performance. Golembiewski found that the clearest indicator of burnout was how the employee was treated by his or her direct supervisor. When people were treated with respect, care and compassion they responded with more commitment and productivity. This research refutes the commonly held belief that individuals burn out because they do not care about their jobs or do not take care of themselves properly. The new way is to stop blaming the individual and look at the relationships at work. Today, many workplaces have been redesigned to encourage both high performance and personal satisfaction. Chapter 2 introduces these new, burnout-resistant work environments.

Many kinds of people burn out—speedy, driven, and passionate people, and quiet, plodding, and calm people. But even though no specific personality type is more susceptible to burnout, we can still explain why some people burn out while others become high-energy achievers, even though they both work in the same environment.

THE BURNOUT EXPERIENCE

Burnout is an end stage of a severe crisis. You do not wake up one morning suddenly burned out. Burnout develops slowly, over time—several months to several years. It is not the same as everyday stress and pressure. While work demands and stress can go up and down—today I feel pressure, tomorrow things will get a little better—the burnout experience does not go away or fluctuate. Once you burn out, major changes are necessary to reverse the situation.

The burnout experience is surprisingly uniform no matter where it arises. Psychologist Christina Maslach interviewed hundreds of burned-out workers. Her Burnout Inventory catalogues three major qualities of burnout:

- *Emotional exhaustion*—feeling drained, not having anything to give even *before* the day begins
- *Depersonalization*—feeling disconnected from other people, feeling resentful and seeing them negatively
- *Reduced sense of personal accomplishment*—feeling ineffective, that the results achieved are not meaningful

Take a moment right now to see where you are in the continuum. Here are a few questions. Think about changes that have occurred in your life over the past six months. Count the number of questions that you would answer yes to. That will be your burnout score:

1. Do you feel generally more fatigued and less energetic?
2. Do you feel less of a sense of satisfaction about your performance?
3. Are you working harder and harder but accomplishing less?
4. Do you feel more cynical and disenchanted with your work and the people at work?
5. Are you getting more irritable, angry, and short-tempered with people around you?
6. Are you seeing close friends and family members less frequently?
7. Are you having more than your share of physical complaints like body aches, pains, headaches, colds, or the flu?
8. Do you feel that you just don't have anything more to give to people?

If you answered yes to more than five of these questions you are in the early stages of burnout. Any more than two yes answers indicates that you should watch yourself; you may be starting the burnout process.

THE LIFE CYCLE OF BURNOUT

Burnout does not come on overnight, although it can build up surprisingly rapidly because you may not be especially alert to the early signs. The burnout process builds through several stages.

Stage 1 is the stage of enthusiasm, the honeymoon stage. Work is challenging, exciting, full of possibilities. You are learning and growing, and feel energized, even if your work demands a lot of your energy. You are involved, learning and feel a sense of accomplishment. When you start a job, enthusiasm happens spontaneously, as you rise to the challenge of a new set of demands. This feeling can fade unless you apply specific skills to maintain it.

Stage 2, stagnation, is very common, but by no means inevitable. Work becomes routine, even boring, as you've mastered the basic skills and do not feel any new challenges. There are no frontiers for you at work, or you are not moving toward a goal or purpose. A variation of Stage 2 is overload, where you simply cannot accomplish what you want. The demands are too great for you to make a difference. At this point you should make changes. If you have from two to five yes answers on the burnout quiz you are probably at stage 2.

At stage 3, frustration, you have fewer and fewer reserves to cope with work frustrations or to get what you want from it. You feel anger and resentment, and you begin to withdraw from involvement with work and your coworkers. You feel like you are disappearing as you experience energy drain. Sometimes a personal, health, or work crisis erupts to persuade you to make the necessary changes. You may be at stage 3 if you have from five to eight yes answers on the burnout quiz.

Stage 4, apathy, is when you simply stop caring and feel beyond help. This is the end stage of burnout, where you are in danger of a major breakdown. If you get this far, research suggests you need more than a remedial program—you need intensive personal help to bring you out.

INSPIRED PERFORMANCE

Burnout is only one side of the story. At the opposite pole is the fired-up, inspired performer. Excited about their work, these workers see their jobs as an opportunity to grow. Their vision and energy are contagious. They are great natural resources for a company, inspiring others to higher levels of achievement and challenging colleagues to reach beyond their expectations.

When we talk about inspired performances we are not just thinking of the new breed of corporate heroes. Of course Lee Iococca coming to Chrysler, and Steve Jobs founding Apple, were both energized, impassioned visionaries. But this book is not about corporate CEOs.

In our work in all levels of corporations, we discovered an incredible fact: All the people we have worked with can remember a time when they were charged up about something in their work lives. All people have a time, a period, or a project, when they work at the height of their creativity, when limitless supplies of energy are available, when they just "know" what they must do, when new ideas flow and everybody pitches in without the need for formal leadership. What this tells us is that everyone is an inspired performer! These times reflect an individual's personal best. Recalling these situations lets you discover conditions that enhance the chances of them happening again and again.

One of Dennis's personal best experiences came in college. In his sophomore year he worked on the school daily paper. The staff all returned a week before school started, cleaned out the building, and put out a hundred-page freshman orientation edition at the end of the week. They built an excited, intense community. When he recalls this time, he can still smell the ink. That energy and excitement, that special bonding period, acted like a fuel to keep the staff fired up to put out a daily paper throughout exam period, cold winter nights, the entire school year.

One of Cynthia's special events was when she was on the faculty of a medical school, working on a team creating a new type of health professional, nurse practitioners, for rural health centers. Her job was to help design the curriculum, teach it, and also to fly around the state and convince rural physicians to take on these new professionals. These were intense encounters, where she felt she was doing work that was deeply important and really changing the health of these communities. By the end of the year she knew every rural area in California. She kept up with each new professional for a year after the training, and even today she is excited to go to family practice conferences and bump into some of her former mentors and students.

Anyone, anywhere, can be an inspired performer. Ram Dass and Paul Gorman, in *How Can I Help?*, a beautiful book on service work as a spiritual path, tell about Albert, a ninety-two-year-old who remains inspired in his chosen work, even though he formally retired over twenty years ago:

> I'm 92 years old, all right. I get up every morning at 7 a.m. Each day I remind myself, "Wake up. Get up." I talk to my legs, "Legs, get moving. Legs, you're an antelope." It's a matter of mind over matter.

You have to have the right spirit. And I'm out on the streets, 7:30 a.m. sharp.

I'm wearing my Honorable Sanitation Commissioner badge they gave me from City Hall. I'm alert, I'm ready, I'm out there. And I got my whistle. My job is I help get parked cars off the street so they can bring in the sanitation trucks and the Wayne Broom, the big one—thirty grand for a broom! So when they show up, I go around blowing my whistle to get people to move their cars. I have a great time.

People are asleep. They're busy with businesses. They're busy taking time off from the businesses. They're busy having a good time. They're busy not having a good time. Whatever, I don't care. I blow my whistle. I'm all over the place.

I don't discriminate either. I go after the sanitation men too. The union got them a coffee break. Some coffee. They're having eggs, they're having bacon, they're having toast . . . they're having French toast. I kid them about it. And I go right into the restaurant and blow my whistle. They love it, they understand. Everybody loves it, everybody understands. It's the whistle that gets them. Sometimes I'm having such a laugh, I can't blow it. Then I get back to work. "Schleppers, get moving, let's go." *

Psychologist Mihaly Csikszentmihalyi spent many years looking at the state of consciousness that people are in when they are fully involved in their work and are working up to their best. He calls this the *flow state*. Interviewing exceptional people—artists, athletes, surgeons, and others whose work requires extreme concentration—he found they described a euphoric feeling of complete clarity of purpose, deep involvement in their work, almost complete loss of sense of self into the moment, and a deep sense of mastery and challenge.

The diagram shows the relationship between skills on one axis and challenge on the other. When you work where your skill level just matches the challenge, that is the *comfort zone*. You are doing what you already know how to do well, perhaps with very little effort or thought. If there is too much challenge, you experience anxiety. With too little challenge, you lapse into boredom.

* Ram Dass and Paul Gorman, *How Can I Help?* (New York: Knopf, 1985), pp. 16–17.

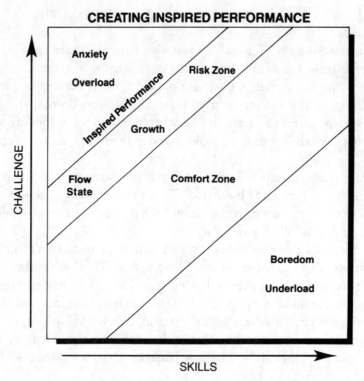

CREATING INSPIRED PERFORMANCE

When you take on a new challenge, move a little beyond your current skills, you enter the *flow state,* or *risk zone.* It arises where the challenge of the work just exceeds your ability. Flow is living at the edge, where you can develop and demonstrate mastery, like a ski run where you are always just on the edge of your ability to stay in control. To move toward inspired performances at work, maximize opportunities to enter the risk, or flow, state. This means slowly extending your sphere of mastery, continually facing new challenges.

HEALTH AND HARDINESS

Personal health, burnout, and work satisfaction are intimately connected. Researchers agree that the most important question you could ask someone to know the most about that person's health is, "Do you like your work?" People that do are far less likely than others to have any type of physical illness.

The same skills and attitudes that lead to inspired performance also seem to promote physical health. Psychologists Salvatore Maddi and Suzanne Kobasa compared groups of the healthiest and the unhealthiest managers at Illinois Bell, a high-intensity work environment. The healthy managers, who thrived under stress, differed from the unhealthy group in four ways:

- *Commitment*—they were more involved in their work.
- *Challenge*—they welcomed change as an opportunity to grow and learn.
- *Control*—they felt a sense of personal power, that they could manage the demands upon them.
- *Connection*—they had a sense of support from and communication with other people, a sense of purpose and meaning in their life.

The people who exhibited these four C's were labelled *hardy,* or stress-resistant. Kobasa and Maddi suggest that inspired performers respond to difficulty with these four attitudes, which promote health as well as high achievements. Perhaps an organization that fosters these attitudes might enable all its employees to thrive under pressure.

Which of the following statements seem to be true about you? This test will give you a rough measure of your hardiness, your strengths and weaknesses in managing work pressures, and your capacity for inspired performance:

COMMITMENT
_____ I like what I am doing and the company I work for.
_____ I wake up eager to start the day's work.

CHALLENGE
_____ I am excited and energized by new projects.
_____ Seeking new opportunities is an important part of my life.

CONNECTION
_____ I seek out other people when I have a problem.
_____ I feel that I give as much as I get from other people.

CONTROL
_____ I look for things that I can do something about, and I do not waste time and energy getting frustrated about what I cannot do.
_____ When there are demands at work, I know that trying my best is the most effective approach.

This test assesses your attitudes toward your work challenges. If you answer yes to more than six of these statements, your style fosters hardiness. If you have three or fewer yes responses, you should think about ways to cultivate these attitudes. The remainder of this book will help you develop the skills of hardiness, to move toward inspired work performance.

Health Promotes Productivity

The personal qualities that promote health also promote productivity. Inspired performers combine high productivity and personal satisfaction with health and well-being. Burnout is the opposite extreme. Burned-out workers experience all manner of stress-related ailments—physical and emotional—and their performance is impaired as well. While some people naturally adopt workstyles that lead to burnout and others are naturally inspired performers, an inspired performer can be put into a work setting that burns him or her out, and a person prone to burnout can be inspired to higher levels of performance. For this reason, organizations are trying to create climates for inspired performance.

There are specific things *you* can do to prevent burnout. You do not have to wait for permission or support to use them. Many of these burnout buffers have to do with your behavior in pressure situations, how you relate to others, and how you think and feel about everyday situations.

The way you set your own standards and look at situations also can help avoid burnout. The burned-out worker tends to be highly self-critical. He or she has a feeling of not doing enough, expects the worst, and has little sense of a personal capacity to make a difference. The inspired, optimal performer has a positive view of himself or herself and of the future, and spends energy where it can make a difference and achieve success. Emotionally, the optimal performer's style is characterized by a sense of connection to other people, comfort expressing and sharing feelings, and compassion and an ability to step into the others' shoes.

Inspired performers approach pressure situations differently from people who burn out. The key skills of inspired performers include:

- Taking care of their physical well-being
- Responding directly to difficulties and demands rather than avoiding them
- Utilizing the help and support of other people

- Focusing energy on mastering some part of a challenge rather than trying to do it all
- Taking time-outs and rethinking their approach when things are not working out
- Effective management of time

Burnout often means you should reassess your life choices and work, or begin a major transition. Today, a person entering the job market, even at a professional level, can expect at least five major job shifts through her or his career. While upheaval can come from external shifts and crises—a failing company, for example—often the need for change comes from inner signals, such as restlessness, boredom, or burnout.

THE PRACTICE OF SELF-MANAGEMENT

You are the key to whether you become burned out or achieve hardy, inspired levels of performance at work. You need to take an active role in how you approach and create your work. Certain critical self-management skills are important no matter what kind of work you do. Since work conditions today place so many pressures on you that lead in the direction of burnout, you need to actively pursue a program to cultivate skills, attitudes, and responses that overcome the early stages of burnout and keep you on a course that leads to continuing inspiration. You need to work to keep the flames of excitement alive.

Shifting to new patterns that keep you fired up takes a while. Change of this depth is not instant. The rewards are great, but the effort to make any major shift is high. We often find that the higher the level of burnout, the more people avoid making the changes they need to make. The more they need it, the less they want it.

Some people need a major crisis—a job loss, accident, lost relationship, or critical illness—to push them to begin to make changes. What seems to be just misfortune is actually the result of burnout. For example, Helen was laid off after a company downsizing after ten years of clerical work. She was shocked, asking herself "Why me?" She had not realized it, but the major reason was that her burnout was obvious to everyone but her. She appeared apathetic, did not take on responsibility, and was not very helpful. The layoff woke her up. She asked what she really wanted to do and then, with three friends, set up a desktop publishing office. She works much harder, but she finds that her energy is higher. People who see her at work now tell her that she seems like a different person: She is alive, energetic, helpful, highly responsible, caring deeply about every newsletter she puts out. The push from her company was the best thing that ever happened to her.

This book brings together basic techniques you can use regularly in moving toward renewal and inspired performance in your work. There are four prerequisites to making any changes.

First, *become aware* that there is a problem. You will not fix something if you do not know it is broken. Each of us reaches this self-awareness at different speeds. You may notice something needs to shift when you are only a little off balance. Or you may have to be knocked off your feet by an illness, accident, or total exhaustion before you begin to see that something is wrong.

The second prerequisite for change comes when you *realize that the problem is not out there, but in you.* This is not to deny that your work environment makes things difficult. But you need to handle your problems directly, not wait for them to disappear. You cannot change other people, but you can change yourself. You must shift from a passive attitude, where you think something is happening to you, to an active role, where you take responsibility for difficulties, and commit yourself to change.

The third prerequisite: *Be open to new possibilities.* When you face early signs of burnout, you discover the old ways of doing things do not bring the desired rewards. You search for a better way to work. In searching out new possibilities, you will draw on the skill of visioning, activating your imagination—your power to dream and invent.

The final prerequisite of change is to engage in *continual self-renewal.* When you become aware that your job has lost its spark and you stop blaming others for your difficulty, then you will be able to see that more than just a few adjustments are needed. This is not a once- or twice-in-your-career realization but something that will need to go on continually. People are continually growing; therefore, they continually need to rethink, redefine, and act differently.

Take a few minutes now to decide whether you are willing and ready to move toward a more exciting, meaningful work and life:

- Are you willing to be aware of your feelings and energy level? To stop ignoring or avoiding them?
- Are you willing to stop blaming your job, your boss, and outside circumstances for your difficulties?
- Are you ready to accept responsibility for making changes in yourself?
- Are you willing to make the effort necessary to go through a personal self-renewal process?
- Are you ready to learn and practice new skills and attitudes in your work and your life?

Many times in this book we ask you to take a few minutes to reflect and to answer questions. These are not rhetorical questions. *Getting the most out of this book means that you will have to work along with us. You will have to look at where you are, what you are thinking, feeling, and doing, what you want, and where you are going. You should expect to change.* If you want to rekindle the sparks of your own work spirit, you will need to take some time to work on yourself.

DEVELOPING THE SKILL OF VISIONING

One of the core elements of taking care of yourself on your job is learning to tune in to your inner guide. Some people call this intuitive or right-brain thinking. This process of reflective questioning and inner exploration is the key to re-visioning your work.

Visioning is the process of allowing your mind to create on its own. The source of this creativity is your unconscious, the deep wisdom that lies outside your awareness. Using your imagination to explore new possibilities is an essential part of creative change. There are no constraints on your imagination. You can imagine yourself doing many new things. Then, after exploring the field of possibilities, you can choose the direction you wish to change. Within your mind you can create and explore an infinite number of new realities.

Visioning is very important to our reeducational program for another reason. Visioning, or imagination, is opening yourself to feelings, thoughts, intuitions, and wisdom that you often neglect or turn away from. We find that high-performing workers are people who are able to tap into their inner experience for access to the creativity, energy, and flexibility that are the keys to inspired performance. The deepest source of inspiration to prevent or overcome burnout is yourself.

Joan, a woman who left a management position to run her own teddy bear store, Ready Teddy, puts it this way. "Being clear about what I wanted has really helped. I started using visualization. If you can picture something and visualize it, it can be yours. Then you have a definite idea of what you want. When it's all mushy, you don't know what it is you want and your energy is spread all over the place. This is what I call my 'inside job.' "

You tap into the creative resource of your imagination by following a few simple rules. The first is that you need to find a quiet place to open up your inner voice. You need to turn your attention from the external world and focus inward. To do this, locate a quiet place where you will not be interrupted. Most people find it helpful to close their eyes. Take some deep breaths, pull your breath deep into your abdomen, and then exhale slowly. You will find that deep breathing releases tension. The more relaxed you are, the more receptive you are to inner messages.

When you have turned attention inward, the next step in visioning is to focus on a thought or issue. This is the message you send in to your unconscious for reflection. It can be a problem or a question, such as the one we will use for this exercise, or it can be a picture or an image. This thought is the focus your creative imagination will reflect upon. Hold this thought in your mind, keeping your attention on it rather loosely, because soon your creative imagination will begin to play with it. You will begin to receive pictures, other thoughts, memories, that are reflections on the seed thought.

As you begin to vision in this way, do not criticize, judge or second-guess what comes up. Many times you are tempted to say to yourself, "That doesn't make any sense," or "That doesn't relate to what I was looking for." You let your practical, reasonable, nonvisionary consciousness work on your images too soon, short-circuiting the process. Of course, later you may want to use your visions for more specific planning and deliberation. But, while imaging and dreaming, let your mind create images just as if you are asleep. Do not interrupt or qualify what comes up.

RECALLING YOUR PERSONAL BEST

Begin now. This exercise will take a few moments. You should be in a comfortable place, where you will not be interrupted. You might close your eyes, which is a helpful way to turn your attention inward. Take a few deep breaths, a signal to your body to relax. Focus attention on your breathing, and imagine as you exhale that you are exhaling your tension and releasing the thoughts on your mind just now.

Recall a time when you were working up to the level of your personal best—a time at work, a project, a team effort, when you felt a sense of limitless energy, excitement, using all your potential. It could be in the past or right now. Let your mind picture this period as vividly as you can. Remember what triggered this period and how it felt while you were in it. Were there any textures or smells that accompanied this experience? Who was with you, and what happened? Think about the people around you—what were they doing, how were they all working with you? Who was in charge?

Now, remember how or why this period came to an end. What made it stop? What were its effects on you? Finally, to finish this reflection, choose three critical elements for this time of inspired work achievement. These could be people, environments, attitudes, or operating principles to remember. What were the elements that made it happen?

You might do this exercise a few times, recalling several projects and times when you were fired-up about work. Write down several of these incidents. After you recall and write down each one, begin to isolate the essential elements for these events again. What do you need to make them happen? Then, thinking about your everyday work life, ask how you could bring some of those elements into your work, right now. This is the first exercise of our process that will lead you to doing just that, creating inspired performance in an inspiring workplace.

We have used this exercise with hundreds of people and organizational teams. Despite the diversity of these work groups—ranging from assembly line workers to physicians—when people recall their inspired performances and define their key elements, their reports are surprisingly similar. They:

- Felt valued as individuals within their work group
- Were given a clear project or task that was meaningful to them
- Had the autonomy to pursue the project to its conclusion
- Had clear and open communication with other team members and with other parts of the organization

- Felt they were using their creative resources and were growing and learning with the project
- Received rewards appropriate to their success

These qualities are the cornerstones of our program for teaching people to expand their capacity for inspired performance. In the next chapter we look at some new workplaces that are modeled on these principles.

CHAPTER 2

New Work: The Shift to Creative Involvement

What is extraordinary about the search for self-fulfillment in contemporary America is that it is not confined to a few bold spirits or a privileged class. Cross-section studies of Americans show unmistakably that the search for self-fulfillment is instead an outpouring of popular sentiment and experimentation, an authentic grass-roots phenomenon involving, in one way or another, perhaps as many as 80 percent of all adult Americans. It is as if tens of millions of people had decided simultaneously to conduct risky experiments in living, using the only materials that lay at hand—their own lives.

—DANIEL YANKELOVICH, *NEW RULES*

This could be the scenario for a screwball British comedy of the 1950's. A young jobseeker enters the factory. Everybody is working intensely on machines that manufacture colored computer wire cables, inspecting each one as it pops out. But nobody seems to be in charge. The workers all seem to be enjoying themselves immensely. When the jobseeker asks some workers what their job titles are, everyone has the same answer: I'm an associate.

A genial grandfather shows the young man around. He says that he started the company but he does not own it. All 3,000 associates own stock in the company. Its earnings are reinvested into the company or used to buy them more stock. The founder does not like the idea of bosses. "Everyone manages themselves," he says, "and things get done just fine." They even choose their own job titles. One clerical worker proudly shows her business card, which gives her title as "Supreme Commander"!

The young man asks, "What jobs are available?" The founder says, "Well, I'm not sure. Why don't you just walk around for a few days and get to know how we do things here. Then find something that needs doing and start doing it. Plenty of the associates need help, and I'm sure a bright lad like you can really contribute here."

Walking around, he sees groups meeting once or twice a day, talking about how things are going, coordinating tasks, and communicating with other groups. The group leaders do not supervise in the traditional sense. As one group member observes, "We manage ourselves. We try to help each other out."

An absurd fantasy? No, this is a description of W. L. Gore and Associates, Inc., in Delaware, one of the most innovative and effective of companies that operate according to a new vision of human nature. Bill Gore, who died in 1986, and his wife Genevieve started the company in the late 1950's. Their work family runs according to Bill's principle that people do their best when they are in charge of themselves, when they feel connected to the whole, and when they share the rewards. The company has a phenomenal growth rate, although no plant is allowed to have more than 200 workers. Then, rather than grow big and impersonal, if they need more people, they open another plant. Small work teams decide how to do their work and are completely in charge of their output. Few control systems are needed; each person pursues his or her own vision of excellence.

The traditional factory or office is quite unlike Gore and Associates. Traditionally, employees are physically present, completing all tasks expected of them, but many are not *really there* at all. They bring a small part of themselves and operate on automatic pilot. Their spirit, their energy, their creative capacities, and even many of their abilities remain hidden. In the past, many companies told employees, in effect: Do your specified tasks, while you are watched over and supervised, and receive your check. Companies wanted their workers to be unquestioning, passive, and uninvolved. The top executives were the thinkers and designers.

The new company values people differently. For example, Doug Green founded New Hope Communications, which publishes specialized magazines for niches such as the natural foods and conference industries, about ten years ago. As at Gore, New Hope employees make up their own job titles. Green recalls, "People were very conservative at first, taking very limited titles. I encouraged them to take larger, broader titles, and at first they were afraid. They felt a great responsibility to live up to the titles they took."

Green's corporate philosophy rests on the assumption that people should manage themselves. Hours, and even meetings, are optional. Sure, he notes, "People come in late. But if they are running late and rush to get here, they really aren't here for the first hour anyway. Besides, if they come late, they tend to stay late." Meetings are listed on a bulletin board, and their purposes are noted. Green likes to see who shows up.

His philosophy is, "If you put the individual first, the company does terrific." This tenet goes beyond employees, to customers. New Hope has a notorious policy of "only doing business with pleasant people." In a frustrating encounter with his biggest customer, Green said impulsively, "I don't think we can do business together. You're just not pleasant." The customer was shocked, but called back later and apologized for his behavior. Ten years later they are close friends. The policy stands, and he says that he has "fired" each of his biggest customers. They usually return, and their attitude often changes as well. He came upon one of his fired customers at a trade meeting, and the customer came up to him, hugged him, and thanked him for making him aware of a personal problem that had been a turning point in his life.

Green also knows how to take care of himself. As a CEO, he feels he owes it to his company to come in only three or four times a month! He is on the road, the company's Mr. Outside, looking for business opportunities. He trusts his people to look after things. Every few weeks, on the road, he takes a "Doug Day," when he just goes off and does nothing. Those days have produced some of his best business ideas.

The North Face Company, making high-quality outdoor equipment, was founded soon after Hap Klopp, a recent Stanford Business School grad, was interviewed by a major manufacturing company. As the interviewer ended by telling Klopp how he would have to fit into the company, Klopp asked, "Why don't they hire me for what I offer them, why do I have to change myself to work for them?" Another entrepreneur was born. He founded his company to manufacture top-quality outdoor equipment. Like Green, Klopp believes that his employees and his customers are linked by bonds of partnership, not adversity. He labels this "partnership marketing," where vendors become his partners and are invited to help develop new products. From the start, he incorporated an ESOP (Employee Stock Ownership Program) to put teeth into his assumption that everyone should share in the value of the company. His management includes little ways that he makes a difference in very routine jobs, such as by creating employee awards like the Golden Shears to reward a pattern cutter or by engraving the name of each employee and the number of years he or she has worked at that machine.

OVERCOMING OBSOLETE ASSUMPTIONS

Today's burnout epidemic stems largely from a "human technology gap"—companies trying to operate on obsolete assumptions about human nature, which in turn kill off human energy, their most valuable and important resource. A company that treats its employees like machines to operate on full steam and then throw away is like a steel plant trying to turn a profit competing against automated new technologies that make better products at far lower cost. It simply cannot do its job. That is not enough any more, either for the company—which needs people to bring more skills and flexibility to meet the shifting demands for new initiatives, high quality, and increasing productivity—or for the worker—who seeks more from work than money and security.

But some people working in more old-fashioned traditional organizations have found ways to renew their energy and commitment to their jobs. They do not accept their work with the attitude, "Well, if that's the way they want it, then . . . ," retiring on the job. Instead, they see their job as something they have a hand in creating. They are not passive, but empowered and creative. Strangely, their companies often come to value and learn from their example. Instead of being reduced to burnout by working there, they become change agents.

While few workplaces operate like Gore, New Hope, or North Face, under the new management principles, almost every organization has been influenced by these ideas. Companies are trying new work arrangements, new types of work groups, and allowing more autonomy and responsibility to each employee. This chapter will survey the new workplaces, exploring some of the values and experiments that are taking place.

WORK AND ENERGY

Think about your work. Some things about it are energizers: They attract you and increase your involvement and energy level. Other factors are de-energizers: draining, frustrating, and negative. Take a few moments and make a list of energizing and deenergizing aspects of your work.

There are several ways to work on this list. First, you can think back to previous jobs or work experiences, and extend your list of energizers at work. If something has happened once for you, perhaps there is a way to make it happen again. Try to think broadly about things in your work, even if they are not directly work-related, that are energizing. For example, you might be energized by something you do with people at work or something your company does. In one company, people remembered the special dinners they all had together after a product was sent into production; in another the branch staff felt energized when they dealt with a customer problem all the way to its conclusion.

Now, put your creative, what-if imagination into service. Think of some of your work energizers. Imagine how you could make them occur more often. Are there some things you do to trigger them? For example, David, a manager of marketing, felt energized when he was able to get his department team together to explore how to respond to a marketing setback. He remembered how exciting and productive the session had been; at the end, everyone almost spontaneously took on one part of the needed tasks, and all he had to do was sit back and collate the information into a new marketing campaign. How easy and satisfying that had been. Yet, faced with another crisis, he tended to keep problems to himself and not bring everybody together. He felt burdened and responsible and began to tell himself that his team did not really care or want to give more to the company. He pulled back. Almost in desperation he called the team together. He was shocked to find that they felt he was not really concerned about them and did not want their help. He had been missing the contributions of creative energy that everyone wanted to offer. How many energizers at work might be under your control?

Now, work with your list in another way. On one side of the page, think about *potential* energizers. These might be things that you expected to get from your job when you started, or things you might like but do not think are possible. In your mind's eye, let yourself imagine them happening. How could you be energized at work? What things could you do that would make you feel energized and excited?

Moving to the other side of the page, take some time to explore the energy drains at work. Left alone, minor energy drains can build up, leading to apathetic, disengaged burnout. Look at each draining situation in turn. Then, let yourself imagine some way that you could make it different. You might think about some new way of approaching the situation or something different that you could say to yourself about the situation to see it differently. If the way you have been managing the situation is an energy drain, you have nothing to lose by imagining alternative ways to deal with it.

What are the common energy drains at work? Few of them seem necessary for good business. They seem more likely to get in the way of people working together to accomplish the company's goals. Here are a few of them. How many are true of your situation?

- I don't feel that I receive credit for what I am doing well.
- I can't see the whole picture. I don't know how my work connects to what the company is doing.
- I have a conflict with someone I work with or a supervisor, and I don't know how to resolve it.
- The rules aren't applied fairly.
- I'm not getting a chance to show what I can do, to really use my skills and abilities.
- I don't get any real responsibility. My work is always being checked and observed as if they don't trust me.
- The rules are absurd. There's no reason for some of the things we have to do. They don't help us reach our goals.

That is only the first part of the exercise. Think about how you and others respond to these energy-draining situations. The most common response is to withdraw, to pull back even further. You think the rules are not fair, or you feel you are not getting the proper rewards. What do you do? Do you try to get things changed? Do you ask directly? Not very often.

Instead, you are more likely to say something to yourself like, "What's the use—people don't care," and accept things as they are.

Every time you do this, you render yourself more helpless.

The energy you could bring to work gets drained away every time you withdraw from a situation without trying to change it. Think about each of the energy drains you encounter at work, and ask yourself if you really try to make a difference. Or do you pull back and go into a pout? Many people who are burned out are upset about something at work that they do not feel they can change.

THE CARING CORPORATION

What do you want from your work? Of course, you want to support yourself and your family. But for most people, that is only step one. Just as you want more from life than air to breathe and three meals a day, you want more than a paycheck from your job. As we noted in Chapter 1, what people want from their jobs is changing today. A few years ago the money, status, and prestige were most important. The talk was of status symbols, external signs of what a big-shot you were.

While we certainly have not rejected the external trappings of success, recent studies of motivation find that people want more. About 97 percent of people say they want to work in a place where they feel respected as people. Over 90 percent want to feel pride in their work and in what their company does. Large majorities of working people say that they want to work in a place that feels nice, that is flexible in responding to their personal needs and family situations, and they want to work with people they like. Well, of course. But the new wrinkle is that workplaces, in order to compete for the best talent, are listening to these demands. And companies have discovered that paying attention helps the bottom line.

People want to feel their company cares about them as people. Reading the many popular "excellence" books, we are struck by how personally involved and caring the excellent executives are. They do more than manage by walking around—they seem to make personal contact with a large number of employees and take the time to really hear from them how things are going. They pick up on problems, and they also see who is doing well.

The president of a small hi-tech company that competes successfully with industry giants says that his management secret is providing employees with a good place to work:

> If this is a good place to work, a place where someone can do really good work and have fun doing it, feel full of excitement instead of full of fear, then we're going to get employees who will stay here longer and be more productive—we're going to be able to put out a superior product on a consistent basis, in a more consistent manner. So you see you can't accuse me of altruism. It comes down to the bottom line.

Caring is a benefit that is passed on to the customer. Service personnel treat customers the way they feel treated in their companies. When you meet a sullen salesperson, you can expect that that person's supervisor treats the salesperson in a sullen way. When people feel part of a team and like each other, that team feeling is passed along to people who come to the company for help or goods.

Human beings are capable of much more than many jobs demand of them. Psychologist Abraham Maslow, in his classic *Eupsychian Management,* prefigured many of the ideas in today's excellence books with a vision of organizations using all of a person's potential. The book was based on his summer of 1964, observing Non-linear Systems, a California hi-tech company experimenting with new management styles. Maslow saw people as having untapped skills, because many organizations—unlike Non-linear Systems—saw people as only fitting prescribed job roles and did not know how to involve people in their work or give them opportunities to participate, grow, and learn. Non-linear was pioneering a new corporate culture.

Maslow coined the term "self-actualizing," to refer to the special people who were passionate, successful, and creative in whatever form of work they did. He noted:

> The only happy people I know are the ones who are working well at something they consider important . . . . [Their motivation is] expressed in their devotion to, dedication to, and identification with some great and important job. This was true for every single case. . . .
> Self-actualizing work is simultaneously a seeking and fulfilling of the self and also an achieving of the selflessness which is the ultimate expression of real self.*

---

* Abraham Maslow, *Eupsychian Management* (Homewood, Ill.: Irwin/Dorsey, 1965), pp. 6–7.

The organization today can utilize an expanding range of human potential. People are capable of so much, and business can learn to channel this potential. The new workstyle evolving today involves employees in ways that challenge their creativity and increase their energy and performance.

Burnout is of epidemic proportions because of delay in companies' responding to the new needs of their work force, or mismatch between what people want from their job and what the job offers them. Burnout signals not that people are working too hard but that they are not used enough. It recedes when the individual worker is empowered to make the workplace different and when the company makes a commitment to serve its employees.

Just as people ask more from their work, companies discover that they need a new type of worker. As every market becomes more competitive, the premium is on having a high energy work force that responds quickly and creatively to new situations and whose pride in workmanship leads to a striving for excellence in everything. Competitive advantage will not flow to a company with apathetic, passive, uninvolved, unresponsive employees.

WHY WORK: THREE FACES OF MOTIVATION

Motivation is a recurring issue. It is what keeps you coming to work each day, and it can never be taken for granted. The most powerful companies have found the formula to make you want to do what the company needs you to do. They take time to inspire employees, and they respect and affirm the people who work there. But motivation is not just something that a company gives to you. It is something that you can help along by looking at your own needs and how your job can help you meet them.

A survey by the Public Agenda Foundation found a consistent pattern of underachievement among workers: Only one in four reported that they worked up to their capacity, and nearly half said they did not put any effort into their jobs beyond the minimum required. What was behind this motivation gap?

There is no single key to motivation. Motivation is affected by a number of factors. Some of these make you feel more deeply connected to your job, while others push you away. When the positive forces prevail, you feel more committed. Many management theorists run into trouble when they try to find one sure-fire way to build commitment in a work team. We have been told that people need (1) to be rewarded soon after they do something effective, (2) to feel like an important member of the team, and (3) to feel creative. Each of these suggestions is right, but companies tend to use only one of these three effectively.

The first motivator, *external reward,* is the traditional motivation of workers—salary, advancement, bonus, job titles, and special perks. There are also external punishments, such as termination. Many companies develop complex systems of rewards and incentives, including commissions, prizes, and perks. These externals allow you to purchase the external trappings of success, demonstrating achievement in the eyes of the world. These external motivators are all helpful, but for increasing numbers of workers these benefits are not of prime importance. A problem arises when a company acts as if they are.

The second, and equally important, source of motivation is a *feeling of importance.* For many people such a feeling comes from being connected to others in a team. Many war heroes, for example, report that their exploits were more about helping and caring for their buddies than about the higher cause. People who care about each other want to do the best for them, not let them down.

It is the same in the workplace: We want to have others value and respect us. When standards are set in a team, and the team rewards publicly those who come through, an important new motivator is created. Companies that emphasize cooperative work, having the whole team get the best results, draw on peer motivators. Yet, many companies inadvertently ignore or even undermine this form of motivation by fostering a hotly competitive environment.

Tom Melohn, the CEO who turned around North American Tool and Die Company, diminished errors, which were endemic to the industry, to almost zero and increased productivity and profits manyfold. His major technique was caring for his employees. The company is deeply committed to helping each worker, through gifts of company stock and through such favors as using company vans to help employees move. Every month there is a company meeting, where people who have had a hand in doing something helpful are honored with a "Super Person of the Month Award" and with cash gifts. Every time a person does something good, it seems, Melohn is there telling that person and everyone else about it. In contrast, a more traditional company had employees who never heard from supervisors except when they had made a mistake. No wonder people learned to avoid each other.

• • •

The third major motivator came into prominence from the work of Maslow and other humanistic psychologists, and it forms the cornerstone of this book: *the sense of meaning, of using one's creative capacity and of growing.* This type of motivation is what is missing for many workers. People want to grow, learn, meet challenges, and participate in decisions. As we noted in the first chapter, this is especially true in the almost one-fourth of workers who are particularly inner-directed and seek self-fulfillment in life. These people seek challenge; they want responsibility and participation in the important parts of their work.

Your connection to your job should optimally contain all three kinds of motivators. Certain people place more importance on one area. Some people prefer external rewards, some peer respect, and others internal validation. Look at what is important to you at work. Which of the three motivators moves you the most? Motivation problems arise when the motivators preferred by your company do not fit with your needs. A company that uses external salary as a motivator may lose creative new MBA's to a smaller company, offering less salary, that says, "You can be part of an important new venture."

Check yourself.

Divide a paper into three columns, and on top of each write External, Team, and Internal. Then list the motivators for your job in each area. Think about the ways that your commitment to your organization arises from each area. Does your company or job emphasize one type of motivation over any other? Now, rank the three areas in terms of which are the most important to you. Does your ranking fit with the motivators offered? For example, are you a team-motivated person working in an external-motivating company?

Finally, think of some potential motivators in each area, especially the one most important to you. How could you create more rewards in an area? For example, if you need more peer recognition, would it be possible to institute some form of team meeting, maybe a lunch group, where people let each other know what they appreciate from each other? One secretary simply kept telling her boss that she needed to hear when she was doing things well. He was surprised, asking, "Aren't I paying you enough?" But he got the message. Eventually, she trained her boss to give her recognition as well as cash. Another possibility is to find a way to take on a special project that will challenge you and help you grow or develop a new skill, in addition to your regular activities. Many times, you can get such an assignment the Gore way, by seeing something that needs doing and volunteering to do it, even if you don't work in the Gore Company.

Motivation is a many-dimensional fabric, not a single thing. If you see motivation as coming from many places, as something you have some control over, you can begin to do things to build your commitment and increase your dedication, satisfaction, and connection to your job.

THE NEW WORKPLACE

A new style is emerging in the workplace. It arises from the need for a company to respond more quickly, and adapt more flexibly, to a shifting environment, including the changing needs of the new workers, who are seeking more internal satisfaction, more self-fulfillment, from their work. The new workplace feels very different from the old, traditional, bureaucratic organization.

Three different workplace styles can be compared to musical performances. First, there are *solo* environments. These are the self-employed professionals, who select their own pieces and play their own instruments. Then, there are the *orchestral* environments. The music is selected by the conductor, and everyone has a part, but the shading, tone, and skill level of the performance are up to all the individuals. Each person plays a different part, but the whole group must be synchronized into alignment. The individuals take deep pride in their personal contributions to the whole. This is the case in a large traditional company, where everyone works for a common goal, and feels connected to it.

And finally, there is the *jazz* group. This style lies in between those of the soloist and the orchestra. There are major themes, but each person has space to improvise. Most companies today, even the large, industrial ones, are becoming more like jazz groups than like orchestras. There is more room for the individual to create within the group themes, and the success of the group depends more on the creative quality of each individual's improvisation. However, despite all this individuality, the most meaningful music comes from a group where each member instinctively harmonizes with the others, and individual contributions fit into a broader whole. From new hi-tech software companies, to clothing designers and manufacturers like Esprit, the jazz model encourages small teams working on their own, with strict accountability and clear expectations guiding their creativity.

The three organization styles offer people different degrees of control. The self-employed soloist has the greatest freedom. The independent professional only needs to please himself or herself. The lure is obvious, and every year people leave organizations to go out on their own. That is one way people restore a sense of personal power and overcome burnout. It is the best choice some people can make.

But becoming an independent professional is not a perfect solution. There are costs. Soloists often do not have enough contact and exchange with others in their fields. The independents are too often lone wolves. Also, while they have more control, they also live with greater uncertainty. How will they get the next client or achieve an adequate income?

Also, the independent professional, the self-employed person, often runs aground because he or she cannot work with so little structure. People inside an organization often see its structures and rules as frustrating limits. What those people often overlook is that the structure and rules also impose order and make many things easy. The organization supplies other sources of widsom to rely on, and it makes support people available. The independent entrepreneur has to make things up along the way and, unless that person has a clear sense of purpose, can face burnout from the overload of too much freedom, too many options, and no firm criteria for success. So, soloists do not have a bed of roses. They face unique pressures and demands.

In contrast to the traditional organization is the new, jazzlike organizational form. The Gore Company keeps its factories small and only loosely controlled, like a jazz group. The old organization had a defined role for everyone and relatively few surprises. The new, improvisational form is not just a new fashion. When the marketplace is unpredictable, when competition is fierce, and when the unknown threatens daily, each employee, at every level, has to be ready to respond quickly and make independent decisions. Many people have trouble because they want to play jazz but they are part of an orchestra, or because the organization acts like an orchestra but the entire melody has been changed. There are often asynchronous conflicts between organizations and people who work in them.

LEARNING AND GROWING AT WORK

One difference between the traditional company and the newer, jazzlike improvisational company is that in the latter people have more opportunities to grow and learn. When you have to improvise, you regularly face challenges, and when you resolve them, you learn. Warren Bennis, in his study of inspirational leaders, found that employees valued the leaders' ability to create a learning climate in the company. "This is a place where we can learn," they told Bennis. They expect to use their creativity in the service of their work.

One of the keys to vitality and satisfaction at work is learning on the job. Even at lower levels, people feel more involved when there are new skills they can develop and opportunities to grow and learn. When a job begins to feel deadly, one of the most certain ways to enliven things is to find something you can learn. A challenge does not even have to be the central aspect of your job; you can think of it as the spice that adds flavor to the whole. If you can find one aspect of your work that lets you grow, other more routine parts are more bearable.

Many people lose energy for their work when they feel they have stopped learning. They may be senior partners or top managers, but the excitement stops when they feel they have learned everything about their job. Similarly, when an organization gets to the point where it is just doing the same thing over and over—marketing the same products in the same ways—stagnation sets in, and energy flags. It is as if nature expects organisms, individuals and whole organizations, to keep growing. Gene Cattabiani of Westinghouse feels that executives must "learn or die." He feels that an executive should *almost* master a position before moving on, rather than stay too long and lapse into boredom or complacency.

Companies become growing, learning environments in two ways. First, they can grow from the creative skills of the people they hire, rather than force people into offering only a part of what they know. One organization whose selection process is designed to fit the person, not the narrow demands of a specific job role, is Cambridge's Lotus Corp. Lotus executives know the skills they desire in new employees, but the creative people who apply for work never fit exactly, and they bring a lot more. Former chairman Mitch Kapor pioneered a method whereby he interviewed all new employees, to see what they offered. Then they created a work agreement to fit their unique skills. A person may have five actual jobs, each one using a different set of skills. A position is crafted for the individual person. Jobs and roles are custom-made, not off the rack.

The second way that a company becomes a learning environment is to create learning opportunities on a regularly basis, for employees to develop new skills. Corporations now spend $40 billion a year on education and training of employees (or more than $100 billion if worker salaries during training are counted). The Carnegie Foundation reported in its recent survey of corporate education:

> The work of the future, especially at an advanced or professional level, is likely to require a great deal of flexibility; not just one set of skills acquired early and essentially good for life, but rather an evolving body of knowledge and new opportunities calling for greatly modified skills. . . . We [must] have a more skillful and adaptive work force than ever before. Lifelong learning is no longer a desirable luxury; it is a vital economic necessity.*

The premium for a company, then, is to have employees that can fill in on many jobs and have several sets of skills. First, if the company's work shifts, they are more likely to be able to shift with it. Second, working in several jobs gives people a broader view of the company, and they develop a better strategic sense of what is needed. That is why Donald Burr, creator of the experimental People Express airline management plan, included the requirement that every employee rotate through several jobs. He would spend time each month checking baggage and making reservations. Although the sale of the company in 1986 demonstrates that positive relationships are not enough to keep a company profitable, the employees of People enjoyed the satisfaction and breadth of experience they gained from job flexibility. They each felt in touch with the needs of the whole, and they understood how one job fit in with others. They felt more comfortable making decisions based on special cases and on improvising when needed.

Another enriching form of organizational learning is cross-training, or learning about other jobs. In one company the service and the sales groups were in continual conflict. They avoided each other at meetings, and each one frustrated the other. Then an experiment was tried: Each person spent a day with one person from the other group. The results were powerful. The two groups came to appreciate the difficulties in each job and get a better sense of why some things were not done. People in both groups felt they could do their jobs better and understand the company better after the learning experience. Another company, one that operated hospitals, had a

---

* Carnegie Forum on Education and the Economy, *A Nation Prepared* (Carnegie Foundation, 1987), p. 128.

long strike. The management and medical personnel had to clean the floors, do the record-keeping, and answer the phones. After the strike, the medical staff had a far better idea of how the hospitals ran and greater appreciation for the complexity of the system. The process of learning about other jobs enriches a person's sense of the whole organization and makes work more meaningful as well as more effective.

Inspired performers report that they enter the flow state when they find a challenge that moves them. It is like the athlete who peaks during the championship game. When you are learning, you are more involved than when work is old hat. Learning unleashes creative energy and excitement. People can rise to demands sometimes far beyond their skill levels.

Robert Leathers is known as the Johnny Appleseed of playgrounds. He is an architect who travels around the country, designing playgrounds for schools and community centers. What is amazing is that he has no employees; volunteers from each community work with him in planning a space that fits their needs, he designs it, and then volunteers come together in the vacant area to do the work. He arranges them into work crews and teaches them as they go what needs to be done. In less than a week the new teams create the play area. It is like an old-fashioned barn raising, with learning added to the experience. Everyone helps, from young children to grandparents. When Leathers leaves, the community has created a high-energy work team, and everyone has been deeply touched with a special work experience.

What challenges do you face? Where is the learning edge for you? If your job has lost the ability to captivate you or challenge you, there are things you can do:

- You can seek out a new challenge. Many workplaces do not expect this, although the new motivation research suggests that this is exactly what many people want at work.
- You can seek extra training or education off the job to increase your skill level to make you available for higher challenges. Many outside educational opportunities can offer you a new view of your own job and new possibilities.
- You can request a new assignment or an additional one.
- You can move around the organization and be curious about what other people do and why they do it.
- You can imagine that you are the CEO and think about what the

organization might need. Then, find a suitable channel to make your suggestions known.

- Learn how to do other people's jobs so that you are available to fill in if needed.

In the chapters that follow, we will have much to say about how to create opportunities for your own growth and learning at work.

THE NEW WORKER / ORGANIZATION CONTRACT

Company mission statements begin with what the company does in the world, what it wants to achieve. But companies that have powerful missions, deeply held by their employees, frequently add a second part to their mission statements: their basic values and how they treat their employees. These principles are reinforced in the rituals and orientations that greet a new employee, that tell what it means to work there and how they will be treated, and in the policies and everyday operations of the workplace.

The new workplace has different values, assumptions, and agreements with its employees. Companies cannot any longer promise lifetime employment, as AT&T once did, or the security of knowing that certain job skills will always be needed. But they can offer respect, group support, and response to inner needs for learning and achievement.

For example, Max duPree, CEO of Herman Miller, Inc., which is consistently mentioned on lists of the best places to work, offers an employee Bill of Rights:

- *The right to be needed:* genuine opportunities to use their gifts. DuPree adds, "If you have a great shortstop, don't ask him to play first base."
- *The right to understand:* regular communication about what is going on in the company and about issues like career opportunities.
- *The right to be involved:* invitations to everyone to contribute ideas, and a guarantee of a response, positive or negative, and a reason.
- *The right to a contractual relationship:* agreed-upon goals, ideas, issues, and values, and negotiation of conflicts and differences.
- *The right to affect one's destiny:* involvement of the people concerned in evaluation, transfer, promotion, and anything that affects their lives.
- *The right to be held accountable:* the opportunity to contribute toward

the company's goals, to share in its problems, to have contributions measured according to previously established standards.
- *The right to appeal:* a check against unfair or arbitrary exercise of power.

These seven ideals set up a culture very different from the traditional company, where the only right was to a paycheck. In companies that are successful today, the level of commitment is much higher than in traditional companies. Not surprisingly, when people are offered more opportunities and more responsibility, they give more.

Adding new style to work has become not only fun but smart business, as well. You will hear more about worker sabbaticals, health promotion programs, job sharing, sending employees to graduate school, equity participation, absence of ranks and titles, cross-utilization of employees, and personal development seminars.

This may seem like a new phenomenon, but in fact over 100 years ago a similar movement was emerging in corporate America. It focused on the improvement—both intellectual and social—of employees, rather than on the wages they were paid. The likes of National Cash Register, H. J. Heinz, Westinghouse Electric & Manufacturing, International Harvester, and Marshall Field were involved in these efforts. They sponsored physical fitness programs, profit sharing, worker education programs, and home improvement workshops. The most notable participant was George M. Pullman, who spent over $8 million to design a model town for employees.

The new workplaces obtain greater commitment by drawing on external, internal, and peer motivators. Power and responsibility are shared, and everyone can make a difference. There is respect for individual needs and for the dignity of each worker.

Why do people implement employee-centered programs? Irwin H. Mintz, of JBM Electronics Co., says, "I like to be liked. The better environment you create for your employees, the more they're going to think of you as one heck of a guy." Second, he mentions competition for good employees: "If salary were all we could offer, we'd never be able to attract and keep really first-rate people." Third, and most important: "If this is a good place to work, a place where someone can do really good work and have fun doing it, feel full of excitement instead of full of fear, then we're going to get employees who will stay here longer and be more productive—we're going to be able to put out a superior product on a consistent basis, in a more efficient manner. So you see," Mintz concludes, "you can't accuse me of altruism. It comes down to the bottom line."

In College Station, Texas, Westinghouse has a small automated plant that represents the best of the new workplaces. With 500 employees, it is smaller than traditional plants and about ten times as productive. The new work arrangements are joined with the benefits of automation, in this case robots that help put together radar assemblies. The employees are organized into small work teams that design their own solutions to work problems and measure their results daily as a team. Individuals are not penalized for slowness or difficulty; instead teams are paid for their effectiveness. Unlike traditional labor arrangements, workers are treated much as management employees. They are on salary. Raises are determined by the number of skills a worker has. Since the company invests in many training opportunities, workers who are there a long time keep increasing the number of things they can do. In addition, training also focuses on general learning skills: problem solving, creative thinking, and teamwork skills. Thus, workers who came from more traditional plants are enabled to work in new ways.

CREATING THE NEW FACTORY
....

Numerous articles have been written about the decline in American productivity in contrast with Japan's achievements. American manufacturing has begun to adopt new workstyle policies producing uniquely American experiments in increased productivity. General Motors, in many ways the prototype of the traditional old bureaucratic organization, has several experimental plants that are remarkable for their high productivity. What these plants have in common is careful organization according to a new set of agreements between workers and management. The new plants assume:

1. People on the assembly line have good ideas about improving productivity that managers do not have.
2. Workers should have a voice in decisions that affect their job, including working conditions, which should improve productivity and quality.
3. Work should be made as interesting and challenging as possible.

4. Workers should share in the rewards for their success as a team.
5. Workers should be treated with dignity, and class lines between management and labor should be blurred.

In factory after factory, the experience of the pioneering Volvo plant in Kalmar, Sweden, is repeated. The assembly line was redesigned to allow work teams to have greater control over how they did their job and to make a team responsible for the manufacture of a whole system of a car, not just one mindless, repetitive task. Productivity, satisfaction, and morale all increased. Today, thousands of plants have incorporated Quality of Work Life programs, that involve greater participation and the increase of responsibility and challenge to the individual worker, with exciting results.

One example is the Fremont, California, NUMMI (New United Motors) auto plant, owned jointly by General Motors and Toyota, and operated under a unique cooperative agreement with the United Auto Workers. Instead of assuming conflict between workers, who want good working conditions and high pay, and manufacturers, who want to pay less and have control, the new agreement states, "Workers and managers together are doing things differently based upon an understanding and respect, rather than coercion and contempt." The new role for labor is signalled by the UAW's "willingness to accept a large measure of responsibility for quality and efficiency at the NUMMI plant."

The difference is that everyone works together to make the plant a satisfying place to work that is able to compete effectively with foreign producers who pay their workers much less. Policies, procedures, and work conditions are decided jointly, in the plant. Every worker at some time has to become a manager, taking part not just in working but in deciding how the work will be done. People who want more involvement have opportunities galore. People who just want to do their job have that option.

The new plant looks strikingly different from the image of the assembly line immortalized by Charlie Chaplin in *Modern Times*. The new assembly line is spanking clean, and work stations are designed so that anyone can stop the line. There are frequent conferences during a week, and people can set their own breaks. The factory has a health club, lounges, lockers, and many things that one would be more likely to find at a community center. Workers feel that the factory is a community as well as a production facility.

BUILDING IN PARTICIPATION

Another quality of the new workstyle is participation. All team members know the company's objectives and needs, and every team member is a part of decisions that he or she must carry out. At first this may seem time-consuming. Instead of one person having all the information and making a decision, why bring a committee into this? The main reason is that people have a natural resistance to doing something they do not understand or feel part of. Thus, many very important new ideas never get off the ground. Often this occurs because the group that does the implementing is not the group that had the idea.

This happens two ways in companies. First, there is top-down innovation. For example, in one company, the corporate headquarters created a task force of key executives from every division. They rolled up their sleeves, looked at reams of data, heard from experts, had long management retreats, and began to coalesce a new direction for the company. They had a beautiful vision. They decided to move on it, and, as a team, they were all in alignment. Problems arose because then a new group of operating managers was given the plan and told to implement it. The style of operation shifted from transformational and participative to traditional directive leadership. The beautiful vision never got into place, because operating managers and subordinates could not participate in the process that worked so well for top executives. Instead, key members of the top management group probably should have convened implementation groups in each of the divisions, spending more time communicating the meaning behind the plans and bringing each division into the process.

The second way one group's innovation can be blocked by another group is via resistance at the top. In many quality circle programs, the worker groups come up with very important new ideas. Then they present them to higher management, often with detailed charts to support them. However, top management feels distrustful or disconnected from the energy that lay behind the innovation, and so the new ideas are not implemented.

Participation is a tool by which the internal motivation of the team is engaged, by respecting the creativity, the experience, and the caring of each team member. Sometimes, participating in decisions builds motivation simply because it shows people care about and respect each other. At other times, important new ideas are added or new information is shared that sheds a different light on plans. The more people who look at a decision, research shows, the more likely it will be the correct one. This is because during the sharing, more important information is brought into the decision process. Also, higher levels of commitment to implementation are generated when more people are part of the process.

Of course, participation is not an unlimited goal. There are some times when people in a work group have to be given a task. Then they may participate in deciding how to accomplish it. There are some kinds of decision that people may decide not to participate in. This became an issue at one graduate school. After a period when the core faculty did all the administrative and governance work for the school, they all felt overburdened. As a group, they decided to delegate some of this work to a dean, who was hired. For two years they felt greatly relieved. Then the pendulum shifted to the other pole, and they began to feel that decisions were being made without them. They become concerned again. Does this story show that work groups will always be dissatisfied? On the contrary. Throughout the whole time, the faculty group came together regularly to review how things were going, look at broader issues, and recommend changes to the rest of the school. In effect, they had a quality circle that always looked at how they were doing. There was no final correct way to do things. The way this faculty kept looking at how they operated, and recommended midcourse corrections, was their strength. When a plane flies, it is on course for only a small percentage of the time. It keeps going off course, discovering it is off course, and taking corrective action. Reaching a destination is a series of approximations and corrections, with the ultimate goal always firmly fixed. The same seems to be true in high-energy work teams.

TWO JOBS / ONE PERSON

Another surprise about the new workstyle is that involvement increases when an employee is asked to do more, and be more responsible, than before. Traditionally, top executives alone were paid to worry. Most workers did not want any more responsibility than just their own jobs. Some people still want it that way. But more and more workers find that a steady diet of narrow tasks with no connection to a wider picture is a prescription for burnout. In the new organization, people at all levels want to see the connection between their work and the big picture, and they want to have a say in some of the larger company issues, especially those that affect them.

The clearest way to increase a team's energy level or to motivate individuals who are becoming withdrawn, in early stages of burnout, is to find a challenge they can mobilize around: a cause or a common enemy. If you feel that your skills are being used and called upon, then involvement follows. Participation in work teams is one way to keep people challenged in their work. If they are always looking at the whole and the future, seeking better ways to get things done, then people maintain their energy and involvement. If your particular job is repetitious, one antidote to burnout is for you and your team to be spending some time looking at how you are doing things and how you could do better.

How does a company accomplish this? The most common way is to create structures that give an employee two kinds of responsibility. We call this the *Two Job Concept,* and we advocate it for everyone. A person's first, or primary, job is the traditional work role—complete a specific task or have a specific operational responsibility. Everyone has his or her own piece of the puzzle.

But work does not stop there. Each employee has a second job, with the opportunity in some way to step out of the narrow role. In Job Two the person deals with the company as a whole, taking a hand in figuring how to do things better, improving the company in general. Instead of being left to feel frustrated because "that's the way thing are," every worker is asked to take some time to think of other ways things could be. Job Two might be participating in a quality circle that reflects on how things are going and tries to design alternatives, a planning group that meets new challenges, or a task force developing a new factory.

The principle behind the Two Job Concept is simple: The worker gains because he or she is able, first, to offer creative suggestions for changing the company and, second, to develop skills and talents that might not be used in the primary job. Working on Job Two also brings the employee into contact with more of the organization and develops a greater sense of what is important and how the company really operates. It makes things more interesting and involving. The company gains because it takes the experience and wisdom of every worker and puts them to work on an important problem. From time to time, a person may take time off from a primary job to participate in a special Job Two project or simply rotate for a term to work in a new area. The goal is to use the second job to broaden and expand the capacity and usefulness of each individual.

• • •

This new concept turns the traditional approach on its head. The old idea was that the designers—engineers, top management, and other creative souls—were the source of new ideas, and the rest of the employees carried them out. But what about unforeseen glitches, or impractical details? Who makes adjustments and changes? The people closest to the work may have the greatest access to new ideas. Innovation and new ideas often come from those who are closest to the customer or the assembly line.

Recognition of this fact led to quality circles, one model for empowering people at work. While they are often thought to be a Japanese concept, in fact they were introduced to Japan by an American visionary, W. Edwards Deming. Now they are coming home once more and are finding fertile soil. The quality circle is a small group of people on a production line or in an office who meet regularly to look at how things are done and to brainstorm, propose, and evaluate ways to do things better. There are several common reports from the many companies that use them. First, they save companies money and come up with a stream of creative ideas. Second, and perhaps more important, the workers who take part in them report that they feel more energized, productive, and connected to their work and the company. Quality circles are appreciated and empowering. People look forward to participating in them and feel that they really can contribute to the company's welfare.

A health products company introduced an extension of this concept. Small groups in every part of the company met to explore every aspect of the company's operations—from customer satisfaction to marketing to new products. Any idea was cricket. They funneled ideas and proposals to the Organization Redesign Group, made up of a cross section of employees who were selected to serve for two years. It met every month and evaluated the ideas from the small groups. When an idea was adopted the group would receive a bonus and notice in the company newsletter.

It is important to note that Two Job performance can be stressful and demanding, as well as exciting. In addition to their regular work, marketing, engineering, or whatever, the Redesign Group had to go over scores of proposals, order surveys, talk to engineers, and evaluate ideas. But all of the members reported that their work was never more exciting. Having the two jobs really made them feel that they were growing and learning the whole business, making a visible contribution. Their hard work did not burn them out. It energized them for more!

ALTERNATE WORK ARRANGEMENTS

Many people are deenergized because their work conflicts with their personal or family needs. In the past, companies did not feel they had to accommodate such personal needs. In the traditional family, the man went to work and the wife was home raising the children. Men moved from community to community, and were available for inflexible hours and overtime. The majority of two-parent families today consist of two wage earners, not one. That is true of the working poor, the middle class, and the wealthiest class, too. Financial need is one consideration, but it is also true that people *want* to work. It is important to them, and not just to make money. They are working for self-fulfillment and personal development. Indeed, whole careers, and exciting ones, are built on volunteer work.

At the same time, many American families are headed by a single parent, often struggling to make ends meet and balance home and work. Single parents need flexibility and support to keep going. The workplace has little choice but to take notice.

When a person feels a conflict between personal needs and work demands, burnout often results. It is hard to concentrate on work if your young children are home alone or if your spouse is offered a promotion in a new community. Workplaces are increasingly accommodating themselves to personal needs. When a company accommodates to such needs, the commitment and the energy of each employee flows to the company more freely.

Flexible work arrangements are becoming common. For example, job sharing and permanent part-time work are available to parents who want to spend time with their children. They do not have to quit a job or give up a career, just slow it down. A person need not leave the company just because he or she can no longer work a full forty-hour week. In several companies, pairs of professional women or a couple share jobs. Two people apply for one job and split it. Companies find that job sharing usually results in about one-and-a-half times the amount of work they would expect from a single employee. And they get the benefits of two sets of talents, two bundles of fresh energy!

Companies use many alternate work arrangements, all based on the decision to allow individual employees to have more autonomy to negotiate the ways to do their job. Some companies, for example, offer flexible hours so that commuters can avoid rush hours or be home when school ends. The Administrative Management Society found that in 1986 nearly 30 percent of companies offered this option, up from 22 percent in 1981.

A flex-time company usually sets some core hours, midday times when everyone must be there and when meetings and other important events are scheduled. Each person or work group has a set of clear goals to accomplish each week. After that, each person or group decides on their hours. People can save hours in the car and the cost of babysitters, as well as worry over their children or frustration at not being able to pursue a hobby. Satisfaction increases because deenergizers and frustrations are reduced, and absenteeism and stress-related illness can be cut in half.

The four-day work week has been successful in other companies, for both company and employee. Companies are more flexible about work at home. Many executives now work like college professors: One day a week they work at a home office or computer terminal. The finding is the same: More work gets done when people do it their way.

These new arrangements recognize a paradoxical situation. Work is becoming both more important and less important in different ways. Work is more important as people ask that it not just offer external rewards but also be a community and a setting where they can learn or grow. They offer more of themselves to the workplace. Yet, on the other hand, work is less important as many people decide they will not sacrifice the family to the job. For example, many executives are reluctant to relocate, because a spouse has a full career and the family is fixed in a community. They ask the company not to penalize them just because they do not want to be corporate nomads.

Another modern solution is the long-distance commute. Every Monday morning in San Francisco the airlines are full of commuters to Los Angeles, 500 miles away, who prefer the Bay Area's quality of life. In other cases, spouses take jobs in cities distant from each other and then see each other mostly on weekends and holidays. Balancing work and family demands creativity, careful negotiations, and much thought. But the payoff in the workplace comes from the fact that nurturing the family helps energize the employee on the job.

Another alternate work arrangement is changing jobs. In the traditional company, moving up was the only reason to change jobs. Anything else was a near disgrace. Many people would leave companies because there was only so much room at the top. Today, companies are trying to stop this brain drain. Instead, they are valuing long service with the company, agreeing with many managers who have decided that their goals do not include lifelong advancement. There is an important place in the company for their wisdom. These senior managers take on second jobs in companies as mentors to younger employees, as keepers of the company tradition, and as members of sensitive task forces.

But, while people do not always need to go up, they do tend to get stale in one job too long. Companies like Castro Travel in San Francisco cross-utilize people by moving them to different jobs at the same level for variety. Maryles Castro says, "They get a better understanding of the overall business that way, so it serves several different purposes." Nissan Motors and other factories offer workers free retraining when they have been in a job for several years.

The heads of Time Inc.'s magazine and book divisions recently swapped jobs. While there was speculation that one job was a demotion, the company noted that it was a "reinvigorating experience that will enable both groups to enjoy fresh perspectives."

The sabbatical has been borrowed from the university as a perk offered to managers who have worked many years. Xerox employees with a certain number of years' service can apply for up to one year of paid leave to work for a nonprofit organization. Leaves have been taken by vice presidents as well as assembly line workers. They offer their energy to the community, and they come back with fresh ideas and renewed dedication. A novel variation on this idea was created at a four-physician family practice. The four partners hired a fifth partner, while not increasing their patient load. Then, each partner took three months off, preferably out of the city, to pursue personal growth. The patients had no trouble adapting to this arrangement, and the partners all felt energized and excited.

Flexibility and alternate job arrangements are something that your company can offer you, but they are also options that you can negotiate for. In your annual performance review, you can ask for more than the obligatory raise and promotion. You might talk about the particular pressure point you feel that inhibits your best performance. You might discuss your personal situation and how you would like to take a day to work at home or experiment with different working hours.

Do your own creative redesign of your work arrangements. Where do you feel the most conflict between your work and your personal/family life? Which of the alternate arrangements might help relieve the pressure and free up your energy to do better at work and feel better at home? Now, think of a way that you could get what you need while respecting the needs of your company or job. Many times, presenting a creative solution to your supervisor or colleagues can be an eye-opener. Everyone gets excited by the possibilities. Or, if you encounter some resistance to an idea, you might suggest a trial period, when your own and the company's performance are closely monitored.

AUTONOMY, CREATIVE RESPONSIBILITY, AND TEAMWORK

The entrepreneur is the explorer of our age. He or she creates something out of nothing and fights skepticism and lack of funding to bring out a product that may be wildly successful. Often to the dismay of subordinates, the entrepreneur exerts close to total control over the new company. But there is no doubt that entrepreneurs are inspired performers, and in the early stages of their development they are able to inspire others to sign on to pursue their vision.

But, how much control and personal responsibility can one employee have in an airline, a hospital, or an auto factory? That is the dilemma within the new workstyle: how to create a working environment where each individual employee feels enhanced responsibility, autonomy, and personal power, while the team, the jazz group, works in harmony. The new workstyle tries to give individuals more creative freedom and also to build more effective teamwork. Quite an order!

As we show in later chapters, this problem is solved when we see that individual responsibility for a task does not necessarily diminish the power of others. In an energized, high-performing work team all members feel responsible for the whole and for their own particular part. But this form of creative teamwork, this synergy, demands new skills from each team member.

Check Your Work Environment
When you enter a company or a work group, almost instantly you feel if it is working. Look around you. Does the space look alive? Do people move with a sense of purpose? Do they have a relaxed or involved expression on

their face and in their body? Is there laughter, informal conversation, kidding around, and a feeling of lightness, alongside a sense of serious purpose? What is on the walls? These signs are expressions of the team synergy, of how well people feel in touch with, valued by, and connected to each other, and how clearly they are working for a common purpose. Their purpose is clear all over the place.

We visited two branches of the same company. In one, the walls were empty, the areas were messy, and everything looked drab and faceless. Another branch had large color posters on the walls, pictures of each member of the team, large score sheets listing how many units were sold, and various slogans and humorous sayings all around. The environment was quieter and seemed much more orderly. Try to guess how people felt in each branch and which branch was the sales leader.

Unleashing Creativity

Gifford Pinchot coined the term "intrapreneur" for the person who works inside a company, taking on a new project or idea and developing it into a practical business opportunity. Intrapreneurs work as change agents within the corporate community, developing innovative ideas and making them real. Try acting as an intrapreneur within your company, not necessarily to develop a new product but to redesign your job to create more effectiveness and energy for you and your company.

Many companies are finding ways to unleash individual creativity. 3M, Kodak, and Ore-Ida all have internal programs that free up individuals to develop a new project. Ore-Ida offers $50,000 to each of five key managers, who in turn distribute it to people who seem to have the potential to make a difference. This gives them time to work on their idea. There is no bottom-line pressure to make it work the first time, because the company knows that people need the freedom to fail. However, the program has led to several money-saving ideas.

In the new workplace, every work group is like the top management team in the traditional company. In the new team, every person is important and is expected to contribute his or her own special expertise, as well as being able to see the whole. Everyone creates the plan about how to do things, and then each individual attends to the job. When the unexpected comes up, the individual is able to improvise and has the authority to act. A person might make a misjudgment, but there is no blame for taking action. Everyone represents the company.

Why Isn't All Work Like This?

Developing the new workplace can be a very long road. Most business schools do not teach this new management style. One exception is the Organizational Management and Leadership Program at John F. Kennedy University in Orinda, California. The program's motto comes from Albert Einstein: "The significant problems we have cannot be solved at the same level of thinking we were at when we created them."

The program's curriculum features classes in emerging models of business, organizational cultures, myths and values, personal power and leadership, and visionary leadership. The purpose is to assist individuals in becoming effective leaders while learning practical methods for implementing change within organizations.

The most difficult part of creating the new workplace is that there are not quick ways to achieve the right mix of creativity, practicality, and fortitude. Labor unions have expressed suspicion of these programs. Accountants and financial advisors are doubtful. It's difficult to make new systems to track widespread financial participation. Traditional managers often feel threatened by these approaches. Because the concept is new, mistakes are predictable, often causing fingers to point and focus on the negative aspects.

But over the long haul the success of new workplace styles will probably depend most on the demands of business itself. Changing work conditions require resourceful, vital, and committed people to respond. You do not get and keep those kinds of people without providing creative, productive workplaces. Jim Pinto of Action Instruments sums it up: "You know, people aren't stupid anymore. They don't like to be used as slaves."

This new workplace fits the model proposed in the excellence books and the compendiums of new management principles. What happens in the traditional company, or the company in transition, when one or more key employees begin to try out new assumptions or to act in new ways? If even one small part of a company acts differently, the whole system may change. Of course, there will be resistance, and things never work out exactly as planned. But one employee who holds fast to a new vision, who courageously, persistently, and strategically suggests that there may be better ways to do things, can have tremendous moral and organizational force.

Think of Gandhi, whose leadership consisted of making his personal behavior completely consistent with his inner values. His example inspired a nation, freed it from British rule, and crystallized a new model of leadership and social change for a new generation of leaders. Your journey, as outlined in this book, is more modest: to redesign your own job. If you hold fast to your personal vision of the job you want, you may unintentionally change your workplace and your organization—no matter what your job is or where in the company you work.

CHANGE: THE FIRST STEP TO PERSONAL EXCELLENCE

CHAPTER 3

MISSION AND VISION: HARNESSING THE POWER OF THE DREAM

I would rather be ashes than dust.

I would rather my spark should burn out in a brilliant blaze

Than it should be stifled in dry-rot.

I would rather be a superb meteor,

Every atom of me in magnificent glow,

Than a sleepy and permanent planet.

Man's chief purpose is to live, not exist.

I shall not waste my days trying to prolong them.

I shall use my time.

—JACK LONDON

What makes you *want* to come to work each day? There's a story about three stonecutters in a large courtyard, each cutting stones with a chisel. A stranger wandered up to them and asked what they were doing. The first one replied curtly, "Can't you see I'm cutting stones." The stranger moved away quickly and approached the second stonecutter. He again asked, "What are you doing?" The second man replied warmly, "I'm working so that my family can live and grow." The stranger then queried the third cutter, who replied with a swelling sense of pride, "I'm building a cathedral. Each stone I cut goes into a house of worship that will last far beyond my life."

Each of these workers performed the same task, cutting stone. But how differently the work felt to each of them! The first worker felt tired, exhausted, and bored by his work, because he was unable to see the larger picture. The second felt satisfaction, even enthusiasm, because he could see what his work would bring to him. The third cutter saw his work connected to a larger whole, full of spiritual meaning and significance. His mundane toil was accompanied by a vision of what his stones would become and how they would enrich other people's lives. This cutter was connected to his inner mission and had a vision of why he was working.

Which of these three workers are you most like? What is the personal meaning of your own work? What do you first think of when you think of your mission and your vision of life? Do you imagine that what you really want to achieve is beyond your reach? May never happen? Is not realistic or practical?

You do not need a crystal ball to see into the future. You can create it. People can use their ability to see into the future to create action-oriented plans for their work and home life. The future is not predetermined. We set out in life in a certain direction, we direct our energy, we orient ourselves toward our own vision of the future. So your daily activity relates to your vision of your future.

People who follow a dream or have a deep sense of purpose about their work are rewarded with an almost inexhaustible supply of energy. They use this energy to reach their goals. This chapter will help you discover your own inner energy source—your deepest personal mission, your vision. This vision forms the fuel for your personal commitment to realizing your goals. People moved by this internal energy source are fired up by inspiration. They are likely to find the energy required to finish the difficult, even mundane tasks that go into any achievement.

We'll look at the basic questions "What should you do?" and "Why do you want to do it?" The answers to these questions are at the root of your motivation to work and change. Your creativity and level of productivity depend not only on the external rewards from your salary but also on connecting your work to an inner sense of purpose. Burned-out people have lost their sense of purpose; their work no longer matters to them. Many of them have in effect retired on the job.

Several things cause this state of affairs. One is a shift in what your job means to you. When you enter a new profession, one of the major motivators is the desire to demonstrate excellence. In the first years of work you develop your skills and begin to experience their rewards. In addition to the external reward of money and status, you have the inner reward of feeling good about doing well. Somewhere along the way, your motivation to be competent can waver. At this point, people report that their work is getting routine, that it does not have the same kick anymore.

The challenge now is to shift from the motivation of learning more new things to something else. Many people at midcareer switch from motivation by competence to motivation according to inner meaning. For example, health professionals we interviewed reported that they shifted from concentrating on their skill in diagnosing and prescribing to seeing more meaning in the relationships they had with patients and feeling connected to the ideals of the healer. The shift in kind of motivation often leads to a shift in style of work or to a new emphasis.

One physician reported to us that a serious illness almost ended his life. At the time he was a busy specialist in a major city. Lying in the hospital he was struck by several thoughts.

I saw the hospital from a whole new perspective, on my back. All of a sudden, I saw that everything I thought was important, all the technical details, weren't really what's important. I wanted to be seen, I wanted my fear recognized. I saw then that's what healing is all about. Sure, I know a few tricks, but what was really important was all the things I never paid attention to.

He gave up his practice and became a teacher in a medical school. Two years later, he received the Best Teacher award for his work with resident physicians in creating healing relationships. He looks and feels healthier, has more time for his family, and feels more effective and helpful as a physician.

Daniel Yankelovich, who has chronicled the emerging shift in work values, describes this shift as from impersonal, technical, manipulative skills toward seeing the sacred, expressive aspects of work. From the "how" to the "why." People seek meaningful relationships, a sense of purpose, a feeling of community with coworkers. Workers want to be valued for what they are, not just what they can do. In our study of 450 physicians in transition, the major finding was that physicians were changing their workstyles so they could feel more connected to the ancient tradition of the healer and rejecting the emphasis on purely technological medicine.

Just as people invest money in a company, so they invest themselves in their work or organization. At every stage a person decides how much or how little he or she has to give. At one extreme, the individual only goes through the motions, turning off the mind and being blind to anything but routine tasks. Fewer and fewer jobs operate with this low level of commitment. Most people want to give more to work. But how much? What makes someone want to work more or want to use more available talents in the service of a company?

One factor is the sense that the company calls upon people's higher selves, broader talents, for an important goal. Feeling part of something larger than themselves, people give their best. The more of themselves they invest, the more exciting, energizing, and fulfilling work becomes. However, no one can just command investment in work. There has to be an inner reason for this commitment. That inner meaning comes from the individual's and the company's mission, vision, and purpose.

This chapter leads you through a process for re-creating and enlarging that sense of connectedness. You will learn how to tie your own inner power and spirit to the work that you do and bring your personal drive into alignment with the mission of your workplace. An increasing number of companies use these strategies to discover the company's own mission, vision, and purpose. One of the outcomes for business is the development of new structures, bringing a new sense of purpose into the entire company. Management and employees use their shared mission to bring new energy and spirit to their work.

FIRST YOU DREAM

Your inner journey starts with a dream: your powerful vision of what might be. T. E. Lawrence, who abandoned the secure life of a scholar to pursue his passion for the unification of Arabia, noted in his journal:

> All people dream; but not equally.
> Those who dream by night
> in the dusty recesses of their minds
> wake in the day to find it was vanity.
> But the dreamers of the *day*
> are dangerous people,
> for they may *act* their dream with *open eyes*
> to make it *possible.**

Daytime dreamers turn their dreams into action. We will show you how to use the power of your dreams to see new ways and guide future action.

Thomas Edison observed that invention was a tiny bit inspiration and mostly perspiration. Success was a combination of persistence and dreaming. But what leads a person to *want* to put in years of sweat to reach a difficult and distant goal? What inspires people to form a company or even just to finish a long-term project? Frequently, it is an indomitable spirit that warms a person from the inside. These long-time achievers were fired up by the power of their dreams, the intensity of their purpose.

Burnout arises when a person, a group, or a whole company loses touch with their personal dream—their sense of where they are going. The soul, the core, the center, is gone. The importance of spirit in the workplace is underscored by a research project conducted by University of Southern California management professor Sherrie Connelly, on what she calls "work spirit." People who love their work exhibit enormous energy, a positive state of mind, and a sense of vision and purpose. They realize that what they are doing fits into a larger picture and can see how what they do makes a difference in the world as a whole.

Think about your *mission.*

What do you think about first? You might think of something deeply

---

* Quoted in Studs Terkel, *American Dreams: Lost and Found* (New York: Ballantine Books, 1981), p. 186.

meaningful to you like, "I want to improve the quality of life," or "I want to help young children learn to read," or "I want to make cities better places to live." People with a mission experience a real drive for what they do, especially when they can feel that their actions now contribute to the mission. Contrast the energy and commitment of people who work on political campaigns, putting in sixteen-hour days ringing doorbells and passing out literature, because they believe their candidate can make a real difference, with employees who are asked to do similar tasks as part of a market survey for a product they think is useless.

Think of someone you know who has a sense of direction, who is able to connect his or her activities to an overall theme. Chances are this person has independently done the kind of clarification we are going to go through. The more people know where they want to go, the greater the chances they will get there; opportunities fall into line. In *Alice in Wonderland*, Alice asks directions from the Mad Hatter. He asks where she wants to go. Alice replies that she really does not know. "Then," the Hatter replies, "any direction will do."

Many people live their lives without a clear sense of their direction. When we ask where are they going, they often reply like Alice. They leave direction-setting to someone else or just find themselves moved as if by giant, invisible magnets. Many of them say they do not set their direction because they fear disappointment.

Think of your mission not as a solid, unchangeable road but as a garden in which your activities develop. All your tasks may seem very different, but when brought together in the garden they all relate to each other. In a garden, each plant is distinct, and no one plant makes a garden, but together all the plants form an interrelated whole. In the same way, no one activity is enough to fulfill your mission. Defining your own inner mission—envisioning your garden—is the first step to maintaining and growing your energy.

On a piece of paper make a list of the things you want in your life. You might divide the paper into two sides, one side for work and one for personal/family life. Make the list as long as you can. Include specific things like "I want to manage a new product campaign," as well as more general ones like "I want to contribute to world peace." Think of the items on this list as the individual plants in your garden. You can discover your mission (your overall visions and your values) by seeing what groups from your list have in common—in other words, what patterns exist in your garden. For example, you might find that several of your wants relate to helping people to learn and grow. So, that is a major value for you. The blossoms and fruits of the plants are the specific activities you do each day to move toward these goals. Take one of your wants, perhaps something like "being recognized as an important contributor to my profession." Now, think about some immediate and some longer-term things you could do to move toward this. Eventually, you can create a blossom for each of your wants, with specific actions.

Defining your mission acts as an emotional touchstone that unleashes a powerful feeling. You might recognize a hidden dream that has been buried for a long time because someone once said it was silly. You probably almost forgot about it, because thinking about it only frustrated you. Why spend time thinking about being a dancer, a newspaper columnist, or an acclaimed chef. You knew that you were "too old," "too short," "too lazy," or "too late." Everyone has some secret desire to go beyond the present situation.

One way to explore your hidden dreams is to remember the roles you have thought about and your role models for them. If you want to be a newscaster, singer, executive, what particular person is most like the person you would like to be? What aspect of this person's life is your goal? Would it be the glamour and publicity, the acclaim for performances, the ability to make decisions that touch many people's lives, or the opportunity to be seen as an authority? There may be very different reasons for each dream role, leading to very different touchstones.

Just as you did with your personal mission garden you will want to look at your particular job or role, and look for the overall meaning. A student was very interested in international health, demographics, and Asian studies, forever trying to figure out how she could fit all these interests together and get a job doing what she wanted. She took a big piece of paper and listed all the things she was currently interested in. She then drew circles clustering her various activities inside them. After a few hours of clustering and erasing she ended up with three core circles of interests. Looking at them she began to see what she was doing in a new light. She then did a visioning exercise where she imagined going up in a balloon and looking at her clusters from above. From this new perspective she saw that the unifying theme was community development. Health was a form of development relevant to her demographics interest. Her interest in Asian cultures gave her that much more focus. With this new clarity she was able to focus her job hunting efforts effectively and eventually found her way into a large corporation specializing in health products, with an interest in Asian markets.

Ralf Hotchkiss is a man with a mission—to design better wheelchairs. He is a major figure in the international network of designers and mechanics who have sparked major advances in wheelchair mobility in the past few years. A wheelchair rider himself, he was most influenced by his experience in third-world countries where riders face major challenges, including dirt roads, stairs, and mud. His designs have resulted in lighter, easier-to-produce and -handle models that give freedom to countless wheelchair riders. His next challenge is to build a squatting wheelchair for the Navajo, to allow easier access to their hogan homes.

Many people get confused and even resist developing a mission because they fear that they need to choose something that will last a lifetime. A mission is not a narrow goal, but an overall guiding picture and sense of direction that can include many goals. Your personal vision is based on your values. Values form the building blocks of your mission. To craft a mission for yourself the first step is to explore your values, the things that you personally stand for.

Sometimes it is hard to distinguish among values, visions, mission, goals, and the concrete actions that make them happen. Here is a model to define each of them in turn. Imagine a pot of stew cooking over an open fire, filled with the widest variety of meat and vegetables. The fireplace surrounding the pot is built with the foundation stones of your values. Your vision is the fire that forcefully heats the pot containing all your goals and desires. The pot containing the stew is your mission.

VALUES: WHAT YOU STAND FOR

Values form the core of your understanding about the world, the basis for your deepest feelings. They act as motivators for your beliefs and actions. You can also think of them as the main themes upon which you weave the experiences of your life. Values feed your passion for the activities that you undertake over the long run. They do not usually change drastically throughout your life, but act as an anchor, allowing you to return to your original purpose when off base.

Your core values tell what you stand for. Many of us, unfortunately, have grown up with the sense that values are like rules—a straitjacket that limits our behavior. Yet, when we look at people who deeply believe in something, we see the opposite. We see people who can draw on vast reserves of energy that seem to flow from their beliefs.

Values are an energy source. A person who believes in something, who acts on what seems really important, always finds the energy to accomplish the task. People disconnected from this energy source find themselves struggling against burnout.

People tend to feel crazy if what they are doing in their work world is drastically at odds with their values. For example, a young man was having terrible stomachaches for reasons his doctor could not isolate. Something was making him feel very sick. He had just started a new job with a telecommunications company, feeling very excited about the kind of high-tech research he would be doing. When asked the purpose of the research he became heated and defensive, saying that it was involved with weapons. He was asked about his values and beliefs concerning strategic arms control and military matters. Slowly he began to say that he had been raised in a religious tradition that opposed military service and was feeling conflicts with his values in doing this new job. He literally made himself sick with the incongruence between his personal beliefs and the mission of the company.

Not everyone experiences this level of conflict, but many people begin to feel less excitement about what they are doing if their personal values are continuously challenged at work. Connecting your personal values with your work efforts is key to keeping your spark alive.

William C. Miller, a corporate innovation specialist and author of *The Creative Edge,* was conducting a workshop on business opportunities for a new flame-resistant material. The group was generating new business ideas at a good clip, but there was something missing. That evening, he recalled hearing about a hotel fire that killed seventy-five people because of flammable furniture. The new material would have prevented the fire, and he began to think of cost-effective ways to have this new product used in furniture.

He told this story to the group, noting that the fire touched his heart, and led him to want to do something. He asked the participants to begin with an important concern of their own about life in general. From the list that was generated, he had people break into small groups to come up with ideas for how this new product could help with these concerns. The energy of the group heightened, as the people were no longer just dealing with a new product but doing something that mattered with it. They generated nearly a thousand new business ideas in the workshop.

Psychologist Douglas LaBier in *Modern Madness: The Emotional Fallout of Success,* writes about the pain of executives who pursue success and end up betraying their inner values. These young men pursue the traditional outer-directed path to wealth, status, and success, only to find an inner emptiness and worthlessness. They reach a crisis of meaning. Their resolution of this upheaval is a new orientation to work, in concert with inner values, and they pursue a clearer vision of what is really important to them. Often, this vision was clearer to them when they were younger, but the pressures of getting ahead at work pushed it to the back burner, as they told themselves it was unrealistic or impractical. Now, they find that reconnecting to their mission is critical to their well-being.

Values are the building blocks for creating strong personal and organizational missions. Because your missions are central to keeping your spark alive, take a look at your individual missions. We use the plural because it is common for individuals to have multiple directions in their lives. Just as you can be both a parent and a manager, you can have several different missions driving different parts of your life. People can get confused by having several missions going in vastly different directions. In that case we encourage people to search mentally for a way to expand their garden until it is big enough to contain all their interests.

A doctor wanted to be involved in medicine and the arts at the same time. He felt pulled in each direction and often trapped and unable to move at all. He worked on designing his mission to include both the practice of medicine and participation in the arts. He could not quite see how to make both of these strong interests fit. After a lot of looking he was able to find a hospital where he could practice medicine with enough flexibility to allow him to attend rehearsals and tour with a theater troupe. The next exercise helped him to do this. See how it works for you.

Find Your Mission

One step in finding your own mission is to use the imagery techniques from the first chapter. First, take some time to get relaxed. Take a deep breath, clearing your mind of all the thoughts and everyday concerns you are carrying. Now ask yourself the question, "What do I stand for? What are my deepest personal values?" Hold that thought, and let your unconscious answer. You will probably get a number of responses. Another way to ask the question is to think about what you would most want to teach your children. What is the most important lesson you have for them? Would it be truth, beauty, freedom, harmony? Allow yourself to formulate these values in any way that makes sense to you.

Now recall a time when you took a stand about your values. Allow yourself to re-create that situation. See yourself acting in accordance with your values. What does it feel like to act in this way? How do you know you are in alignment—what are your inner signals? If you have more than one value, imagine them lining up; take a moment to consider each of them in sequence. Allow your mind to wander back over all of them, and select one value that seems to be at the center of all your values.

Now let your imagination create a symbol that represents your value. It could be an object, a sound, a color, a smell, a texture, a person, or an animal. Be willing to be surprised by what your imagination produces. Just accept whatever comes to you. Do not be judgmental. Just allow yourself to watch. This symbol will act as an anchor, bringing you back to this core value whenever you need it. Drawing a picture of your symbol will give you something to grab when you may have lost touch with your core value. It may then inspire you with something new to do in the situation you face.

People in our workshops come up with a range of symbols, everything from a high mountain to a shining stone. Each person creates a unique way of representing the core value. Take some time now, or later, to draw or find a picture that represents your value.

You may wonder, Why a picture? Images have a special quality; they give a shape and form to your value and can be used as an anchor when you want to return to them. They do more than just *state* a value, they become personally meaningful, adding an emotional identification to an abstract concept. Symbols and pictures *move* you.

One woman whose basic value was in growing and being open to new experiences came up with the image of an acorn in a first inner imagery exercise. At first this seemed tiny and insignificant in relation to her large dreams for her life. What changed her understanding was looking more deeply into the image and seeing that the acorn has all the energy to blossom into a huge tree. She used the emotional feeling of the tiny acorn giving birth to the huge flowing tree to remind herself of the energy she had inside to accomplish her dreams. She found a tree branch and mounted it on her desk to remind herself that the big tree started as a dream of the acorn. This branch reminded her to connect her regular work activities with her own personal growth.

Sharing pictures of values can be a powerful experience for a work group. We once conducted a workshop for people who were the survivors of a company that had been gutted by economic reversals. They were in pain about the people who were gone and about the frustrated expectations they had for the company. The question for the team was, How can we begin anew? We talked to each of them about working according to their deepest values and bringing these values to bear on the organizational crisis. Each person drew his or her value and talked about how to activate it at work. One person drew a set of scales and talked about how she was trying to balance realities with what she wanted to do. Another drew a head and a heart, and talked about trying to accomplish layoffs with caring. The pictures led each person to see new facets of the others. They also led to new ways of doing things and creative discussions of how the new team would work. They decided to try to create a team symbol that reflected the most important values of each individual. As a result, their commitment and involvement in the plan were much higher than they would have expected for this crisis time.

ENTREPRENEURIAL VISIONS

There have always been people who have had vision, that ability to see beyond the present, to imagine what is to come. This ability is not always welcomed. Some people who see ahead are thought to be a little crazy. Consider how Leonardo DaVinci was received in his day when he drew sketches of flying machines. On the other hand, some leaders have visions and dreams of a better future that inspire millions of people. When Martin Luther King, Jr., made his "I have a dream" speech, it ignited a sense of possibility and hope across the country.

The ability to see into the future and guide an endeavor on that imagined path is exemplified by William Paley. When he took over CBS in 1928, it was a bit player in its industry. It had no stations of its own, was not financially secure, and was completely overshadowed by NBC. But Paley had the uncanny ability to sit in his small New York office and see, not his desk, but the millions of Americans who were out in the hinterlands, without anything other than the radio for entertainment. He could see ways of reaching them. He knew his network had something for them. In his mind he created the link between the TV station and the audience through advertising. He generated a strategy to develop programs that would bring in larger audiences and thus larger revenues. Within ten years, CBS had 114 stations and was earning $27.7 million. These results would not have come about without hard work and tenacious strategy. But these factors themselves, without the vision, would not have netted the outcome Paley experienced. With a vision, the leader provides the all-important bridge from the present to the future for organizations.

Today, the ability to set a vision for others is much in demand. This is the era of the entrepreneur, a person who can take an idea and shape it into a working organization. Entrepreneurs are today's frontiersmen, seeing the possibilities, engaging investors, designers, and marketers in the adventure. In the past, the motivation for such empire building would have been earning millions, great personal power, or social status. Those values have not entirely passed away, but today's entrepreneur is just as likely to drive a beat-up car, live in an unfurnished house, and not have time for the social whirl.

Bob Schwartz, founder of the School for Entrepreneurs at the Tarrytown Center in New York, finds entrepreneurial motivation to be different from what it was a generation ago. The company creator today has a powerful vision and wants to validate it in the marketplace. More often than not, the entrepreneur wants to see his vision affecting other people. So, computer creators want to see people influenced by their portable machines, while others want to see their management principles or sense of how things could be in action. As is true for some of the new business leaders, the external rewards are less important than the opportunity to actualize a vision. That vision in turn recruits hundreds of others, who are persuaded and join the caravan. A new business is not a building, or a product, but a group of people who share a vision and make it happen.

Another aspect of mission for entrepreneurs is that their product excellence comes from their deep caring for what they do. Anne Robinson, for example, founder and president of Windham Hill Records, did not set out to create a $40-million-a-year record company. She and her partner cared about a new kind of music that was not released by the larger companies. They paid attention to detail, quality, and meaning in their records, and they supported their artists. Those hallmarks remain now that their New Age music has moved into the mainstream. Even as they grow, she has not changed her style. "I know where I'm comfortable, and I don't go outside that," Robinson notes.

The entrepreneurial path provides an alternative to a traditional career path. Today, many people use their professions or the first stage of their career to build their skills and set the stage for creating their own business. Some people come to build their own companies when they find they are misfits, need more control, or just do not fit into traditional jobs. Rather than compromise, they take the risk to create their own work.

For example, Gail Chrystal was a rising star in the marketing department of a large advertising agency. Like many talented women in traditional organizations, she was faced with a situation where she could not develop her fullest ability. She was told to be a team player and not challenge her boss. Good advice for some, but to others it is just impossible to be shackled. After being fired for "inability to comply with the corporate mode," she looked at other job offers.

They did not seem right. After a few weeks, she saw that what she really wanted was to start her own company. That same month, she became pregnant. She found, however, that the two new responsibilities meshed well, because, for the first time, she was office-bound and had time to meet with her clients. Her new agency prospered because she could run it her way, using her energy and talent to the fullest.

There is another wrinkle in the new company game. Many families have two-career couples, working at jobs that do not fit them. Many couples have some exciting hobby or interest they share and find that their time off is not enough. So, couples are finding that they can actualize their visions together. Banana Republic was started by the Zieglers, who wanted to combine their interests in design and travel, and who founded a chain of stores that featured a creative catalogue that was their travel diary. Another couple, a television announcer and producer, quit their jobs to create their own syndicated magazine show. It was a thousand-to-one shot, but their show, GEO, is broadcast widely. Mrs. Field's Cookies, Esprit, Maxi-Care Health Maintenance Organization, and scores of other businesses were created by couples who wanted to work creatively together.

These new businesses are started by people who are willing to risk all for their vision. They devote their time, an almost inexhaustible supply of energy, and their own money—and they often temporarily pull back from friends and family—to make something happen. In each case, the experience is more meaningful, real, exciting, and energizing than anything they have done before or since. Their visions in turn inspire legions of coworkers, who are motivated by their example.

Etta Allen is a reluctant entrepreneur. Twenty years ago, when her husband died, leaving her to support their children, she took over his sheet metal contracting company. She became the only woman contractor in the state. Her employees are proud and protective of her, and her customers are invariably satisfied. Is her mission putting heaters into walls? Not at all. She says, "I've always been concerned about home comfort. I feel connected to the home, and I know what makes people feel comfortable. That's what we do—create comfort. If I see a room, I know just where the heater belongs; I don't just put it on the most accessible wall." By creating a broader vision and connecting it to something deeply personal, she inspires her company.

PERSONAL VISIONS

Visions are not just for leaders. People use visions every day to produce striking results. Cynthia's father always wanted to sail on the ocean. He could see himself facing into the wind, feeling the spray of the waves. All this despite the fact that he lived in landlocked Arizona. He had this dream early in his career, when he had a young family and little extra income. In place of finances, he used his dreams to make his vision live. If he could not have the boat he could have a piece of it. He built himself a boat trailer, the kind that would fit the boat he had in mind. People often thought he was a little strange to be doing all that work for something they felt sure he would never have. But "Crazy Scott" had a dream and along with it came the fishing poles, the boating classes, and the years of anticipation. One of his proudest moments came when he was able to hitch up his boat trailer and drive to the boat factory in California. He watched his boat being lowered ever so slowly onto the trailer. His first ocean adventure took him along the coast of Mexico. His way of nourishing his dreams stuck with Cynthia. She learned that you can keep your dreams large and work toward them step by step, and that without a vision all you have is a shell of fiberglass and some welded metal.

Visioning is using your imagination to create a picture of what you want in your life. You can see a project completed before it is even started, imagine the possible as accomplished. Human beings have this ability to create the real from the unreal, and to hold visions that are separate from present reality. Many things that are real today once existed only as someone's inner vision. Visions sustain people in moving to the future. Visioning is the ability to see beyond the present and into the future. It is the answer to the questions, Where am I going? and what will it be like when I get there? It is a combination of your dreams, your hopes, and your values and beliefs.

Everyone can have a mission. A project of the New York Public Library is illustrative. The library will clean 3.5 million books in the next five years. The library has enlisted, not squads of technicians in matching jump suits with oxygen tanks on their backs, but a team of cleaning women headed by Nonna Rinck, a Soviet emigré, using masks, ammonia, paper towels, and hand vacuums.

Mrs. Rinck, who is about fifty, was a librarian in Moscow, where the books are "not so dusty," but "the only books available are the ones officials want you to read." She said she was well paid and had a good job but left "for the same reason zoo animals that are safe and well fed walk out when the cage door is left open."

There is nothing difficult about using creative visioning. Chances are you are already using it every day, whether or not you are aware of it. Most children use their imaginations quite easily in their everyday play. They create imaginary characters, go on fanciful adventures, and use their toys to build complete dream worlds. Along the way many of us were told to keep our dreams to ourselves, to stop daydreaming, to forget such crazy ideas. Mistakenly, many people associate daydreams and visions with inaction. Maybe this is because many people who do dream do not think that they could make their dreams real. These beliefs about dreaming may have dampened your ability to use visioning spontaneously. What we know is that people who do take their visions seriously become the activists and achievers who create projects that were thought impossible. They are the people who mold our world.

You use imagery more than you think. Take a moment right now and think about the last time you did something that felt very important and meaningful to you. Remember the event as vividly as you can. You may be able to experience your memory with all five senses. Now, imagine yourself doing something meaningful that you would like to do in the future. Experience it as if you are doing it right now. That is a quick example of how you can use imagery to create a possible future event.

Anytime you imagine, What would happen if? And how would it be if we did it this way? you are visioning. Visioning is one way to see the outcome before you start—it creates a blueprint that helps clarify where you want to go and how you can get there. The most important thing is to know how to harness your inner ability and connect your vision with your goals.

Why do some people use their ability to work from their own mission and vision and others not? You might think that you don't have the ability to do something like that. That only famous people have missions, not you. But everyone can have a mission, and needs one. The challenge comes from creating a theme that encompasses what you are doing.

An Indiana man had been a butcher for twenty years until he got an ulcer and sciatica so badly that he had to quit. He was fifty-five years old and he decided he wanted to start a stonemasonry business. His family thought he was crazy. But he had a feeling that as soon as he started his business his health would improve. And indeed, as he found himself working with stone, the aches and pains seemed to melt away. He felt tied to history, that what he was doing was good, making some kind of meaning in his life. The most striking observation came from his son, who said, "My dad was an old man fifteen, twenty years ago. Today he's a young man."

In *Working,* Studs Terkel interviewed scores of people about their "search for daily meaning, how they got recognition, as well as cash." One of the most interesting challenges you may face is how to make what some might call meaningless work into art. Terkel tells about Dolores, a waitress, who does just that. She moves among tables with a special gracefulness. She pretends she is Carmen, a gypsy, holding out a tambourine waiting for coins. She found it very tiring to keep saying, "Would you like a cocktail?" over and over. So she uses different approaches. One time she will ask, "What's exciting at the bar that I can offer?" and another time, "How can I make your day brighter?" She rephrases what she says enough to make it interesting for her. Making up new dialogues each evening makes it seem theatrical, and she feels like a different person every night.

Dolores has found a unique way of making meaning in her work. At the end of the night she feels tired, but she has avoided the burned-out feeling that comes from doing work that she does not believe in. Dolores has discovered Rule number 1 about making work meaningful—she puts a part of herself into everything she does. This way she turns what could be dull work into her own personal theater.

People who are able to make meaning in their work avoid feeling trapped. Making meaning is one of the keys for keeping your spark alive. Your personal mission adds meaning to even the smallest task.

Going back to your original sense of what you wanted to do can be very instructive. Think back to the first time you heard about the type of work you do, the first time you said to yourself, "I could do that." How did you see that job? What grander vision did you see yourself accomplishing? What did you see yourself actually doing? Sometimes the spark dims when the reality of the work we do has totally disconnected from the vision we were seeking. At that time, we face a choice: Do we give up the vision, the ideal we were seeking, or do we change the reality today? Too many people give up their dream, and their work becomes empty.

A group of minority recruits to the San Francisco Police Department all said they had wanted to be police as far back as they could remember. When asked why they said it was for personal growth and to show people it could be done. Their dreams helped them put up with the rigors of the academy. It also helped when the realities of daily police work became more bureaucratic and routine than their ideal. But the sense of participating in one of the most important roles in society, and the encounters in which they really made a difference, kept the meaning alive in their work.

In recalling their early vision, lawyers might remember a visit to a courtroom, and doctors almost invariably have an image of being a healer, saving lives, and having access to almost magical powers. Early visions fuel the choice to enter a profession, putting up with years of schooling, competitive exams, and going into debt. After going into practice, or spending years getting to a respectable job in a company, the ideal may begin to tarnish. At that point, it is vital that you reexamine where you are and think about how you want to change your daily work. Do not give up your personal vision!

MAKING IT REAL

Taking your sense of personal mission and combining it with your work is the next challenge. Many people wish they could operate in a larger world of possiblities but just do not know how. They see others go from nothing to something but are not sure how. The pitcher Joachim Andujar, the only son of a sugarcane factory worker, escaped poverty by his single-minded focus on baseball. His overall mission was to do something in the world; baseball was his vision of how to accomplish it; and the hard work and practice the outcome of his commitment. Talent and a lot of hard work were the steps on his way to the national recognition that came from his daily focus on his dream.

Connecting your mission and vision to your work is not instant. It takes some reflective and active time to put your plan into action. We have looked at a number of people who have harnessed their mission and vision to create meaning in their lives. Barbra Streisand is another good example. She has a reputation as an uncompromising artist. She starts her *Broadway Album* with a series of interviews with her friends, all saying the album is not commercial, will not sell. (Ironically, this became her most popular album in years.) Then she sings a Stephen Sondheim song about how "art isn't easy." The song tells about the painstaking effort that goes into making a vision a reality, and it can be a warning to anyone who is trying to make a vision real. Now it is time to take what you learned about personal mission and vision and create that connection with your work.

Think of your personal mission as the link between your vision and the people, things, and activities that will make it happen:

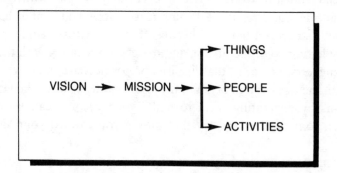

The first step in taking your mission into your work is to make it portable. Distill your mission into a few words. These words will act like an emotional touchstone, enabling you to remember your larger purpose in an instant. Take a few moments right now to put your mission into a short phrase. Ask yourself, What is it about my mission that makes me most excited? Is it the creative fulfillment, the fame, the money, the chance to help people, the closeness to nature? Find the kernel of meaning at the center of what you want to do. Some examples are "news that serves" for a publicity service, "creating harmony through training" for a management development company, "the best damn truck in America" for a truck manufacturing company, and "hellos are good buys" and "someone is alone until you phone" for Southern New England Telephone. A touchstone needs to be brief—and often exciting, because it takes people right back to their core mission. What have you come up with? These phrases become handles, which you can use to carry your mission into your everyday work. Take a moment right now to write down your phrase.

Now bring your mission down to earth: Discover the people, things, and activities that will make it happen. Keeping a clear focus on your vision, expressed in your mission statement, begin to articulate the specifics of what you will be doing to express this vision. You want to be a healer: Will you work in an urban clinic, or do you see yourself creating a new-style health system in a rural setting? What do you have to do to reach your goals?

Take a lot of time and care with this planning, because it will be your guide. If you work in a company and your job seems fixed, try to reconceptualize it from the perspective of your ideal vision. What could your job be if you and the company would let it? Practicality *follows* visioning; too often we get practical before we let ourselves dream and create freely.

Musician/educator Robert Fritz observes that there is always a distance between an ideal and reality. Likening it to a stretched rubber band, Fritz talks about "structural tension" between the two. Most people resolve the tension by letting go of the dream, and thereby not dealing with the discomfort. He suggests, however, that inspired performers are those who are able to live with the tension and begin to move the reality toward the vision. You can do this by generating ways to make your visions real. If you try to accomplish something every day that moves you toward your vision, and

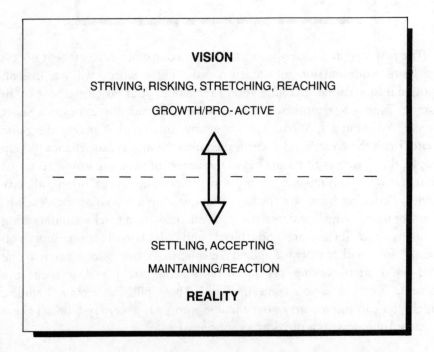

VISION

STRIVING, RISKING, STRETCHING, REACHING

GROWTH/PRO-ACTIVE

SETTLING, ACCEPTING

MAINTAINING/REACTION

REALITY

you take time each day to congratulate yourself and feel good about this accomplishment, you will find yourself energized by your work toward your vision.

A person can be motivated by his or her current reality, the status quo, or by a vision of what can be. People connecting only to current reality are committed to a steady state. They are reactive, they settle for or accept the way things are. In contrast, the more you are motivated by a vision, the more you are stretching, risking, striving, and reaching. You are growing toward your vision, and you need to be creative, because you are continually trying to make reality more like your vision.

ORGANIZATIONAL MISSION AND PURPOSE

Just as individuals need visions, values, and missions, so do organizations. In recent years, management theorists have linked the success of an organization to its ability to be meaningful for the people who work there. When people feel that the organization they work for does something worthwhile, they are willing to give more of themselves. They also have more to give.

The challenge to find meaning in what you do is at the core of the new work ethic. Employees want more than just a paycheck from their work. They want to feel connected to their organization's mission and vision. They look toward the organization as a place where they can grow and accomplish their own personal vision as well as the organization's larger purpose.

An organization is a group of people engaged in a common enterprise. Individuals join the enterprise with the hope of receiving rewards for their participation. These rewards are often largely economic, but also include psychological, social, and physical benefits. Increasingly today employees are adding to the list of rewards they want the opportunity for recognition and the ability to make a contribution. They also consider the health of the working environment and the company's support of their own well-being. People also join organizations because they want to be part of them; they want to identify with what the organization does.

Just as the individual worker strives to gain rewards from the organization, the organization also derives rewards from individual contributors. When an organization has a clear sense of its purpose, direction, and desired future and when this image is widely shared, the organization and the people who work there all benefit.

John Young, head of Hewlett-Packard, reflects this connection when he says, "Successful companies have a consensus from top to bottom on a set of overall goals. The most brilliant management strategy will fail if that consensus is missing." Another way of putting this is that all people in the organization are aligned with a shared purpose. Individuals who experience alignment feel empowered, because they are able to see themselves as part of a larger worthwhile enterprise. When people feel this sense of connectedness they feel they can make a difference, and usually do.

Russell Ackoff, a prominent management theorist, describes mission as "a very general purpose that can endow everyone in an organization and all they do with a sense of purpose. . . . It can be to planning what the Holy Grail was to the Crusades." * People who are aligned with the corporate mission feel very different from those who feel forced to go in a direction not in agreement with their own aims.

Ackoff goes on to say in his book *Creating the Corporate Future* that companies and individuals create their own social framework when they attach significance to certain actions and beliefs. On this framework of meaning and context the stakeholders can base their commitment. This sense of mission provides members of the organization with a way to behave toward each other. It serves as a control mechanism, sanctioning or prohibiting particular kinds of behavior. Mission forms the overriding direction guiding the organization forward.

One of the most noticeable innovations of the new workstyle is companies' involving their employees in the creation and re-creation of the mission and vision. Traditional management starts with the assumption that employees need and want clear, strong direction. The new workstyle starts with another assumption: Good employees will act in the best interests of the company if they are provided with the information, the tools, and the opportunity to use them, and if they participate in connecting the company mission with their individual missions. They can help create their own direction.

* Russell L. Ackoff, *Creating the Corporate Future: Plan or Be Planned For* (New York: John Wiley & Sons, 1981), p. 107.

BUILDING ALIGNMENT WITH COMPANY MISSION

Observers of entrepreneurial leaders have noticed something they call "entrepreneur's disease." This takes root in a company where the leader thinks that he (it usually is a he) is the only one that has any ideas. At first, people are excited about working with this fountain of energy and creativity. But nobody can be right all the time. Employees begin to see mistakes, unexpected difficulties, and new possibilities. But the entrepreneur thinks he is the only person allowed to be creative—the others in the company are there to listen. This attitude begins to alienate loyal supporters, who begin to withdraw. In many companies, the creative leader is supplanted by a new CEO, who is more able to bring others into the process.

One new CEO came into such a company. He was hired because of his experience in another industry, but he had strong ideas about what needed to be done in his new company. The first thing he did was to call meetings of small groups of managers. He would first share his vision, his sense of the future. Then he said, "But I really don't know much about this industry or this place. So, I want to hear from each of you. What do you think? Go ahead and tear up my ideas—better to do it now than to have the marketplace tear them up for us." The sessions were very helpful, and everyone in the company got involved. Everyone felt a part of the resulting mission statement and business plan, and it represented the best of everyone's ideas. It was hugely successful.

Increasingly, companies are hiring workers based on a set of values. They seek employees who share their vision. The head of an engineering company points out, "If you don't do this, you'll be sitting on a time bomb." He would rather have an employee with half the academic credentials and twice the team spirit, because without that he has nothing.

Creating Synergy

Everyone in a company needs to be aligned with the company's mission. The result of such alignment is synergy. Synergy develops when you know where the company stands, where it is going, where you stand within it, and how your own work connects to the goals. In the traditional team model, the leader, executive, or manager says, "This is what we are doing. Here's how we will do it. OK, let's go." Then what happens? People silently ask themselves why. They say to themselves, "I think it could be done much better," or they just do not see how what they are doing connects to the whole. Usually the members of the team will find themselves distancing, lowering their energy, bringing less than their full selves to work.

Why does this happen? First, people need to see the connection of their work with the organization as a whole. In Warren Bennis's study of visionary leaders, he noted that their employees always knew where they stood. Even though the company grew and changed, there were certain basic principles that the leader and the group stood for. In some companies, it is easy for employees to say, "This is our kind of product," or "This is our kind of marketing campaign." In contrast, some companies, especially large conglomerates, found themselves drifting because they had no overall theme or corporate purpose. Some, like Transamerica and Quaker Oats, pared themselves back down, to keep their business in areas where they are known.

But more is required for synergy. In a work team where everyone feels trust, respect, and personal power, but does not know what the group is doing and how, the members might all take off in different directions, producing chaos, or at least working at cross purposes. For example, in one company Bob starts planning a project, while Jerry is working on something overlapping and Sue is doing something completely unrelated, but counting on Bob and Jerry to help her. Real confusion, and not much of a group. In traditional work teams the leader would coordinate and keep people on track.

What if everyone in the team knows in a personal way what the team is trying to accomplish? They then see clearly how an effort fits into the whole. People are empowered to make decisions and connect them to the overall effort. They know when to coordinate and when to check with others on the team, but do not feel constrained when immediate action is needed. The whole team is in a state of synergy. People are empowered to act as individuals, but they know enough to fit their activities into the whole team's mission, without a boss looking over their shoulder or checking up on them.

James MacGregor Burns, the political scientist and author of *Leadership,* writes of a new phenomenon, *transforming leadership,* which he sees emerging:

> The transforming leader seeks to satisfy higher needs, and engages
> the full person of the follower. The result of transforming leadership
> is a relationship of mutual stimulation and elevation that converts

followers into leaders. . . . Their purposes, which might have started out as separate but related, become fused. Power bases are linked not as counterweights but as mutual support for common purpose. . . . The leaders throw themselves into relationship with followers who will feel "elevated" by it and often become more active themselves, thereby creating new cadres of leaders.*

Creating and disseminating the company mission statement helps insure a connection between individual and company mission. In the old style, top management wrote the mission statement. This left a number of employees —the implementers—out of the process. Another problem with this strategy was that the statements were long-winded and often dealt solely with the economic side of the company. The new workstyle encourages a process that involves the greatest number of employees.

A large-scale employee involvement effort, such as a company-crafted mission, takes commitment and careful implementation. Because this is often a new style for managers, they need coaching in the new values that this approach assumes as well as skills in creating participation. People will not all of a sudden begin to participate if they have not been encouraged in the past. They need to believe that the company and their supervisor are really serious about wanting their opinion. At mission-generating meetings the focus is on how the values and mission of the individual fit with the mission and vision of the company. These conversations can lead to a release of individual spirit that money cannot buy.

This special energy and spirit are noticeable from the very beginning in working with a new-style company. When we entered the Nissan plant in Tennessee we saw all the workers dressed in what appeared to be identical blue pit crew suits. This was not just the attire for the line workers, but for the office workers and managers as well. Everyone's name was embroidered on his or her pocket, creating an instant nametag. This meant anyone could talk to anyone else without feeling embarrassed about not knowing a name. It also created an atmosphere where it was hard to tell "them" from "us." This simple policy created a spirit of camaraderie. The uniforms also re-minded everyone of the main work—building trucks. The suits helped show that the company worked hard to connect the individuals' feelings about their work to the larger corporate mission.

* James MacGregor Burns, *Leadership* (New York: Harper & Row, 1979), p. 78.

Developing a mission involves the review of the organization's purposes, goals, and values, not just at top levels but throughout the entire organization. When we consult with a new company, we ask employees at random what the mission of their company is. If a large percentage do not know, they are not being as productive as they could be. This clarity is not the result of clearly written memos, circulated widely, but of a group process in which a manager or supervisor leads a discussion, like a quality circle, asking team members what they think the mission is. This process sets in motion a way for employees to find how their personal values fit with the values of the company.

L. L. Bean, a mighty mail-order outdoor equipment distributor, is another company that powerfully transmits its mission. Bean achieved this level of efficiency by motivating even temporary employees with its vision. With many seasonal employees, it is surprising that Bean invests up to one week of training for everyone who works at the company. This process includes a film on the history of Bean, introduction to the quality circle process, the values of the originator, including L. L.'s favorite sayings—such as, "A customer is not dependent on us, we are dependent on him." Going through orientation, new employees also learn about the performance management monitoring system, in which vital statistics, such as how often customers are sent orders, are posted daily. Productivity and accuracy records for each stock picker and packer are maintained. Bean uses them to decide how much each worker should be paid. This attention to imparting the values and communicating with workers creates an intense sense of loyalty and high productivity.

This process can be critical to the future involvement of employees. A branch manager in one company and his entire management team formulated a mission that excited them. The branch manager was asked ahead of time to review corporate communications relating to the purpose and values of the company. He collected a substantial pile of papers, memos, annual reports, and a famed "mission statement." Many important values were expressed, but the volume of communications was so great that managers were confused about what they were to be doing. The session started with a quiz: "In 20 words or less, what is the mission of your company?" Everyone's ideas went up on the board, and this started a discussion of the purpose of the company, the task of the branch, and everyone's roles and responsibilities. After several sessions they reached a condensed statement of the branch mission.

Long-winded mission statements are hard to understand and do not tend to carry the emotional "goosebumps" that allow everyone to feel excited. We ask groups to distill their purpose to a three-word phrase that can be said almost as if it were a cheer at a sports event. This branch group came up with, "Sell like hell, collect like heck, have fun!" That was what was left from all those memos and statements. Everyone could understand it. It helped them focus their work and made them laugh at the same time.

Individuals can buy in to the company mission, but in some ways individual missions do not overlap with that of the company. For example, a person can have professional goals—perhaps involving recognition and achievement within a professional group—that may be only partly connected with their company work. A company could often ignore these areas of non-overlap, or allow a person time off for professional development or to do community activities as a job benefit. But more recently, companies have begun to work to integrate personal goals with organizational goals. For example, many midcareer managers pursue graduate degrees while they work. The company can invest in their development, even if it is not directly job related. Some companies even find ways to help managers do research projects for their M.B.A.'s on topics that are helpful to both the student and the company. They contribute released time and some company resources to the project.

The company has much to gain by working to integrate the personal/professional goals of its people. These accommodations are all ways to help the individual invest in the company. They say that the person matters for who he is, not just what he is producing. Yankelovich notes that this feeling of being valued for oneself is one of the key shifts in the new work agreement he sees evolving. One company that goes far in promoting this integration is Wilson Learning Company. The staff of one division gets together each week, and each person talks about his personal learning goals for that week and how his work will help accomplish them. Expanding the company to fit the personal goals helps the staff feel involved enough to contribute the highest level of creative energy to the company.

CHANGING MISSION

Feeling connected to the larger company mission is an important component to enhancing motivation. People work with more spirit when they feel connected. Recent research on motivation shows that the first reason people choose for coming to work is not how much money they make but how they *feel* working there.

Shared values and beliefs are the glue binding individuals to the organization in the new workplace. Companies often think that this mutuality occurs automatically when you receive notice of employment. Companies thereby misuse one of the most powerful opportunities for introducing employees to the values and beliefs of the organization: new employee orientation. This is the time for the employee to grasp the overall picture of the new work community. Companies can neglect this opportunity to communicate fully with their new workers by mistakenly focusing the orientation narrowly on personnel issues, like salary, retirement, vacations, sick time, and filling out forms. What this format says to the new employee is that this company values policy and procedure over the individual's contribution. The first step in creating the new workstyle is to use this opportunity to illuminate the corporate mission and vision and show how the new employees can be part of them. Most employees are looking for a way to connect to the values and beliefs of the company.

While going through a shift in mission, from service to marketing, a large utility company was hiring new workers to supplement their existing crews. They wanted to find a way to spread this new marketing spirit through the company. As consultant, Cynthia reformulated new employee orientation to be a learning event about the values of the company. This was the point where the new workers had their first glimpse of the company. If they learned from the start about the new direction as well as its core values, they would understand their jobs in a new way, as part of a larger vision.

Senior employees participated in the orientation, sharing stories about the company that embodied the strong spirit and values that formed the foundation of the company. A retired line foreman told how the crews had pulled through difficult storms, restoring the power to stranded residents in rural areas. These stories represented the service value that the company had grown its roots in. They provided a mythic way of translating the past mission to the new recruits, more effectively than any memo. To seed the new direction, the division manager led a discussion with the new employees about the direction of the company and how they could be part of building it. The old values were celebrated and the new values introduced.

Employees' satisfaction is closely tied to their feeling of support on the job. Most people came to this utility not knowing one other person in the whole company. This division alone had 3,000 employees. An important goal of new employee orientation was to introduce them not only to the mission of the company but to each other. Taking time to get to know one another emphasized the company's interest in teamwork and the importance of pulling together. To accomplish this we asked the new employees to create a picture of themselves on the job, using colored markers, magazine pictures, stickers, and imagination to create symbols of their work. Each person stood up, introduced himself or herself, and talked about the new job, using the picture to illustrate the presentation. The new people told what they did, how they got their jobs, and what was exciting for them. They then taped their pictures onto a wall-size chart of the organization, showing everyone where they fit. This became a map of new life for the organization. It was left up in the cafeteria as a recognition poster, until the next set of new employees went through orientation. This introduction ceremony gave each person a chance to meet thirty other people who were also learning the ropes. It set up an informal network between employees in various divisions. They now had someone they could call when they had a question about another part of the operation.

There is no cut-and-dried way to create a mission shift. Each example is unique to the company that invented it. Strategies are created to match the company culture and reflect its values. Copying anyone else's style of transmitting company mission and vision will not work.

Visioning can be a creative process to help a company discover some important points about itself and its direction. Wayne Silby, founder and chairman of the Calvert Social Investment Fund, the first socially responsible investment group, has a business card that reads "Chief Daydreamer." Part of the way he sees his job is to help everybody who works there use visioning to see the company differently. For example, his desire to explore people's inner creativity led him to an experiment, creating a corporate logo using the ancient Chinese oracle *I Ching*. Another project to help the company explore its inner visions involved hiring a consultant to interview employees about the history, myth, and tradition of the company. The interviews went from the normal business history to talk about people's own inner pictures of the company, including questions like "If the company was an animal, what would it be?" The resulting booklet is given to all employees. Silby sees such interventions as part of a continuous process of corporate self-discovery.

SHIFTING WORK GROUP MISSION
· ·

Work groups can work their way out of burnout to create a renewed sense of mission. The need to bring a work group through a shift in values is going to be increasingly common, with the increase of divestitures, mergers, downsizings, and consolidations.

Any time a major change is undertaken there is always the hazard that values and beliefs useful in the past will become obstacles. A prime example of this is AT&T's transition from a service-oriented telephone utility to a market-oriented communications business. This transformation required that one out of every three of the million jobs in AT&T be changed. Some of the deeply held values of the organization—such as "We never lay anyone off" and "There will always be a place for you in the Bell System"—were challenged. The organization began operating under different values—such as "Performance matters" and "Accountability at all levels." Many employees felt they had been abandoned, and indeed they had. The company they had signed up to work for was now gone. The basic values that guided the organization were under revision. The social architecture was now being rebuilt to support a different direction.

The first wave of this massive reorientation was set in motion when Chairman John DeButts went on intracompany TV to announce to every employee, "We will become a marketing company." Then he found that saying it did not necessarily make it so. A shift of this magnitude in the culture of a company that had developed such a strong architecture is like trying to shift the shape of the pyramids overnight. The process of creating a new mission and realigning the employees is a massive project.

These shifts happen in educational institutions as well. Cynthia spent three years on the faculty at a prestigious health sciences campus as part of a team redesigning the mission of one of their primary care programs. For years the mission had been to provide staff for underserved, rural areas. This particular program had trained over 500 new health care providers, among whom 80 percent had stayed in their rural location.

The health care system was just beginning to accept these new professionals, and increasing numbers of people were interested in becoming nurse practitioners and physician's assistants to participate in primary care in rural and urban areas. In addition, the values of health care were shifting to include greater participation from the patient and different modes of professional training. The demand for nurse practitioners and physician's assistants increased as the program was successful. The school needed, as in any business, to adapt to new markets and settings. This goal required the re-visioning of the mission this new health professional would play in the health care team and rethinking of the mission of the entire department.

They began this shift with a values exercise at a re-visioning retreat. The consultant chose several sets of contrasting values, like patient-focused care and professional-focused care, and asked each faculty member to stand on an imaginary line, at the position indicating how he or she felt about each set of values. After people took their positions, they looked around the room to see where their colleagues were. They told the people next to them why they were where they were. They all had to decide where they stood and to see where their colleagues stood before deciding where they were going. Just as in the business examples cited earlier, it was very important that the group feel aligned with a vision.

For educators it was important that personal values match the values of the proposed curriculum. To change the curriculum, the faculty had to discuss differences that had shown up on the values voting. A few faculty members who held different values had difficulty proceeding in this new direction. After extensive reflection they decided to opt out of further participation in the new program. The process gave them the chance to see that their values did not fit the new direction. A similar thing happens in most organizations that go through a reorientation of values. Some people will leave based on values and mission disagreement.

Many companies do not know how to harness the power that comes from aligning the mission and vision of the individual with those of the organization. Many companies settle for surface indicators of agreement and ignore the deeper values and beliefs. Many of the more entrepreneurial companies are experimenting with ways to create value-based organizations. The new work ethic and workstyle management strategies bring this clearly into focus. In our Visionary Manager seminar we have found that the same techniques that are successful helping individuals develop their mission and vision also work for groups. The exercises in this chapter for defining mission and vision can be done with individuals or work groups.

Management groups have embarked on wilderness adventures, jumping out of airplanes and scaling mountains, in efforts to produce this team spirit. It takes single-minded agreement to get a whole team up a mountain using ropes. Reaching this focused alignment often transfers back to the work setting. We use a less strenuous approach, engaging work groups in visioning processes where they create an overall mission and vision for their work group and then for the whole company.

Organizational success takes more than clear mission and vision. It takes *commitment* to translate new values into personnel policies and succession plans. It takes *perseverance* to create new products that fit your values and mission. It takes *stamina* to sort through new employees, making choices based on their values as well as technical skills. It takes *tenacity* to reorient a group of employees to a new corporate mission, involving them in the process, so they feel committed to the new direction.

CHAPTER 4

GROWING THROUGH TRANSITIONS: BECOMING A CHANGE MASTER

I heard one unhappily perceptive young man say of his work that he felt as though he were at the Twenty-third Street subway station and could see all the way to Seventy-seventh Street—and that he hated the notion of a life-trip spent entirely in a subway tunnel. Such distress is not the decree of fate, but a signal. For those of us who have already committed years to one profession, feelings of terror are likely to accompany that signal; a feeling that starting over is now impossible, or that "giving up what one has" would cost too much. Such are the pains of growth and transition.

—RICHARD GROSSMAN, *CHOOSING AND CHANGING*

Life today has many transition points, job changes, forced shifts, and choices. Today, a person entering the job market, even at a professional level, can expect at least five major job shifts before retirement. While upheaval can come from external shifts and crises—a failing company, for example—often the need for change comes from inner signals such as restlessness, boredom, or burnout.

Both you and your job are probably changing. The changes can be unexpected, sudden, and extensive. New ownership, direction, procedures, and economic and regulatory climates change the face of your company. Some people welcome these shifts; some are apprehensive about them. Whatever your feelings, you can learn to cope with these transitions.

This most likely will not be the last major change for you. As futurist Alvin Toffler predicted twenty years ago, we live in an age of accelerating change, or future shock. Change has been increasing in intensity in the last fifty years. Americans have been experiencing future shock more and more as change takes place at a faster pace than ever before. Toffler said, "Change is avalanching upon our heads and most people are grotesquely unprepared to cope with it." People who develop the skills to manage in the face of drastic, even continual, transition will be the most successful. You cannot afford to ignore these skills.

Job loss in smokestack industries is widespread, along with the realization that those jobs will never return. Twelve million workers lost their jobs because of plant closings or cutbacks between 1979 and 1984. In 1985 a downturn in the semiconductor industry resulted in the elimination of over 60,000 jobs.

Being in transition affects you as well as your company. What do these transition times mean for you? How can you plan for the uncertain future? The information in this chapter comes from the experiences of many organizations during change and from research on people who perform well during transition. It is designed to help you learn the key skills for becoming a *change master,* not a change victim.

When going through transition, it is natural to wish that the current changes never happened. You may have intense feelings about the disruption. But you cannot wish them away. You can, however, plan and manage your own way through times of transition. This chapter will help you stay afloat, and manage the effects of change on you.

People become burned out and disconnected from work when they are out of sync with changes taking place around them. Burnout is often an avoidance of changes that need to be made. The signs of burnout—feeling deenergized, a low sense of accomplishment, and estranged from your work —often emerge to cover up the fear of making a change. A person coming to such a shift point cannot simply change work or life situation. Transitions demand major inner self-renewal and restructuring. The personal stress of change, research has shown, affects one's health. The individual must allow time and space for the emotional shifts, because emotional reserves are often exhausted by a change.

Many people do not allow themselves time to recover from a layoff, a personal loss, or a crisis, and then they wonder why they cannot sleep or why they cannot be fully effective at work. In a company undergoing a major downsizing, we found the effects of the layoffs to be evident in the surviving workers for many months. Supervisors and managers needed special briefings to understand the normal signs of transition and assist their employees through this process.

Burnout can be the signal for a major life transition. The person who is burned out can be the last to discover it. Often family members or coworkers discover that your spark of excitement is lost and your performance has gone flat. Environmental adjustments, such as rearranging your office or taking a vacation, are not enough. Completing the renewal process usually includes shifts in attitude as well as activity.

One way that people attempt to make sense out of transition is to examine the rubble on which the new structures are built. The notion of building on the old is ancient. The nine cities of Troy were each built on the ruins of the city before them. The challenge facing our culture today is to navigate the changes and shifts toward the future without losing the roots of where we have come from.

This becomes the question not just for our society but for each of us in our personal and work lives. How do we reclaim the initial fire and passion from the rubble of our personal and work foundation and use the masonry to reconstruct the new workplaces and relationships?

CAREER AND WORK CYCLES

Human beings are not static; they are growing, changing creatures. Therefore, as your skills, interests, involvements, even values and sources of satisfaction change at different stages of your life, you will find yourself looking for different ways to connect to your work. Your connection to work depends on your being able to find a harmony with your changing life stages and needs.

Think of your entire life as a ruler. The first section is childhood, then a period of formal education, then work career, with retirement around age sixty-five as the goal, and a retirement stage to conclude. That is the traditional life cycle.

Many changes have transformed that neat sequence into a relic. More often our lives are made up of increasingly smaller and smaller segments of experience, which move more in a spiral fashion, turning back around in yet a different form. More and more people move from one kind of involvement to another. Parents move in and out of the work force and care for their children. People interrupt school with work and work with school. Transition periods may last different periods of time. A job loss may lead to a year traveling, or it may be the impetus for a new family business. People also switch from the nonprofit sector to the profit sector and then back again. People do not retire but start new interests. Many artists and craftspeople learn their trades after their first retirement. Life is becoming less like a ruler and more like a spiral.

Mitch Kapor, the founder of Lotus, the large computer software company, is one example. His early career included several periods of schooling and part-time work ranging from being a meditation teacher to a disk jockey. Then he took up the hobby of computer programming and sold a program for just under a million dollars, what seemed like a fortune. He could have retired, but he looked for a new challenge, as many members of the new inner-directed workforce do. He created an integrated software package called 1-2-3, and founded Lotus, a company that embodies the new workstyle. After the company grew and went public, and after a period of soul searching, he did what is characteristic of many of the new seekers at work today, but what was unthinkable in the past: He just quit and walked away from it all. He had recently married and had a small child, and there was much that he wanted to learn. In an interview with *Inc. Magazine* (January 1987), Kapor says about his decision to leave Lotus:

> I did not jump, nor was I pushed. Fundamentally, my leaving was a function of the company's growth, of my own growth. I will always be somebody who is highly motivated by things I regard as challenges, and I tend to be terribly unmotivated by—if not outright resistant to

—anything else. And because Lotus grew so large so fast, it rapidly ceased to play that central role in helping me give meaning to my life. And therefore, the honorable and responsible thing for me to do— and the best thing for me and for the 1,350 employees and for several million customers and all of that—was to remove myself from the company sooner rather than later.

While many people are pushed into transition, just as many, like Kapor, create their own changes. They find that what was fulfilling at one stage is no longer best. It is hard to imagine oneself leaving a job to do something else, or leaving a university teaching job to go to law or medical school, but that is what people today are doing. They are starting small businesses and moving to new environments. As people come to live longer, parents are making career shifts when their children are grown. One psychologist went to graduate school when her daughters were grown, after her own divorce, and received her doctorate a year before her daughter did, from the same school.

Create a picture of your own life cycle on a piece of paper, noting the turning points, the unexpected and chosen shift points. Think about each major shift and what started it. Envision what shifts you may want to make in your near and far future, and which ones you may need to make. One way to design your life and your work is to anticipate change, to face your life transitions with as much awareness as possible. Most people face a major transition every five years!

LIFELONG LEARNING

Lifelong learning is increasingly the norm. A recent estimate by an executive at General Motors is that GM employees need complete retraining every four years. What we learned in school is right now becoming obsolete. No more are we trained for life. Since work is shifting from industrial-based and labor-intensive to service- and information-based, we will need to shift from traditional work patterns. We will have to make, sell, service, and operate new products and new machines.

Lifelong learning strains our traditional education system, which is by and large geared for younger learners. Organizations are finding that they are benefiting when they set up their own "corporate universities," complete with curricula, diplomas, and commencements, to renew the skills and visions of their workers.

These corporate learning centers have two functions. First, they train and retrain the work force. Second, and in keeping with our Two Job concept, the most innovative of them are also teaching managers the new workstyle and how to learn. One example is the corporate college of American Medical International, one of the nation's largest hospital corporations. AMI perceived a need to rethink the whole way that the organization was designed. How could that be accomplished? Not with an edict from the CEO. No, the key managers of each hospital had to agree upon and learn about the new values and the new style of management. AMI assembled a faculty that included Warren Bennis as dean, and many of the foremost management pioneers as designers of the curriculum. Then, key executives came to a week-long retreat, followed by a program at their home hospitals. The college has been a systemwide success, helping AMI create and carry out a complete redesign of the company.

This is a preventive way for an organization to manage transition. Similarily, individuals are seeking seminars, training programs like est, and other personal development experiences to help them learn the skills of change. If your company does not have a corporate college like AMI, you may have to create your own curriculum to prepare yourself for challenges you never were taught to face at school.

Increasingly people are finding that they want to make some turns at midlife. The Fielding Institute, in Santa Barbara, California, and Saybrook Institute in San Francisco, are specially set up to accommodate the needs of professionals in this phase of life. The average age of students in these graduate programs is forty-three. The programs are designed to fit the mid-career student with work and family obligations. Their external degree model enables the students to work in geographic clusters on learning plans that fit their personal and professional goals.

Many people in transition feel like they are falling apart. They need a structure where they can explore their values and goals in both their personal and professional arenas. Frequently people turn to outplacement services for this process and find themselves in groups writing new resumes. This midcareer discovery is being treated in a special way at the newly formed Mid-life Development Institute (MDI), headquartered in Santa Barbara, California. Situated in seventy-five cities nationwide, this six-month-long program provides a format, with other people in this same stage, to explore and grapple with core values, mission and vision, and the process of translating insights into meaningful work. It is important to take time during these midcareer transitions and not try to create a quick fix by abruptly changing jobs, marriages, or geographic locations.

WHEN IS IT TIME TO CHANGE JOBS?

Americans change jobs about every four years. Even then, some people wait too long. There are risks for leaving too soon as well as staying too long. One way to think about whether you have been in one place too long is to ask, "Have I had four years of experience with my current employer, or one year of experience repeated four times?" If you find yourself at the top of a career ladder maybe it is time to find a new ladder.

First take a look inside your department. What happens to people who work there for a long time? Can you anticipate a promotion or a lateral transfer into another area of your interest in the next two years? Are you reporting to someone who will not be retiring for years and years? Have you been passed over for a promotion? Do not get caught standing still while others are moving. Are you ready for more responsibility while you find yourself stuck in the slow lane? Have you been able to establish a mutually valuable relationship with your boss? Occasional disagreements are predictable, but if there really is not a way for you to work together then it is time to move on.

Is your body giving you signs of dissatisfaction? Have you had unexplained depression, accidents, insomnia, irritability? Your body will start "voting" for coming in late, taking a lot of sick days, and getting ready to leave early.

If this sounds like you, take a moment to answer these twenty questions below to see if you should in fact leave your job. There is no specific number of "yeses" that means you should move on; only you can decide when you have reached your quota.

1. Have you been in your current position for more than three years?
2. Have you failed to gain new responsibilities in recent months?
3. Have you learned nothing new in the last six months?
4. Do you find your days routine?

5. Do you think you are in a dead end job?
6. Is your workload too demanding?
7. Do you feel a lack of challenge?
8. Are you feeling overwhelmed and anxious and tense?
9. Do you hate to get up in the morning?
10. Has your salary been frozen, or have you had difficulty getting deserved raises?
11. Do you no longer care about your work?
12. Do you find that values that were important to you earlier have shifted?
13. Have you been given extra work because of layoffs?
14. Do you find you have a difference in workstyle or a different philosophy from your boss?
15. Have you had difficulty getting along with your boss?
16. Are you working for a workaholic who wants you to be one also?
17. Does your boss give you negative feedback and little or no praise?
18. Do you have a hard time getting coworkers to cooperate with you?
19. Do you sense you are being left out of the informal political network in your company?
20. Have you stayed in situations before too long, even if you were unhappy?

Reviewing these questions will help you decide when it is time to move.

THE NEW RETIREMENT

The idea of retirement is going through some important rethinking. Not everyone dreams of retirement at the end of a long work career. Retirement can have an adverse effect on the health of people who were accustomed to active lives. Increasingly, people are not waiting for retirement to renew themselves. They are taking a sabbatical break at midcareer for rest and renewal. Once the privilege of tenured university professors, a paid leave away from the regular job is being offered to employees of more and more corporations. Lawrence Livermore Laboratories encourages midcareer professionals to take time off for renewal. Participants in this program have taken up gardening, climbed the Himalayas, and joined VISTA as ways of finding renewal. The program has paid off in the retention of highly creative professionals within the organization, and it has minimized the occurrence of medical and behavorial problems.

DANGER AND OPPORTUNITY

Transitions are opportunities for growth. Each one represents a stepping stone from which you spring on to the next level of life experience. This concept is embodied in the Chinese character for change, which combines the symbols representing danger and opportunity.

Burnout can be turned into a positive signal to initiate a transition from one endeavor to another. This is often the case with individuals who have lost sight of the original reason that they went into a particular field. For example, Bill, a human resources executive, had been a fighter pilot in the Navy for a number of years before entering his present field. He took great pleasure in the freedom of flying and missed the excitement very much. After a particularly challenging position as director of human resources, Bill entered a slump, feeling that his work was not fulfilling and that he just could not face another day. He applied for a disability leave because he was having numerous physical complaints. Both his body and spirit were burned out.

Bill's renewal process led him to explore his original mission in entering the human resources field and the satisfactions that he drew from it. Revisiting his original dreams and seeing how they were not being nurtured were important parts of his recovery.

He also took time to reconnect with friends that he had become "too busy" for and recognized the importance of his work relationships. The third part of Bill's renewal was taking time to listen to himself and his needs. He yearned to "fly free," unencumbered by a large corporate structure. The human resources activities were not wrong; his work environment was.

This realization encouraged him to leave his position and move into a setting that allowed him more independent judgment and initiative. Renewal is not instant. It requires self-examination and willingness to make changes. Just as burnout does not suddenly appear, neither does the renewal process finish overnight. There are many paths to renewal. Most important is to spot burnout before the flames consume the whole spirit. There are many opportunities to prevent burnout before it takes hold.

NORMAL RESPONSES TO CHANGE

Nothing ever remains the same. Everything is in perpetual motion. There may be short rest periods between life changes, but sooner or later there will be another wave of change. Change affects the workplace. After an acquisition or a major policy or administrative shift, there is often a climate of mistrust and suspicion. People do not know where they stand. They get worried. Rumors fly, and clear information is scarce. People do not know whom they can trust. They worry about being blamed and feel like it is every man and woman for themselves. Work often becomes paralyzed as people are not sure what to do or whether their work will mean anything.

The stress of change leads to:

- *Physical signals,* such as major pain, headaches, rashes, flu, or, in contrast, increased energy and vitality
- *Emotional signals,* such as anxiety, anger, fear, frustration, or, in contrast, excitement and exhilaration
- *Mental signals,* such as worry, confusion, distraction, or, in contrast, increased questioning, personal planning, and clarity.

These signals influence job performance. They may lead you to take time off or withdraw emotionally while on the job. You may consequently make poor, impulsive, or ill-considered career choices. On the other hand, you may switch into high gear and move yourself ahead in a new way.

HOW CHANGE AFFECTS YOU

Not every transition is voluntary. You may enter a transition when your job is phased out and you are laid off, or you may need retraining because you want to undertake a new career. People do not welcome such transitions. They bring on all kinds of feelings: worry, doubt, anger, and shock. This is predictable, because a transition marks the ending of one phase and the beginning of a new one. Any time you go through a separation or a loss of any type, the uncertainty causes concern.

Any merger, acquisition, or other organizational change has many effects. Like a rock thrown in a pond, change ripples throughout the company, causing disruption, excitement, distress, and sometimes crisis. Your usual ways of doing things, your expectations about your job, are now in question. In place of clarity there is uncertainty. At first, nobody can say for sure how things will turn out.

Organizations often undertake special efforts to make the transition easier. They engage in team building to rekindle work spirit. They sponsor celebrations that mark the change and acknowledge the new positions and organizational structure. For example, one large bank sponsored a series of commercials in acquired banks, where they showed a single person rowing a boat in a large current; then they showed a twelve-man sculling shell breezing along. The message was clear: the new organization had a larger team that you could call on for help.

In times of change, there are also things that *you* need to do, to take care of yourself and make sure you land on both feet. Personal change management can help you avoid illness and distress, and can make you more effective throughout this period of transition.

Continuing work while your job is in transition involves managing situations that are uncertain and sometimes confusing. While change affects everything and everybody, it does not affect everybody equally. Some people come through it easily, while others get sick, become immobilized by worry and confusion, and have problems maintaining an adequate level of performance.

And, most curiously, some people come through change with major increases in their performance level. They grow and thrive within the transition. You can become one of these change-hardy people, if you develop the skills of change management.

YOUR BODY LETS YOU KNOW

Managing transition is not just a performance issue; it is a health issue as well. Studying thousands of people starting just after World War II, physicians Thomas Holmes and Richard Rahe explored the connection between life changes and illness. Their found that after a major life change, or a series of minor changes, people are likely to experience some type of illness or an accident. Adjustment to change demands a lot of our energy. This is true of positive as well as negative changes. A promotion, a move to a new, bigger house, while exciting, also calls on our attention and energy. Too much good, like overeating a great meal, can strain the body.

A recent study by Cognos Associates on the high-tech layoffs in Silicon Valley showed that two-thirds of people recently laid off reported some physical effects, and 20 percent reported health problems requiring a doctor's care or hospitalization. The solution to this difficulty is not to avoid change but to maintain yourself carefully through the change process.

RESISTANCE TO CHANGE

While change is continual, it is hardly ever welcome. Resistance is natural and predictable. Letting go of the old ways is a kind of death. You need to say goodbye, and even go through a kind of grief and mourning for the old ways. Some companies have even had goodbye ceremonies, or organizational wakes.

Some of the reasons people resist change are:

1. Your expectations are disrupted, and therefore your sense of security. All of a sudden you are not sure where you stand.
2. You are reminded that your power is limited. Experiencing that sense of powerlessness sometimes brings up anxiety.
3. You secretly doubt your ability to make it through.
4. Changes can make you look and feel awkward, like a child learning to ride a bike. You may feel embarrassed to say that you do not know something.

If resistance to change is natural and to be expected, what can be done? You can plan for and acknowledge these resistances. Keep yourself focused on what lies ahead, not what has gone before. It is important to acknowledge the normal feelings of grief, anger, and loss that accompany transitions. Many companies pretend these feelings do not exist and consequently have to deal with resistance to the new organizational forms expressed in unclear ways.

For example, some people quietly stop asking any questions and just try to do the minimum and not be noticed. Others resent the changes, and they subtly do everything they can to mess things up. They would deny this if they were found out; they may not even do it consciously. Still others are so paralyzed by fear that they simply cannot work up to capacity, and so they appear much less competent to their new superiors.

MAPPING YOUR TRANSITION

One of the key predictors of how people will manage change is how they think about change. What is often most disorienting about change is that the "meaning" of the change is not clear. Many people can endure great hardship when they understand the purpose and meaning of the change. But other changes do not have clear and easy meanings. People ask "Why me?" or "Why did this have to happen?" Sometimes, people have to create their own meanings for events that seem unfair or unnecessary. Pain and anger block people from planning their next steps.

To better understand this confused feeling in the middle of a transition, imagine that you had decided to take your sailboat out for a spin. You set sail from one mooring toward a destination further down the coast. Everything is going along smoothly until, at a midpoint in your journey, you realize that the port toward which you were navigating is not where you thought it was. Looking back, you see that your starting point is lost in fog. You are in the middle, moving forward and not able to go back. Many people in transition feel as if they have let go of one way of understanding their life and work and are not yet sure of the new pattern. Seeing transitions as welcome times of growth, occurring periodically all through life, enables you to harness your energy to make the best of these times.

Transition happens through periodic accelerations and transformations, with periods of disorientation and reorientation. In nature, change often moves along slowly until suddenly the bank erodes away or the branch blossoms. The signs of our own personal transitions may be less clear than in nature but nonetheless exhilarating. Anticipating these disruptions and shifts allows you to move through a natural process of self-renewal and rebalancing.

Change researcher Bill Bridges notes that it is not change that is hard, it is the time of transition after the change that calls on our creativity. "In transitions we come to beginnings only at the end, when we launch new activities. To make a successful new beginning requires more than simply persevering. It requires an understanding of external signs and inner signals that point the way to the future." Each time your world or something inside you changes, you have to rethink who you are, where you are going, how you will do things, and what you want to do. In effect, you remake yourself during each transition. This is what we call *self-renewal*. The ability to reform and rethink your life contributes substantially to your ability to benefit from transition.

Terry was in the midst of a very profound transition. After many years in the television industry, he was laid off, like many of his colleagues. He was devastated and went into shock and grief. He began to look for a similar job, when something inside him began to say "Whoa!" His inner voice said, "This is the time, maybe the only time in your life, to do something really new."

He entered therapy and, with his wife, began to explore new options. As he was doing this, he had a brainstorm. There were no resources for people like him, yet people needed help with the transition after layoffs. His television work and contacts came in handy: He would make a videocassette to help people move through layoffs. He called upon several friends and colleagues who could help. Everyone volunteered time and equipment, and he was able to make a professional product at almost no cost. The cassette is now circulating, and he is launched on a new career, making educational videos. This was a creative response to a personal crisis.

TWO RESPONSES TO CORPORATE CHANGE

Jerry and Eileen are both tellers at a savings and loan that has just been acquired. They each have several years on the job and had looked forward to a career at their present bank. They each sit through a meeting describing the upcoming changes. They face the same new realities, but they adopt very different coping strategies.

Jerry responds with silent terror. He puts on a brave front, but inside he feels that his whole world is crushed. He does not know where he stands, what to expect, or what to do next. He is furious, thinking to himself over and over, "This is not fair, this isn't what I expected." His motivation sags, and he begins to make mistakes he never made before. He withdraws and stops talking to even his closest friends. When he does go out with coworkers, he spends the time complaining about how unfair and bad things are.

Jerry "retires on the job," waiting for "them" to decide how things will be. He catches the flu, is out for a week. When he returns, he is summoned into his supervisor's office and, just as he expected, informed that his job has been eliminated. He leaves bitter, angry, and feeling less confident in his own abilities than he had a few weeks before.

Eileen too is shocked and worried about what the changes mean. She is quite upset, but she knows from talks with coworkers that such feelings are shared by everyone. She certainly does not like the changes, but she decides to make the best of them. She tells herself, "They still need people to manage this branch, and I'm as good a teller as anyone, so I'll see what happens."

She does a little personal planning. She talks with everyone she knows, trying to get a sense about what the new management has in mind for the bank. She researches the history, management structure, and performance of the new bank. She calls a friend who went through something like this and discusses his experience. She also checks with other banks in the area and finds that she is employable elsewhere. Eileen works energetically, even though sometimes she feels unrewarded and is not always sure she is doing the right thing. Several weeks later, her supervisor invites her in and offers her a choice of challenging new positions.

THE TRANSITION CYCLE

We find predictable stages that apply to both individuals and organizations in transition. These stages were first mapped by psychiatrist Elisabeth Kübler-Ross, who looked at the emotional shifts in dying patients. Other studies of survivors of loss, and other emotional trauma, document similar changes. Individuals go through this cycle after job loss, or even when they start work after a promotion, as well as in family and personal changes. Whole organizations go through these phases as they steer through layoffs, mergers, acquisitions, and other organizational growing pains.

Change affects the glue that ties you to your organization. It disturbs the connecting links and basic agreements that help you work. If you are caught in a changing company, or a changing life, knowing the stages of transition will help you figure out what stage you are in and help you move to the next step. After working with numerous companies in transition, developing the Mastering and Managing Change Program, we see five major phases in their transition cycle. These apply to individuals as well as to the company as a whole.

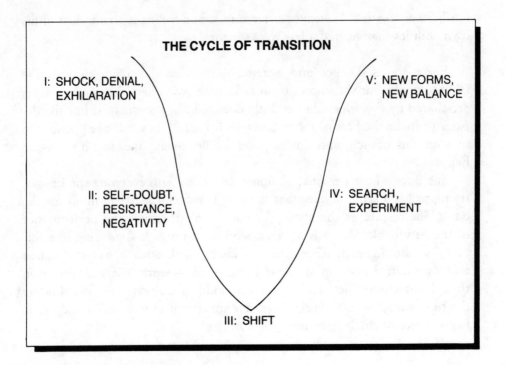

THE CYCLE OF TRANSITION

I: SHOCK, DENIAL, EXHILARATION

V: NEW FORMS, NEW BALANCE

II: SELF-DOUBT, RESISTANCE, NEGATIVITY

IV: SEARCH, EXPERIMENT

III: SHIFT

1. Shock, denial, exhilaration
2. Self-doubt, resistance, negativity
3. Shift
4. Search, experiment
5. New forms, new balance

The first response to unexpected change is shock, a general refusal to let the information in. This protects people from being overwhelmed. Common elements include:

- Denial—"This can't be happening"
- Ignoring it—"Wait till it blows over"
- Minimizing—"It just demands a few minor adjustments"

You may try to go on as before, but sooner or later the impact catches up with you and you have to respond internally.

In the second phase—self-doubt, resistance, and negativity—things seem to get worse. Your personal distress level rises. You may spend time looking for someone or something to blame and complaining about the new organization. You may get sick, feel all sorts of physical, emotional, and mental symptoms, and even doubt your own ability. In this phase, you are mourning the past, not preparing for the future. Many people want to avoid these painful responses and pretend they are over them, sometimes by moving back into denial. Just know that by acknowledging your feelings at this stage you will move more quickly on to the next phase.

Shift, the third phase, comes after a period of struggle, when individuals and organizations emerge from their negativity, breathe a sigh of relief, and shift into a more positive, hopeful, future-focused phase. A change occurs that lets people know they are going to make it. It can be as subtle as just feeling better or more obvious like sleeping through the night for the first time since the transition started. The sense of shifting differs for each person, but you will know when it happens. It is a real, definite experience of the load's getting lighter. It happens after you have let yourself feel deeply the period of struggle and doubt.

New directions do not emerge full-grown. Rather, what emerges is the energy to put the fourth phase—search/experiment—into action. You begin to explore and discover new ways. You start clarifying goals, assessing resources, exploring alternatives, and experimenting with new possibilities. You feel motivated to swing into action, without trying quickly to find the "right" way. You should resist stopping too soon by accepting something less than you are capable of. This is a period of high energy. Your creativity will be at its peak.

Finally, the organization or the individual grows a new face, discovers new ways of doing things, and adapts to the new situation. The phase of commitment to new forms/new balance begins when you decide upon a new course of action. This could be a new way of doing the job or finding a new job. When you have successfully reached new balance, there has been growth and adaptation.

Just when you get through one transition cycle another one is likely to begin. The cycle of transition never ends. Think of yourself moving in a rhythm of change as long as you live, facing new challenges and crises. You may even find a new transition occurring before you have completed the previous one. It is common to have several transition rhythms going at the same time. It is important to know how many personal and organizational transitions you are going through at any one time, so you can be careful not to overwhelm yourself.

GETTING STUCK OR DENYING

Organizations, like people, run into trouble in two ways: They remain stuck in one phase, never able to move on through, or they try to breeze across the curve like Tarzan, pretending that they do not have to go through all the lower half of the transition curve. People and organizations have to be alert to counter the tendency to say, "We're managing it fine," "We're back to normal," "Things are over," when in fact they have barely begun.

The Tarzan Swing,^{SM} going immediately from shock to commitment, is popular within organizations, especially at top management levels where they are often already through their adjustment to the transition when the rest of the company has just begun. Top management often has a hard time understanding why people cannot stop moping around and get to work. They want people to skip across the top parts of the transition curve and have very little toleration for employees in the lower phases. But, as we say, "The tenacity with which you insist you've made this leap is proportional to your denial."

People always ask how long this process takes. It is impossible to make an exact prediction. You are likely to go through this transition as you have gone through other griefs. If it took you a long time to get through your last transition you may find the same pattern repeating itself, or you may have learned some key strategies and be able to help yourself along more quickly. How you go through this transition will depend on the severity of this change and your personal experience in handling other major changes.

In our experience, moving through the phases can take anywhere from several weeks to a number of months. The more you are able to acknowledge your feelings and get support for being in transition, the more quickly you will move.

One manager, who had been laid off three times in the past year and a half, was asked how he managed these difficult times. He confessed that he went home, lay in bed, cried, and ate lots of chocolate for about two days each time, and that seemed to get him quickly to the shift stage so he could start his job hunting again. The sooner you go through your shock, denial, negativity, and resistance the sooner you will be moving up the other side. Go easy on yourself if you do not feel you are handling change as quickly as you think you should. Everyone moves at his or her own pace.

Think of the current major or minor change you are facing. Take a moment and find where you are in the cycle of transition. Note on the transition cycle on p. 112 where you think you are right now. If you just recently heard about the change, you are probably at phase 1 or 2. You may think, or wish, you were at phase 4, but it takes more than a few days, even for the most practiced change master, to reach new balance.

You may find that you personally are at one phase, while your organization is at another. In many companies, since the top management has been living with the change longer than those at lower and middle levels, they may be farther along the transition cycle. Therefore, the top managers may be ready to experiment and explore while the people they supervise are struggling with denial or negativity. The lack of coordination of stages, with top management being impatient and lower levels struggling with difficult feelings, often complicates the task of managing change.

CREATING CHANGE-HARDINESS

Often there is very little we can do about changes in the outside organizational climate. In these cases the only area we have control over is how we perceive a situation. Sometimes your mind can be the most potent buffer you have. Look again at what made the difference in what happened to Jerry and Eileen. Each approached change differently. Jerry experienced change as a defeat and became a helpless victim. Eileen, on the other hand, while not thrilled with the change, approached it actively and began to seek out others and to make alternative plans. She was ready to take advantage of the opportunities that the new situation offered.

Eileen utilized some of the key inner skills that researchers have found are characteristic of people who thrive in times of high stress and change. We noted in the first chapter how Salvatore Maddi and Suzanne Kobasa compared employees in a high-stress company who were extraordinarily healthy with employees in another office who experienced many major and minor illnesses. The hardy, or stress-resistant, employees had the following qualities:

1. They saw change as a challenge and as an opportunity.
2. They focused their energy and attention on things they could control.
3. They were committed to their jobs and felt their work was meaningful.
4. They received help and support from coworkers and felt a sense of connection to them.

These four C's—challenge, control, commitment and connection—are the keys to being an effective master of change.

HOW YOU CAN AFFECT CHANGE

An effective response to change at your workplace involves several key skills and new attitudes.

First, you must recognize that, when a company is changing, you have only limited power to influence the outcome. Organizational changes are more powerful than any single individual, and no one person, in any position, can affect things as fully as he or she might like.

Sometimes, when people realize their influence is limited, they assume that they have no power to make a difference. That is a serious mistake. There are many specific skills and attitudes that can help you manage the change.

Here are some areas where you have some direct choice:

1. You can control your inner or emotional *response* to the change, your attitudes toward it, and how you will act with others. Recognize when you are feeling uncomfortable. Know that you will probably have times that you feel anxious and have your old fears awakened. Find someone to talk to about how you feel. This will help you feel not so isolated and alone.
2. You can *influence* the change process. You can make suggestions. Being actively involved will help you feel more in control.
3. You can gather *information* about what will happen. Planning your next step becomes easier, the more information you have. Do not act for the sake of action. Making a successful transition takes time.
4. You can *take care of yourself,* and deal caringly with your internal reactions to the changes. Take care of yourself in little ways. Eat lunch

with the same people, go to your friend's house for dinner, maintain a few familiar patterns and habits as you go through your change.

You increase your control by taking responsibility for your own response to change—that is where you, and only you, are in charge. You are in charge of what you think, what you feel, how you take care of yourself, how you act, and how you relate to your coworkers and supervisors.

The remainder of the chapter will outline a survival guide of key skills to help you manage life and work transitions, to land on your feet. There are three areas where your change skills make a difference:

- You can create a positive *internal climate* to manage change. Chapter 5 will continue to show you how to manage your attitudes and internal awareness.
- You can take *direct action* to increase your information level and personal control over the future. Chapter 6 will suggest additional ways to mobilize personal power.
- You can *mobilize and increase the support* you get from the people around you. In Chapter 7 additional ways to build support will be presented.

CREATE A POSITIVE INNER CLIMATE

When situations change, the first thing you need to manage is yourself. You need to take care of yourself—physically, emotionally, and mentally—to create a positive internal climate. Five things you can do are:

1. Practice physical self-care.
2. Recognize your feelings.
3. Respect yourself.
4. Give up old expectations and prepare for new ones.
5. Look to the future.

1. Change demands energy, and your energy derives in part from the proper care of your body. An eighteen-hour day, a seven-day-a-week schedule, with fast food snacks, too much caffeine, and hours of worry, will drain your energy and not allow enough recharging. When you are under stress you need to eat regular and nutritious meals, get a good night's sleep, exercise regularly, and take time off for personal renewal. Recharging your inner

batteries helps when you are waiting for some of the changes to sort themselves out.

2. You worry about where you stand when you go through a major shift. Everyone doubts himself or herself sometimes, and worries. As psychologist Irving Janis discovered, there is a valid role for worrying, provided there is neither too much nor too little of it. In small doses worrying can prod you into searching and exploring.

If you do not recognize your feelings you may find them expressed indirectly as accidents, careless mistakes, loss of energy, or sickness. The best thing to do about such feelings is to admit them to yourself and discuss them with others. Once you recognize and accept your painful and negative feelings, they go away faster.

3. The key resource in managing change is yourself. Look at how you treat yourself. Are you expecting too much? Some people are cruel and negative and treat themselves to all sorts of negative self-talk, doubting their own ability or forgetting what they have already accomplished.

A positive attitude begins with an attitude of respect and caring for yourself. Expecting yourself to have the new ways mastered in a few days only adds to your burden. Thinking about all the "what ifs" is not helpful either. Remember to recognize your strengths and accomplishments, and reward yourself for your achievements. Do not wait to be recognized by others, because in times of change, people often have their attention turned elsewhere.

4. A transition represents a disruption in your set of expectations—how you will be treated, what you can expect, promotion policies, performance evaluations, indeed everything about the way things are done. Many people waste valuable energy bemoaning the loss of the old ("When we were ____, they wouldn't have done this," or "This isn't fair, we never agreed to this"), or comparing old with new ("The old way was much better, this way is dumb").

At many times during the shift you will find yourself holding on to the old set of expectations or feeling upset about saying goodbye to the familiar. Let yourself feel the loss, but in your mind prepare to let go and move on. The new ways are probably neither right nor wrong, better nor worse than the previous ones. They are new, and they need to be practiced and learned, then judged on their merits. Most often, you will not know enough about how a decision was made or why something is done the way it is or how it will feel when you are accustomed to it, to really evaluate it.

5. Things are not going to return to "normal," because there is no normal to go back to. Waiting for things to settle or go back is just wasting precious time that you need for learning new skills. There is never enough time, so do not waste the time you have.

Some people respond to changes in their companies by feeling that they have to do everything they can to save their jobs. If you have worked for a company for a long time, you have a considerable investment in staying. And, since you have not been in the job market for a long time, you may not know how employable you are. Nevertheless, people can't take risks and learn new ways if they are holding on to their jobs for dear life. The fear of losing your job will cause you to make mistakes and will make it hard for you to see clearly. While there may indeed be a place for you in the new form of the company, to assume at the start that this is the only place for you is to close off important options. You may find you do not fit the new company style.

PREPARING YOURSELF TO TAKE ACTION

The second set of change-mastery skills focuses on outer strategies and initiates the process of strategic action planning. Get started by:

1. Getting a clear vision and setting goals
2. Reassessing your priorities
3. Conducting a personal resource/liability review
4. Experimenting with new options
5. Actively seeking what you need

1. Ask yourself what you want out of the change. The best way to do this is to take some quiet time and create a personal vision of how you would like things to turn out. Do this right now. What would be the best possible outcome of this change for you?

Now translate your best possible world picture into specific goals for this period of transition. Write your long-term (five years plus) goals. Next, note your short-term (one to three years) goals and, finally, what you would like to achieve in the next six weeks. Be specific (not "I want to get the best possible job," but rather things like "I would like a supervisory position or a move to another department or branch"). The important thing in planning is to have a clear idea of your own direction.

2. One of the pitfalls of setting new goals is setting more goals than it is possible to accomplish in the time available. It is very common for people to look at someone else's achievements and not see all the work that has gone into them. Because of this tendency not to see the whole picture, you may set your goal too big, and when you do not reach the goal within your time frame, you make your dream smaller. You take this "failure" as a signal that the original dream is wrong. However, the part that is wrong is the time frame. When people lessen their dreams they dampen their spirit in a dangerous way, starting them on the path to burnout. People should not make their dreams smaller but should create a more elastic notion of how long it will take to accomplish the dreams.

An executive whose main dream in life was to go hiking in Nepal, a complete wilderness trek, was convinced that this was only a dream. He set a goal—trekking in Nepal—without breaking down his dream into doable steps. In this way he remained frustrated. Thinking about going to Nepal only made him feel hopeless and disgruntled. To help him get to his dream he wrote out all the tasks he needed to do to go to Nepal. He quickly filled up two pages listing passports, vaccinations, proper clothes, etc. He then picked out a task on that list that could be accomplished in five minutes in the next week. At first he could not find anything that small. Then he found one by breaking down one of the tasks into smaller bits. Yes, he could make a phone call to order the passport application in five minutes. The amount of exhilaration that he experienced in taking that small step set in motion the momentum to continue his dream plans, step by step. What he had been missing was a way to make his dreams operational. It was a real treat to get a postcard from him two years later, mailed from Katmandu. Accomplishing your dreams is not always easy, but with enough elastic and the snap that goes with it, big dreams are possible.

3. When shifting, it is important to take stock of what you have to offer, as well as what you need to learn. Chances are, others at your workplace are aware of your strengths and weaknesses, and there is little sense in pretending they do not exist. You may want to involve people you work

with in this process. Some people have a hard time assessing themselves in a positive way. You will probably discover that you have more to offer than you initially gave yourself credit for.

Take a piece of paper and fold it in half. On one half make a list of your personal strengths, skills, and resources. This is what you have to offer to your new employers. Include personal qualities, experience, and achievements. Then, on the other half, list the areas where you are aware that you need to learn and grow: skills you would like to acquire, areas you need to improve.

How could you acquire the skills that you have targeted as needs? Create your own development plan. There are often many community resources and business groups that specialize in professional development. Do not wait to be asked what you need; do your own self-assessment and craft your own plan. Often people wait for the company to know magically what they need and offer it to them. When this does not happen, people become angry and resentful. Do not wait for another person or your company to give you what you need, especially if you do not know what it is or have not asked for it for a long time. Don't wait. Clarify and move ahead.

4. As you enter a new phase of the change cycle, allow yourself to suspend decision making, hold back on commitment, and spend your energy exploring options. One aspect of exploration is trying things that may not work. That involves taking risks. People who manage change well report that they take risks frequently, and that many times the tries do not pan out. Babe Ruth was both the home run king and the strikeout king. He tried more often and hence made more mistakes as well as more hits.

Managing change means operating in a situation where the outcome is uncertain, where important things are unclear, and where your power is somewhat limited. Since the outcome of any single strategy is impossible to determine, the most effective approach is to have several alternatives available in every situation.

5. The one response to change sure to backfire is to sit, wait, and stew. Opportunities do not get placed on your desk; you need to find them or create them. Locating an opportunity or proposing something that will help the organization is more likely to succeed than holding back and offering nothing. If you do not clarify your goals, and let people know what you are looking for, you are less likely to get what you want.

People who are change-hardy develop their sense of personal power by having an active approach to change. They look for what they can do, and they do it. If one avenue is blocked, do not conclude that nothing can be done. Just try something else. As you take action you will discover new sources of energy and new possibilities.

BUILD POWERFUL SUPPORT NETWORKS

Other people are a key resource who help you deal with change. They can help you as you:

1. Gather information
2. Check out rumors
3. Renegotiate your relationships with important people
4. Get support outside the workplace

1. People who manage transition well seek out other people. Other people can help you to gather tremendous amounts of relevant information. By talking to people in the organization, you will know what is going on—if a new position is available, what a new executive is really like, plans for a division. Other people are also sources of emotional support. Having someone to talk to, sharing difficult and stressful effects of change and brainstorming new ideas, is often very helpful. You feel better about things and see them differently when you talk to others. The feeling of camaraderie helps you all move along the change cycle.

One of the things that plagues people in transition is their lack of information about what is possible in the work world outside the company. Their ideas are limited when they think about new ways to work. People often get stuck in options that they learned early in life. Many areas for work that exist today did not take form until recently. Contemplating change with only your internal dialogue to advise you may sell yourself short.

When looking for new options, start gathering information from the outside. You need to contact people within and outside of your normal work environment to see what opportunities exist. Take yourself on a safari for new ideas—consider unmapped areas, follow wild leads.

Bill, that personnel executive we talked about earlier, suffered from just this problem. Because he was in transition he was not very articulate about what he was looking for. That made him not want to talk to people, lest he look "flaky" to people in his field. Bill found a creative way around this problem. He decided to call a meeting of his "board of directors" to help him gather information. This board was made up of colleagues and people that he played sports with outside of work, but they were not people he would normally feel comfortable asking for advice. To make himself feel more comfortable, he called an evening "meeting," complete with a tray of sandwiches and beer, and ran the "meeting" as if it were a formal process. The agenda listed was:

1. Reviewing past accomplishments
2. Exploring existing options
3. Looking into new territory

Emerging from this meeting were a range of contacts and ideas that amazed everyone there. Having gotten over his hesitancy to ask for help, Bill got a much-needed shot in the arm for his transition.

Bill's renewal was not instant. He needed to explore his values and beliefs and examine his willingness to make changes. Pushing past his initial embarrassment, he learned to ask for outside assistance.

2. A brushfire is nothing compared to the rumor mill during times of organizational change. People's fears often lead them to believe the most outlandish stories. To plan your response to change, you must act on reliable information. Therefore, when you hear something, before you go into a panic, try to check it out with other people. Help cool the flames by not passing inaccurate information, but rather by asking for and seeking clear information. Sometimes, information you think is sensitive or confidential is readily available if you ask the appropriate person.

3. During change important working relationships need to shift. If you try to operate as you always have, strain results. Stress comes from not clarifying how the new situation will affect your relationship with coworkers. In times of change, people need to check in more and redefine how things are done.

Every relationship involves people who expect certain things from each other. These expectations enable you to work together without checking in about everything. Things go along well in times of relative stability, but when things change, your relationship falls into flux. What each of you expects from the other needs to be shifted, not just once but frequently. When things are changing really fast, you may have to check in with your friends and colleagues quite frequently and be willing to renegotiate expectations and job roles.

4. The changing workplace can become a pressure cooker. If you spend all your time and energy inside it, the stress can build up. You need an outlet for release. One way you can diminish the pressure is to make sure you seek out the people you know—friends and family—outside the company. They will help you regain perspective and see that the company is not the whole world for you. They can also help you see alternatives you may be missing. Finally, and perhaps most important, they can help you see that you are a good, worthwhile, competent person, no matter what is going on in your company. This will build up your energy reserves, and enable you to go back into the company refreshed and renewed.

MOVING ON

You now have some understanding about how change affects you and a number of ways to manage change successfully. There are general principles and skills that are useful in change, but each time you will be in a unique situation. There is no simple list of things you must do. This chapter offers you some guidance on the change process. It presents you with a storehouse of some of the important skills for mastering change. The process of letting go of the old and finding your way to the new forms is both exhilarating and confusing. Each transition has its own rhythm. The next move is yours: You need to look closely at yourself and create your personal map for navigating your transitions.

CHAPTER 5

LISTENING TO YOURSELF: USING YOUR INNER RESOURCES

There has appeared in the past two decades a tendency to balance the awareness of the world around us with a growing emphasis on the world of inner experience. That new awareness includes the sense that the individual is by no means as separate as we ordinarily take ourselves to be, that under certain conditions we may become directly and intuitively aware of our oneness with others and with the universe and of a lack of limits to the potentialities of that oneness.

—WILLIS HARMAN AND HOWARD RHEINGOLD,

HIGHER CREATIVITY

A major disaster hit the CCD&E ad agency: Video Warehouse, one of the city's largest advertisers, just announced that it would take its account to another agency. There had been few signs of dissatisfaction. The new CEO of Video said it was time for a change. Three key CCD&E executives had responsibility for the account. Betty was the account executive, who planned overall strategy. When she heard the news, she immediately blamed herself. She thought of scores of things she had not done, ways she had been inattentive, and things she might have done. She had had her chance to prove herself with this account, and in her mind she had failed. She became depressed and thought about quitting her job.

David, the art director, saw it differently. He blamed everyone and everything—the writers who did not talk to art directors, the agency for its conservative strategy, and so on. He became furious, sure that once more the agency had shown how it stifled creativity. He thought about handing in his resignation. Betty blamed herself, while David blamed the agency. They were both demoralized.

Leonard, the division vice president responsible for the overall coordination, took a third approach. He was upset and saw ways that he and the agency may have erred. But he neither punished himself nor looked for others to blame. Maybe, he thought, this was good for the agency. They may have been overconfident, too conservative, and they may have lost some of the creative dedication that marked the agency's first years. Leonard decided to use the event as an occasion for exploration of new directions. He visited the Video Warehouse and talked to its president. He learned some things he had not been aware of, about limits and difficulties in his agency. He made some changes in the style and strategy of CCD&E. Within a year, the agency sent a new, unsolicited proposal to Video Warehouse, detailing a new approach to their advertising. They regained the account.

Betty and David eventually shifted their attitudes, but not before months of frustration and demoralization. It is unlikely they would have renewed their commitment to the agency if it had not been for Leonard's persuasive, facilitative leadership. Their problems were not with their own competence, motivation, or dedication, but rather with they way that they saw the company and themselves. Their beliefs and expectations about themselves and the company limited, deenergized, and frustrated them.

The differences between high-energy, turned-on managers and burned-out, turned-off ones are obvious in everything they do: how they approach new tasks, how they work in groups, how they relate informally. But these outer effects are only the reflections of a climate that begins deep inside them. Energized workers see the world differently—not necessarily with rose-colored glasses—because energized workers can be tough and realistic in a way that gets them into constructive action and keeps them there until they can make a real difference. In contrast, burned-out workers feel trapped in a cycle of negative, self-limiting or even catastrophic expectations that keep them from even trying to make a difference.

It is often what you bring to your work, not what the work brings to you, that makes it exciting, meaningful, and challenging. True, certain companies and projects can inspire and excite you. But, more often, you bring the feeling of excitement or deadness to the job. High-energy workers approach each job in a positive way, because they have a positive sense of themselves and their job. Attitudes create or scatter the energy that fuels the excitement and satisfaction of working well. Each person brings a web of expectations, judgments, and attitudes to work—a belief system. Like Betty, David, and Leonard, people with similar jobs can experience completely different work worlds, because of their views of what they are doing, why they are doing it, how they can or cannot do it, and who they are.

This chapter explores your inner world. We will challenge the inner limits you bring to work and show you how to transform them into inner prescriptions for achievement. Many times it is not the nature of the job itself, but the inner baggage of negative and limiting beliefs and expectations, that turns off the energy and excitement you could have at work. You will learn to program yourself with positive, energy-releasing, action-producing beliefs, expectations, and attitudes that lead toward realizing your potential.

Your inner world also includes a vast storehouse of images, memories, feelings, physical sensations, and intuitions. That capacity to create, plan, and imagine makes the human being unique. You can learn to use these visions of the future to modify or track present behavior.

A MODEL OF THE SELF

To conceptualize the many important facets of your inner self, you can use the model of the self in the diagram on page 128.

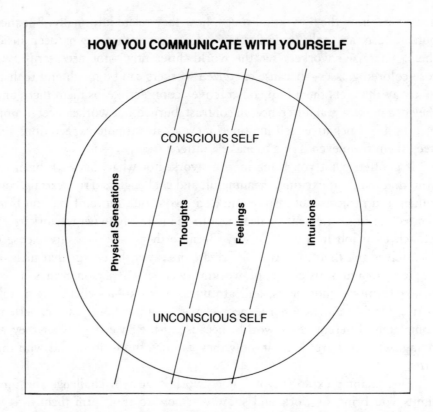

The circle represents the inner self, divided by a horizontal line. The top half of the circle represents the conscious self—aspects of the self accessible to awareness. However, there are also vast dimensions of the self outside of awareness, the unconscious. The unconscious includes not only the repressed feelings and memories, but also the potential skills, the creative wisdom, the intuitive faculties that may be dormant but that lie within everyone.

The diagonal lines mark off the four major pathways of internal communication. First, there are physical sensations, or body talk: the messages you receive from your physical body. Next, there are feelings, which can be either conscious or unconscious. As we become more self-aware, more of our feelings become conscious. The next band is thoughts. These include beliefs, expectations, and the internal conversations you hold with yourself almost every minute. Finally, there are the creative, intuitive aspects of the self, the inner wisdom that lies mostly below the surface of consciousness but that, as you will see, can bubble up if conditions are right. All four paths come into play to enhance your relationship to your work.

WORK AND BELIEFS

. . . .

Dennis took his son Oren to the zoo one day. They looked at an elephant. Oren saw that the elephant was tied to a pole with a tiny piece of rope. "How," he asked, "can that little rope hold that powerful elephant? Why doesn't he break away?" They asked the trainer. "Well," he began, "when this elephant was very little, we put it on a huge rope. The elephant tried to get away, and learned he couldn't. As he got larger, we used smaller and smaller ropes. Now, he just looks down, sees the rope is there, and never pulls on it."

In a lot of ways, people act like the elephant. A challenge or an obstacle keeps you from something you really want. Like the grown elephant, you say, "I can't do that," or "It hasn't worked before." Then you give up before even trying.

The elephant is trapped by his belief that the tiny rope will stop him from getting what he wants. The belief is a relic of an early experience and is no longer true. People often trap and limit themselves by hanging on to old beliefs rather than testing them out and perhaps changing them.

Every day at work you live behind the shield of your many beliefs, expectations, and assumptions about the way things should be. This shield interferes with your ability to see things as they really are. For example, many dedicated and idealistic young professionals came to community action agencies because they desired to make a difference. Two of them, Andy and Walter, began work at the same time. They had similar jobs, similar talents, and came from similar backgrounds. But each of them had very different beliefs, expectations, and assumptions. Andy stayed only a year, and left in bitterness and frustration. Walter became head of the agency and went on to a distinguished career.

How did Andy get into trouble? Andy came to the job with a load of unrealistic expectations. He thought he would make a huge difference to people's lives, and the community would respond to him immediately. He started work after a long string of successes in school. At school, people work alone, and succcess is immediately rewarded with good grades. Not so at work. Andy's expectations of the job were so high and unrealistic that they couldn't be met. He expected far too much from himself and from the environment. To further complicate matters, when he stopped living up to his high expectations, he became highly self-critical. He felt he was a failure. He thought he hadn't done the job, even though others would say he was doing just fine. He burned out, not because of the job pressures, but because his beliefs and expectations never let him start fresh.

In contrast, while Walter too wanted to make a difference, his initial approach was "Let me learn what is possible here." He sought out other people to help him discover what he could expect and what could be done. His first expectation was that he had a lot to learn before he could make a difference. He believed that he could learn to be effective, not that he should be effective from day one. These attitudes not only maintained his energy and dedication to the job, they brought him into contact with others who helped him succeed.

Management theorist Warren Bennis, for many years professor at the Sloan School at MIT, talks about the "Wallenda factor" in his study of eighty successful leaders. Carl Wallenda and his family of acrobats lived their lives on the high wire. Into his seventies he would go up and perform, without a safety net, until the tragic fall that cost his life. A year later his wife told Bennis, "You know, he never thought about falling. It never entered his mind. Then, just a few weeks before the fall, he talked about it for the first time. I knew then that something was wrong."

Bennis tells us that successful leaders do not consider the possibility of failure. This is despite the fact that they all do fail, and fail frequently. Successful entrepreneurs have an average of five business failures in their past. But they do not see these as failures. They never even use that word. There is a different attitude.

Losing a business can be a cause for self-criticism—telling yourself that you are stupid or that you should never take that kind of risk again. The successful leader, in contrast, is more likely to say after such a setback, "Well, that didn't work out as I expected, but I really learned some things about the market, and now I know how to do it right." Their way of seeing obstacles is different and leads them right on to the next challenge. They do not have failures, they have learning opportunities. For example, Abraham Lincoln is thought of as a natural and confident winner, who listened to his inner voice against public pressure. But before he won the presidency, he had been defeated in six previous runs for office. He obviously was not ready to give up his mission or call himself a failure.

EXPLORING BELIEFS

One way to explore your beliefs in operation is to listen closely to the words you use when thinking about a topic. For example, think about your reactions to the word "boss." You might say to yourself things like:

- "Bosses are hard to please."
- "The best bosses are fair."
- "I never had a boss I liked."
- "Bosses don't really care about who works for them."

These responses reveal attitudes. You can predict how a person with one of these attitudes would behave in relation to a superior. Your prior experiences shape your beliefs and expectations, and your beliefs and expectations shape your current behavior. If you never had a boss you liked, what would it take to turn your inner world around? You might approach a new boss suspiciously or negatively and receive a negative response in return. "Another lousy boss," you might say to yourself.

Connection to work relies on two kinds of beliefs. First, there are beliefs about yourself. These are the expectations about your own capacity, the type of person you are, how you should act. These beliefs may be negative or positive, expansive or limited, accurate or inaccurate. Yet we rarely evaluate them. They are like the background music, always there but never really listened to.

The second type of beliefs are about your organization and your particular job. They are often shared by others. When a group of people in a company share beliefs and expectations of each other, these beliefs and expectations become company norms. Together, these norms make up the corporate culture, the way things are seen and done inside the company. Company norms can frustrate the people who work there and limit the company's potential. As you will see, you can do your part to change, question, or modify these norms.

SELF-ESTEEM: VALUING YOURSELF

The images and expectations you have of yourself form your self-esteem, the value you place on yourself. Your beliefs about yourself can be off-base in three directions. First, you may think too little of yourself, and be excessively self-critical and demanding. At the other extreme, you may be too easily satisfied with yourself, and stop short of what you could become. Third, you may have an unrealistic, or misplaced, set of beliefs.

A frustrated and highly-stressed factory manager was feeling thoroughly demoralized because, "They were asking me to produce design changes in days, that needed weeks of work." "What did you do?" we asked. "The situation sounds impossible." "Oh," he said, "I gave them the designs they wanted, but they were so rough I was ashamed of them." It was clear that, even under the pressure of production, he held himself to far higher standards than his superiors expected. They knew they were asking a lot. They were paying for his experience, and they trusted his hunches, what he called "rough work." But his inner standards prevented him from feeling good about his quick, effective hunches. He felt like a failure, aiming a barrage of negative self-evaluations against himself. He burned out because he did not modify his internal standards to fit his actual work situation. This high-performance manager lived in a hell of self-criticism. Once he realized this, he shifted his expectations of himself in a more positive direction.

Do you dilute your good feelings of accomplishment with a highly critical internal system? Do you demand more of yourself than any supervisor or coworker would? How many times, for example, when something good happens, do you negate it by saying to yourself "Yes, but . . . ," or "I should have done better"? Your inner set of self-expectations can diverge widely from external reality. Unrealistic expectations dim your positive energy at work and take away the pleasure of doing things well.

Many people work without a clear sense of what they want to accomplish. Such people are critical of themselves, but they do not know where they want to go.

What do you want? Think about your job. Set some personal goals, and then think of a reward that you will give yourself when you reach each one. You should have a goal for every month-long period, as well as longer-term goals. Being clear with yourself makes it less likely you will set standards that no human being could meet.

Ethan is one of the best-liked branch managers in his company, unfailingly supportive of his people and always willing to listen to them. However, his caring does not extend to himself. He does not treat himself the way he treats the people in his branch. He never takes time for himself, never lets himself off the hook. When he is sick, he is still at work. He never stops, praises, or rewards himself. Clearly, Ethan has a double standard that leaves him with less than anyone else. Why? It turns out that he believes that he will not be noticed or liked unless he is doing things for others and that he himself does not merit very much. That was how he felt in his family, where his mother was always sick, his father was never home, and he was the oldest of four children. Ethan acts in his branch just like he did in his family. Eventually, Ethan develops a serious illness that forces him to take time for himself.

Take a moment and turn your attention inward. Reflect on how well you are doing at work. Ask yourself, "What beliefs do I have about my work in general, my specific job, my own abilities to perform? Do I generally feel positive or negative about these areas? What judgments do I make about myself and others?" While you reflect, allow another part of your consciousness to act as an observer of how you are thinking about your performance.

When you observe your mental processes, you will probably notice an internal conversation. You are always talking to yourself, prepping yourself for action, anticipating consequences, fearing others, telling yourself what you will do, or going over things that have already happened. You are always the coach and the player, the actor, the director, and the critic, all rolled up into one. This is your *self-talk*.

Think about some of the things you expect of yourself. What do you think you should accomplish at work in order to feel satisfied and successful? Write them down. Many of your expectations may be what we would call "myths," highly overblown extensions of reality or reasonableness.

For example, a woman manager may suffer from the "superwoman" syndrome. In order to be effective at work she needs to be the best, in the shortest amount of time, and make it look phenomenally easy. Then, she may return home and assume the traditional roles of wife and mother, trying to nurture and take care of everyone. Her inner world operates on the belief that "all good mothers and wives should always be there for spouse and family, all the time. Sure you can work, but you choose it, so don't complain." Such beliefs, rather than actual life and family pressure, become her greatest burden.

A woman physician had a prestigious medical practice. She felt obliged to come home every day, and cook dinner for her physician husband and her five children, then put the youngsters to bed, while her husband relaxed with a drink and played with the kids. She never questioned how much she expected of herself, until she began to feel deenergized, her motivation flagged, and she experienced some of the early signs of burnout. Her burnout resulted from her self-expectations.

Many of us bring similar unrealistically high standards to work. The mythology is that these high expectations spur us on, that self-criticism leads to higher performance. That may be so in a limited sense. However, the down-side is that a highly critical person never feels he or she has done a good job, can never rest and feel good about success. These people see only their mistakes, not their achievements. Pretty soon they tire of this diet of pressure without relief. But they cannot say this to themselves consciously, so their bodies deliver the message indirectly, in the form of illness, burnout, or diminished energy.

The external pressures that lead to burnout may not be there at all. When you blame something outside yourself—your boss, your company, your lack of ability—for your difficulties, look again. The energy drain comes from what you believe about the situation or about yourself. Many people are their own severest critics, continually putting themselves down for imagined deficiencies or mistakes. Nothing is good enough!

This self-criticism not only causes you considerable pain, but it also keeps you from paying attention to what you need to do to reach your goals. Many people have clear missions and beautiful visions, but they keep themselves from achieving them. They live in a state of continual deprivation. They are not able to get their energy flowing to move their dreams into the world of reality.

LIMITING BELIEFS AND SELF-FULFILLING PROPHESIES

Some people who do not get what they want from their work suffer not from expectations that are too high but from ones that are too low, too negative. Negative expectations are very seductive. If you do not think you can do something, you are not likely to get it. Then, when you do not, you can at least take comfort in the fact that you were not wrong. That is a major reason for the persistence of negative beliefs. People can always be right about what they cannot accomplish. Many individuals, and whole companies, become paralyzed and demoralized when they find themselves caught in this type of negativity.

Limiting beliefs about ourselves can lead to self-fulfilling prophesy. Harvard professor Robert Rosenthal, in a famous experiment, separated members of a junior high school class into two groups identical in ability, achievement, and motivation. However, he told teachers that one of these groups was made up of high-potential students. By the end of the year, the students who teachers believed were in the high potential group were actually making higher grades and doing much better than the other identical group, who were not blessed with the teachers' high expectations. This experiment showing how beliefs determine outcomes has been repeated many times. A person who believes something behaves in ways that bring it about. In this case, beliefs helped bring out performance gains in a group of average students.

Many people have been saddled with school achievement or aptitude scores that told them how smart they were. Many creative and intelligent people, like Sylvester Stallone, were told by teachers that they were too dumb to expect much of themselves. Tragically, too many people internalize these expectations and then begin to expect less than their best from themselves. A "fear of success" has been found in people who are afraid to succeed because doing so would go against their expectations.

You can become programmed for failure or only limited success. In response, you set lower goals and move away from what you really would like to accomplish. You may then find yourself, years later, working in a way that denies or ignores your potential. You can finally burn out at work because you slowly grow to realize—just on the edge of awareness—that what you are doing is much less than what you could be doing.

Sören Kierkegaard said, "Our life always expresses the result of our dominant thoughts." The things people expect, believe, and tell themselves determine what they accomplish. Negative, limiting beliefs erode your motivation and your faith in yourself to accomplish what you want. If you want to make significant accomplishments at work, your thoughts and conversations with yourself need to contain visions and beliefs that support these achievements.

Limits are not just about negative thinking. They are built into your perceptions. People see what they look for. It has been said that "if you have a hammer, everything looks like a nail." That is why, for example, for several years auto executives in Detroit simply did not perceive the public's shift to a desire for smaller, fuel-efficient, easily fixed cars. Leaders in the auto industry expected people to want what they had wanted in the past and believed that major U.S. manufacturers could continue to dictate consumer taste. They are still recovering from their mistakes.

Let us look more closely at the nature of a negative belief. By definition, it is a conviction that something is not possible. Famous examples from the past were demonstrated by the people who told the Wright brothers that people could never fly, the scientists who said breaking the four-minute mile was physiologically impossible, and the marketer who said that electric light was an impractical fad. In all these examples, people closed off the possibility that the future could be decisively different and instead projected the past to continue indefinitely into the future. In contrast is the realization that the only sure thing is that things will change. And the rate of change is increasing.

Limiting beliefs involve the irrational assumption that things will not change. Their effect is to keep people from trying, from looking, from taking risks, and from attempting the "impossible." More mundane and more personal examples can help illustrate how limiting beliefs can keep you from the achievements you are capable of at work.

SHIFTING THE CORPORATE CULTURE

One common company belief that dims the spark in many creative employees is, "This company will never change." People used to say that about the giant, regulated monolith AT&T. Then, with one court decision, everything changed. Now, all the deregulated telephone companies are plunging into new products and new markets, and they are trying new management styles. The reason—they have to. Their survival and success depends on it.

Massive external shifts force other giants to change as well—tobacco companies are threatened, food manufacturers are challenged to find new marketing ideas, camera companies struggle to keep up with new technologies, and products like microcomputers are widespread where a few years ago they were nonexistent. Too often, companies are hampered from adapting by their outmoded beliefs. In one such company, we worked with managers who were asked to take on new, more marketing-oriented roles. Some of the managers who were most highly stressed told us they did not know how to make the required changes.

Every company is threatened by the belief that nothing can change and that the way things have been is the only way they can be. Companies, as well as individuals, need help to discover new possibilities, not to justify why things must remain the same.

Limiting company beliefs are true in one sense and not so in another. They are true in that most people in the company share them and limit their behavior accordingly. These people do not try new things, and they often act in rigid ways. However, these beliefs are also untrue in that unexpected things happen when they are disregarded. For example, one commonly accepted belief in your company might be that women can never make it to top management. The exclusion of women may exist today. However, as conditions change, no one can be sure when that "truth" may change. Maybe affirmative action regulations or new values have made the company more receptive to new behavior. Acting as if the limit does not exist, or questioning it, might lead to new standards. A pioneer is the person who is first to question or disregard a limit.

Negative beliefs keep people from making the contribution they are capable of. Remember David in the ad agency. He saw ways that he could make a difference, be more creative, and give more to the company, but the agency prevented it. Blaming the agency assumes that the limitation lay outside of David himself.

For example, when David says, "They won't let me try anything new," or, "They don't want what I have to offer," and gives up, what is likely to be the long-term outcome? The self-fulfilling prophesy operates, limiting any attempts to probe further about why his suggestions are turned down. At one company, a person with such a negative belief inquired further and was told by a mentor that there were some things about the way he presented his ideas that turned people off. He never asked others' opinions, he never took time to explain things fully to people who could be helpful, and he never appeared to be willing to really help other people with their projects. Now, instead of an erroneous belief that kept him from going further, he had some clear information. But he had another dilemma—what to do with all this feedback. What he did next was to embark on a personal program to develop the areas where he was weak. Since then, he has become an innovator and sparkplug for new programs.

One key to being turned on and re-energized by work is to move beyond the limitation of negative beliefs about yourself and about your workplace (including the people in it). Inspired performers focus on *possibilities* rather than limits. Every time you say to yourself, "I can't," or, "This isn't possible," you need to shift your focus by saying, "How can I find out exactly what is possible?" or, "I need to learn_____to do this," or, "I need to explore this area to discover how this might be possible." There are no absolute impossibilities, if the goal is real and important enough for you to commit to it.

Here is an exercise to explore your beliefs. Make a list of the limiting beliefs that you hold about yourself and about your workplace or work team. Start with, "At work, I can't. . . . My company can't. . . . My team or my colleagues can't. . . ." Take time to become conscious of negative or limiting beliefs that interfere with your effectiveness and energy at work. You will use this list in the next exercises. Think of things you say to yourself in times of frustration. Or look at the situations at work where you feel the most pressure, and think about how these difficulties might be related to internal beliefs about yourself and about your workplace.

Most people make fairly long lists. Curiously, even though each list is very individual, when managers share their lists, the nervous laughter that greets each statement suggests that the items are also very common. Many people labor under similar sets of negative, self-limiting beliefs. When members of a work group share their lists of negatives, most groups discover that the items on the lists usually contradict the company's stated values. For example, we have yet to encounter a company that does not say that it values innovation and allows open communication. Yet, companies often act differently. Managers may actually be discouraged from talking about problem areas or told not to ask difficult questions. While the limiting items are almost always agreed upon, they are rarely talked about. Yet, it is only by talking about them and evaluating their effects that their negative consequences can be shifted.

Our training as cultural anthropologists taught us important lessons about changing the direction of a company's culture. Like changes in developing countries, organizations undertaking change must understand that they are shifting deeply held beliefs and values. The first lesson of change requires that the belief system must be shifted to incorporate the new way of operating. Just as individuals have belief systems, so do organizations. Studying how individuals change beliefs is a key to understanding how organizations can change them.

Communication and training are the keys to shifting beliefs and values. Often people are unaware of what values and beliefs are operating before they try to change them. In one office it was assumed that a messy desk was a sign of hard work. Another belief was that long hours in the office meant a lot of work was being done. The values clearly emphasized quantity and not quality. To change the office culture, we began with a meeting to look at current values and belief systems. The people found they focused on quantity and not quality. They listed behaviors that reflected quantity or quality. We decided on a strategy of experimentation. They would practice using behaviors from the quality list. To take this another step into the company, we set up more meetings to see how the emphasis on quantity was embedded in the larger company policies. We found in the next discussions that some of each perspective existed in the larger organization. Because we could not change the whole organization overnight, we chose to focus on promoting the quality behaviors. This was our way of seeding the quality focus throughout the company.

CHANGING BELIEFS

How can you change limiting beliefs? One of the most effective and common tools is your imagination, which can create new beliefs and expectations. Here is an exercise to turn around one self-defeating belief.

Select one limiting belief about yourself that you would like to modify. Repeat it aloud to yourself and then you may wish to close your eyes and imagine clearly what you believe you cannot achieve. See a picture of yourself achieving this. Take enough time to let the picture become clear. You cannot do anything that you cannot first imagine yourself doing. See yourself doing every step of what you want to achieve, not just the final outcome. For example, if you want to become a leader in a project team, see yourself doing everything that you will have to do to achieve what you want. Imagine not just the outcome but the whole journey toward your goal. If you are imagining a skill or capacity that you would like to develop, see yourself doing the things that you will need to do to learn that skill or unleash that capacity. The more precise you are, the more precisely you have begun to program yourself to achieve your goal. As you generate the mental picture of the goal, you will also have some positive feelings that go along with the accomplishment. These feelings will be pleasurable and, more important, they will be energizing.

Now you have the seed of a new belief.

Another way to shift a belief is through actual experiment. Take one limiting belief about yourself or your job. Get a clear picture of what the belief implies will happen. Then imagine a way that you could test it out. For example, your belief might be that your supervisor only wants things done his or her way. For your test, you might select an idea to improve production that you have been harboring for several months. Your limiting belief might be that your supervisor will not listen, but your experiment leads to a plan to present your new procedure. Clearly, tactfully, but assertively, you make your case. To your surprise, while your supervisor is indeed a little resistant, he or she is persuaded by your idea and agrees to the change. Reality testing has taught you that the limit is not as absolute as you assumed. You feel more freedom and more satisfaction with your work than you have in nearly a year. (There is, of course, a risk that your supervisor will refuse. Risk is explored in Chapter 6.)

Beliefs about yourself and what can happen always control you, acting as internal organizing structures, mobilizing or limiting your psychic energy and attention. Now that you have isolated some beliefs that keep you from your goals, here is a powerful method for realigning your beliefs with your personal mission. This process is called *affirmation*. The affirmation process is a way of changing behavior by consciously changing beliefs. Instead of being limited by the set of beliefs that you developed unconsciously and inadvertently, you initiate a process of creating beliefs that lead toward your personal goals. By creating internal energy centers around these positive beliefs, you begin to mobilize the drive to move forward.

Look at your negative beliefs about yourself and your workplace. Select another one that you would like to modify. For example, you might select a limiting belief about your own capabilities, such as "I can't get any further in this company," or "I'm just not a person who can stick to anything." Now, begin by turning the belief around. By this, we do not mean to turn it into its opposite—for example, "I can become the president of the company," or "I can accomplish anything I desire." Rather, turn the belief around by exploring the other side of the limit—what you want from the situation you feel limited in. You might find, for example, "I want to advance and be recognized by others as a high-potential manager," or "I want to complete one successful new product campaign." Notice that you are not just turning around the negative belief but also making it more concrete and specific. One reason that negative beliefs defeat us is because they are so overpoweringly global. You want to formulate a positive statement of a goal, what you want to do or accomplish. This is a second method of changing beliefs.

Draft your affirmation this way. Write a sentence that describes your goal as already accomplished. As you write it take a moment to see in your mind's eye what you want, and to feel the feelings that are associated with it. The sentence that forms your affirmation should be short and positive. For example, you might say to yourself, "I am a respected and much-praised manager, whose supervision and results are a model for others in my department."

There are several additional guidelines you can use to strengthen your affirmations. First, the affirmation should be about what *you* want to have done, not something that others do. It should be about *your behavior* and its effects on others. Second, it should be stated in the present tense, as if you have accomplished your goal. It should focus on what you have done or achieved. Third, it should be something that you can really see and feel yourself doing, an assessment that pushes you beyond what you have already done, but not so far ahead that you will be setting yourself up for failure. The affirmation might include some of the excitement you will feel when you reach the desired goals. Look at your affirmation and see if it meets these guidelines. Then, go down your list of negative beliefs, and turn each one around into an affirmation that sets you in the direction of something new. Do not limit yourself to what you have done or not done in the past.

To make use of an affirmation you must repeat it to yourself daily. Repeat your list of affirmations to yourself several times, and feel the effect they have on you. You may want to write them on a card and place it someplace where you will see it regularly—on your mirror or refrigerator door. It may be helpful to pare your list somewhat and pick one or two affirmations to focus on for a period of time. Take a few moments at the beginning of each day and repeat them to yourself. In your mind's eye, see them in action. Then, explore ways that you could move toward those goals in your work that day. Do not just plan a bunch of things or make a list, but let your inner sense of what you need to do come out. Try to make a commitment each day to do something that moves you toward realizing your affirmation. Ask yourself at the end of each day what you have done to move you toward your goal.

For example Teisha changed her inner beliefs about work as the first step of what has become a total shift in how she works. She was a probation officer, one of the most burnout-prone occupations. People in her agency almost universally went around hating their work and feeling helpless to change the vast bureaucracy. A psychology class led her to an experiment. She learned about how people could see the world in one of two ways: either as coming from inside themselves or as coming from the outside environment. Clearly, most probation officers felt that control lay outside of them.

She decided that her anxiety came from feeling that she had no control. She created an affirmation for herself:

> I was always asking "What do they want?" not "What do I want?" I decided to change my attitude first, by saying to myself, "I love my job." The others thought I was crazy. So did I at first. But things began to change, and it became easier to work. Then, somehow, I heard that they were looking for a volunteeer director. They would reassign one officer to develop links to local colleges and to find volunteers to help out. I thought it would be very exciting, and I decided to go for it. Forty others were interviewed. I got the position. They said that my answers were so positive and I seemed so excited that they had to give it to me.

An affirmation and some new beliefs led to a chain reaction of events that has since propelled her into a series of new and more exciting jobs.

INTUITION: THE SOUL OF CREATIVITY

Your inner voice offers more than just limiting beliefs. The unconscious or subconscious mind is also a source of wisdom and creativity. Think of the times in your life when you had a hunch or suddenly saw things in a new way, that helped you accomplish some important task. The history of invention is filled with moments when a person, after working on a problem fruitlessly for a long time, had a sudden breakthrough. In *The Soul of a New Machine,* about the creation of a new computer, Tracy Kidder talks about the "golden moment" that designers, scientists, and artists have when the "scales fall from the designer's eyes and the right solution is suddenly there." * In Kidder's example, there was a breakthrough moment when the leading engineer came up with a solution to a design problem that made the new computer not just another product but a genuine innovation. He came

---

* Tracy Kidder, *The Soul of a New Machine* (Boston: Little, Brown, 1981), p. 80.

up with a new way to design the internal architecture, the information storage model for the memory chips, that was far more efficient and made the product faster and more efficient. Just a little shift in how it was done had a profound effect on the product itself and energized the whole team.

Where do these breakthrough moments come from? Actually, they are frequent occurrences for everyone. Think back over your life. Have you had a hunch that you should be doing something or making a shift? We all do. However, our training is to ignore hunches or to distrust them as irrational. Yet, these insights often reveal unexpected, creative ways to approach issues and struggles.

At work, these moments can turn a project around. One company was having difficulty coming up with a useful marketing plan for a new product. The whole group felt they were just going through the motions, but since they were doing all the right things, they just kept going. Then one person said, "It just doesn't feel right. Nobody seems to really have a sense of excitement about what we are doing." Everyone agreed, and they began to talk about their feelings, to look inward and see that their energy was blocked. The conversation became more intense, and people began to pay attention.

The group discovered they were all ignoring their feelings. Then, one member had a breakthrough. He looked at the sales of their last product and said, "Maybe we should just look at what worked last time." Instead of creating a huge comprehensive marketing plan, they discovered that what worked in their small company was a plan that targeted the special customers who would appreciate and purchase their products. It sounds like a simple shift, but until the planning team stepped back, looked at their feelings, and consulted their inner voices, the breakthrough hunch, and the resulting shift, could not have occurred.

These hunches can also be called intuitions. Intuition was long considered synonymous with superstition and not worthy of serious attention. However, psychologists like Carl Jung began systematic study of intuitive events. Jung and others looked at the creative moment, the act of seeing something that is wholly new and unprecedented. Jung defines intuition as a mode of knowing that bypasses the senses, mind, and feeling. Intuition seems strange to us because it comes instantaneously and directly from the unconscious, complete in itself. Creative scientific breakthroughs, artistic and poetic visions, as well as organizational possibilities come through intuition.

Management professor Weston Agor studied intuitive processes in hundreds of managers. A disproportionate percentage of managers at top levels of organization utilize intuition in their most important decisions. These are not impractical visionaries who reject rationality or scientific data. They go beyond the rational, and their achievements are clear and useful. Agor, in *Intuitive Management,* reports that intuition is a process that top managers bring to important decisions *after* they have digested all the data and have come to a dead end using traditional methods.

These top managers are not any more intuitive than anyone else. Every person has intuitions all the time. Think of the hunches you have had recently—the times you had a sense that you should or should not do something. Did you listen and consider these intuitions or disregard them? Often, people reject them and later recall that they had a sense that the correct event would happen.

Here is an exercise to stimulate your intuitive processes. Take a particular problem or challenge that you face now, or focus on a person who is difficult for you to work with. Find a quiet place, and prepare yourself to enter the inward, reflective state you have already practiced. Take some deep breaths and relax yourself deeply. Deep relaxation is the way that you open the gates to your inner self.

Now, in your mind's eye, create a picture that represents the problem or person you wish to focus on. The picture might be of yourself working on that problem, or of that person as he or she actually looks. Or, your imagination may present you with a symbolic or fanciful picture that it connects to the person or situation. Just allow yourself to be open to what comes. Do not be judgmental or tell yourself that you have the wrong picture. Just accept whatever images come up, whatever happens in this exercise.

Let the picture that is emerging get into clearer focus. Now, imagine that the mental picture can talk to you and that you can reply. Ask the image what it wants to tell you or what you need to learn. You will be surprised to discover that the image will give you a response. The response may take the form of words, or the picture itself may simply change or shift. Just allow the response to emerge; do not try to create it or prompt it into being.

You may want to continue to converse with the image in your mind, asking more about why it is a problem for you, or asking what it can suggest to help you deal with the problem. Do not think about whether what you are seeing, hearing, or feeling makes any sense. You will interpret the message later. Take as long as you want on the exercise. Now, slowly bring yourself back into ordinary awareness.

The images and responses you received in this exercise are ways that your unconscious, intuitive mind works on the challenge you present. Do not expect a full-blown solution. The intuitive faculty offers you a new way of seeing a situation, to illuminate possibilities that you missed or neglected. Intuition uncovers additional, partly hidden possibilities. The challenges most of us face at work are such that old solutions, and rational planning, are not enough. We need to develop our capacity to have breakthroughs, to see things differently.

You can apply intuition to any problem, in any number of ways. If you do not have spontaneous intuition, you can help it along by using the reflective process we have just taught. The most important thing to remember is to relax and to accept, without judgment, the images and responses you get to a situation. Then afterwards, you can see what sense they make, and how you will use them.

To give one example of how this exercise can work, an airline flight attendant, fighting a serious case of burnout after twenty-two years on the job, focused on what she would do about her work pressure. She asked for a picture of the pressure, and she saw herself in the form of an old, hunched-up bag lady, carrying her few possessions in a dirty paper bag. When she asked what she needed to learn, the lady turned into a more youthful mountain hiker, in shorts, carrying a walking stick, and the bag turned into a knapsack. She straightened up and climbed the mountain. She felt a tremendous release of energy. What did she make of this? The message was that the job was killing her, and she could not wait the three years for full retirement. Her decision was that it was necessary to leave the job now and attend to her own personal development.

A charge of energy is liberated in all intuitive exercises and indeed every time you pay attention to the messages of your inner self. Burnout dams up your energy, because you are expending all you have to keep from listening to yourself. Burnout is like flooring a car when it is not in gear—it gets you nowhere but causes grave harm to the engine. When you listen, you really gun your inner energy engine, but this time you are in gear and moving. The energy is focused, and you find that you are moving toward your goals.

FEELINGS: YOUR INNER WARNING SYSTEM

People talk about marching to the beat of a different drummer. In many ways, what separates the high-energy worker from the burned-out worker is the capacity to listen to messages from inner voices. These voices come in many forms: feelings, body symptoms, and intuitions. Your inner self sends messages that are important to your capacity to be effective. When you learn to unravel these messages and pay attention to them—not to the exclusion of other messages and demands—then you also make tremendous energy reserves and inner sources of wisdom available that can make your work so much more powerful.

It is surprising that many managers who are masters of the external world—who supervise hundreds of employees and deal with millions of dollars in resources and complex processes—spend almost no time learning about their inner world. Perception is turned outward, toward mastery of outer processes. When it comes to self-mastery, the ability to balance, pace, and renew one's inner resources, the manager is often lost. In American culture, especially at work, the primary way that people think they manage pressure is by ignoring it. But pressure then builds up, day by day.

How do you handle the pressure? Early in life, especially if you are male, you learn that you are expected to push through. Keep going, don't give in. If you feel pain, you probably take an aspirin, smoke, have a drink, or eat when the tension builds up. We call these habits *quick fixes,* because they bring the illusion of relief. After a while, even the slightest pressure message triggers these responses.

Now, what do they actually accomplish? Physiologically, each quick fix masks the tension. Alcohol, nicotine, food, and aspirin all separate you from the experience of your tension, even though they do nothing about the source of tension or about the negative effects of constant tension inside your body. Body tension remains in the form of tight muscles, increased blood pressure, secretion of stomach acid, and activation of stress hormones that cause your body to work on "hyperdrive." Under the influence of a quick fix, all these continue outside of awareness.

They produce a sort of numbness. What was once a responsive and expressive body, capable of a wide range of responses, eventually becomes closed. In effect, you say to yourself that *how* you operate in the outer world is important but *what* and *who* you are is irrelevant. The consequences of numbness are more serious even than burnout—your life may be at stake.

Here is an example. If you touch a hot stove, the pain response is a warning sign that cannot be ignored. Besides pain, there are other signals that are capable of registering various tensions and levels of distress. If you use drugs, food, or smoking to numb yourself, it is as if you are keeping your hand anchored to the stove, while taking a shot of Novocaine for the pain. The result is a continual drain, destructive wear and tear in the body. Minor signals are ignored, creating conditions for a major breakdown. That breakdown can be burnout or serious illness.

Dennis had a vivid experience of this when he worked at UCLA School of Medicine, in a residential program for key executives recovering from heart disease. Many were overweight and had alcohol problems. He asked how they handled stress. They all said they did not let it get to them. These were all people who had been hospitalized for heart trouble! Then, he hooked them up to biofeedback equipment that measured their muscle tension, and he told them to relax. When they experienced themselves as relaxed, their actual muscle tension was about fourteen times normal. Even in the hospital, not working (sometimes for the first time in many years), these people were under incredible tension—and they were unaware of it. Over the years, in managing their work worlds, they had almost completely lost touch with themselves.

They had to overcome a lifetime of using quick fixes to manage stress. Using quick fixes—believing that if you do not feel pain then things are fine —can lead to a personal crisis, sometimes through a health breakdown, sometimes from loss of energy. When you get hit over the head—when you reach the crisis—you have to do things differently. If you do not listen to early warning signs, you may need a major crisis to claim your attention.

The basic principle is: *Listen to the message and discover what it is trying to teach you.* When you are not feeling energized by work, there is a reason for it. If you take a drink and try to ignore it, you will have missed the opportunity to learn how to approach things differently, and you will simply be continuing your past mistakes.

Listening to your inner voice is "following the energy." If you feel charged up and excited, you are on the right track. You will find that things at work are easy. As you work, while you may become tired, the tiredness at the end of the day is different from exhaustion. You will feel, along with tiredness, the sense of satisfaction and accomplishment that marks achievement.

But, if you are like most people, many times you feel the opposite. You begin to feel drained, apathetic, bored, disconnected. Common feelings, but what do *you* do when you begin to feel them? These are all messages about your work, that you need to pay attention to. Burned-out people have one experience in common: They had these negative feelings for a long time, and they either ignored them, turned them off, or just gave up.

These negative and positive messages offer critical information about the emotional concerns that may be hidden from your awareness. You may feel angry or upset about something, or excited and happy. Emotions are direct and basic; they are your inner evaluation of a situation as good or bad, threatening or helpful. In many American households, especially among men, feelings have very bad press. Men are often taught not to show feelings or even to recognize them. If they are angry, hurt, excited, or upset at work they are taught that feelings are unprofessional or unsightly. So they hide feelings, not just from others but eventually from themselves. Emotional men are looked down on.

The feelings are still there, deep inside. You may be angry, hurt, threatened, or joyous inside, even if you are not aware of it. But when you suppress feelings, you in effect act against yourself. You create an inner conflict—needing to do one thing, but actually doing another. It has a way of catching up with you.

For example, Barry, an office branch manager, felt drained at the end of every day. He tried all sorts of things to feel better—getting more sleep, working out, watching TV—but nothing worked. At the office, he was the picture of congeniality and even temper—always helping out, never complaining. He had even gotten into the habit of doing work that properly belonged to others but never asking for help. His people liked him, in part because he did a lot of their work and was not very demanding. Barry will always help us out, they thought.

What were Barry's actual feelings? He was furious, resentful, and really wanted others to pitch in and help him. But he could not acknowledge to himself that he had those feelings, and he therefore never took them into account. He never let himself *consciously* feel aggravated. He was in the early stages of burnout, ignoring inner messages. He worked for everyone else, not himself. Burnout was a message from his *feeling* self—saying, "Hey, what about me?"

Think about the purposes of the messages Barry was getting from his inner self. Barry seemed very easygoing. Was he? Or was he angry, resentful? Actually, neither was true. People are not all angry, or all easygoing. People have a vast range of feelings. Sometimes they are angry, sometimes kind and caring, and sometimes, as in Barry's case, both at once. Think of Barry's exhaustion and anger as a message to him, a warning, much like the pain from touching a hot stove. What was the warning? His anger was telling him that he had gone overboard, giving himself away to his job and his subordinates. He was not looking out for his own welfare and was creating a dangerous imbalance. If he paid heed to his feelings, he would hear, in effect, "Maybe you've done enough for them. It wouldn't be a bad idea if you asked them to do something for you." The negative messages were attempting to bring him back into balance. By ignoring and denying them, he set himself up to burn out.

Information comes in from the environment through our senses. Then our mind looks at it and makes a judgment. You have seen how the mind brings its own blinders to the evaluation of information—beliefs. Feelings also affect the interpretation of information. Feelings are keys to what it means to the whole person, to inner needs. Ignore feelings at your peril!

BODY TALK AND THE TYPE A TREADMILL

If you ignore feelings they may create physical distress. An intense feeling can cause you to tense up physically. Even if you do not recognize and take the feelings into account, they still act on your body. Over time, you may become aware of physical symptoms: *body talk*. Daily language recognizes how your body can communicate with you. A person may say something "makes my flesh crawl," "gives me a headache," or "makes me sick." These expressions reflect ways your body responds to stress.

If you have a headache at 3:00 every day, or if you wake up one day too sick to go to work, you should do more than just take an aspirin or stay home. You need to ask, "What is triggering these responses?" Many physical illnesses may be the long-term results of ignored inner messages.

You have probably heard about the Type A behavior pattern, identified by cardiologists Meyer Friedman and Ray Rosenman. Type A activity is related to the development of heart disease. Type A behavior is defined as "a continuous struggle to accomplish more, achieve more or participate in more events in less and less time, frequently in the face of opposition—real or imagined—from others." *

* Meyer Friedman and Diane Ulmer, *Treating Type A Behavior: And Your Heart* (New York: Fawcett Crest, 1984), p. 33.

• • •

The Type A person not only has "hurry sickness" at work, but feels more and more resentful of other people. Over time, these tendencies get worse, because the feelings and inner responses are ignored or denied. Finally, the struggle gets expressed in the body, in the form of illness. Initially, most Type A people deny that they are angry and resentful. Their neglected feelings move to their body, aggravating illness.

Friedman and his colleagues helped several thousand Type A people become more aware of the inner messages of their bodies and their feelings. For a year, at weekly sessions, Type A people were taught to moderate their behavior. They learned that their impatience was accompanied by anger and hostility, feelings that they could not identify at first. They practiced slowing down and learned time management. But, most important, they began to explore the possibility that they wanted more from their lives than simply to get more done at work in less time.

The encouraging findings suggest that Type A behavior can be modified and that, when that happens, the incidence and severity of heart disease are decreased as well. When Type A people learn to attend to themselves, the self-destructive pattern is broken.

Friedman's program to change Type A behavior involves learning to listen to internal signals and changing from a narrow focus on control to a broader focus of concerns, involvements, and attachments. But the program never talks about *controlling* the self. That would be self-defeating, because the Type A person is already overcontrolling. Rather, it talks about acquiring more *freedom* in life. The former Type A person learns to live with more possibilities. The ten freedoms that Friedman's program cultivates are:

- The freedom to overcome insecurity and regain self-esteem
- The freedom to give and receive love
- The freedom to mature
- The freedom to restore and enrich the personality
- The freedom to overcome and replace old hurtful habits with new life-enriching ones
- The freedom to take pleasure in the experiences of friends and family members
- The freedom to recall the past frequently and with satisfaction
- The freedom to listen
- The freedom to play
- The freedom to enjoy tranquillity

These ten freedoms form an effective framework for building zest in life and renewing your relation to work. How do they accomplish that? They include many activities in which you tune in and listen to your inner self. They include caring connections with other people and deep relationships. And they add an element of balance to life.

BALANCING WORK AND LIFE

One of the most common experiences reported by burned-out people is that, despite the lack of positive energy and good feelings from work, they try to work more and more and to move away from nonwork attachments. They do the opposite of what their feelings suggest. By the time burnout makes it impossible to work, a person may be cut off from any other meaningful activity and relationships. A surprising report from charged-up workers is the opposite: They tend to take time for personal and family relationships, and to have outside hobbies and involvements. They have lives that are in balance.

To look at the degree of balance in your own life, imagine an energy wheel that represents how your energy is distributed between work and personal life, and between giving to others and receiving back. Use the

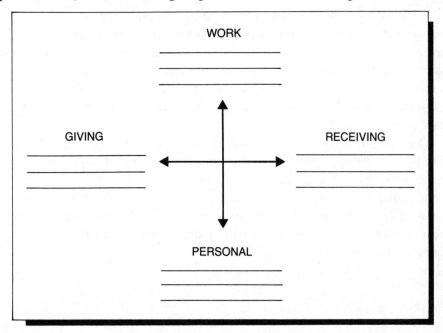

diagram on p. 151 as a model. Fill in each of the blanks with activities that fit into each area, and see if there is one part of your life that is unbalanced or undeveloped. Then, imagine some things you could do in that area.

When you begin to lose energy and motivation at work, sometimes it is the result of an imbalance somewhere else. As a child you probably had many interests claiming your energy. As you grow up, building a career, your lens narrows. Sometimes, the message of feelings, the drain of energy, is a signal that you have become too narrow. For example, one executive talked about how he had been a gifted pianist before college but had given up music to concentrate on more practical concerns. Now, as his company faced a difficult takeover threat, he had no way to relax. He mentioned that he had had a dream about playing the piano, something he had not done in years. Soon, he bought a piano and started to play again. He began to look forward to an hour or so of music at the end of each day, rather than a cocktail and watching the evening news. He felt more refreshed each day, even though his work pressure was greater. His wife also noticed that he was more genial and energetic at home. He had renewed his connection to an activity that gave his life balance and tapped into his creative, inner reserves. Most surprisingly, he found that after playing the piano, he sometimes had some very powerful and helpful intuitions about his work situation.

In the focus on work and career, many people forget about youthful passions or do not allow themselves to pursue potential new interests. "I'm too old to do something new," or "I don't have the time," are the standard excuses. Yet, sometimes, the message that comes from listening to themselves is that they need more breadth. They need to open up time to let more personal relationships in or to take up old passions once again or discover new ones.

You will have to practice the skill of listening to yourself. Almost everyone has learned the opposite—to turn inside messages off. Over time, hearing these subtle messages can help you discover or recover your energy for work, offering the organic wisdom of your inner self. This innner wisdom sometimes points more clearly to what you need for health and well-being than does your conscious, thoughtful, reflective mind. Learn to pay attention, or you will get the message too late.

PART III

Taking Charge— High Tech Meets High Touch

CHAPTER 6

CREATING PERSONAL POWER: THE SKILLS FOR GETTING WHAT YOU WANT

The adaptive corporation needs a new kind of leadership. It needs "managers of adaptation" equipped with a whole new set of non-linear skills.

Above all, the adaptive manager today must be capable of radical action—willing to think beyond the thinkable: to reconceptualize products, procedures, programs and purposes before crisis makes drastic change inescapable.

Warned of impending upheaval, most managers still pursue business-as-usual. Yet business-as-usual is dangerous in an environment that has become, for all practical purposes, permanently convulsive.

—ALVIN TOFFLER, *THE ADAPTIVE CORPORATION*

People dream of making it to the top. Sometimes, the allure is for the wealth and prestige such a position would bring. But, most often, people dream of being at the top because they think that is where they can really get things done. At the top, they will finally have *power,* so they can do what they want. Before then, they expect to be frustrated and powerless, because they are so far down in the organization, or in their profession or career.

Talk to any chief executive and you will find that the myth is far from the reality. People at the top feel all sorts of limits and frustrations. Richard Neustadt points out in his classic book *Presidential Power* that the first thing every new U.S. President discovers is that even he cannot make anybody do anything or cause anything to happen. Presidential power rests in having the ear of the country and being able to persuade and educate others to do something. It rests, as our Declaration of Independence notes, with the "consent of the governed."

This is true in organizations as well. In the mid-'60's when all organizations were in turmoil, a group who worked at low levels in a mental health center decided, in the wisdom of youth, that they could do a better job than their superiors. To their amazement, they got a grant and a mandate to set up an alternate mental health service for young people. Dennis was one of three directors. So in a few weeks, he leapfrogged from the bottom to the top of the heap.

Many things happened, most painfully the discovery that even the directors of the program could not change the mental health system overnight. They could not get the many volunteers and counselors to do what they thought was needed. The directors were increasingly frustrated and angry. The staff perceived them as autocratic and power-hungry, even though the directors actually felt helpless. Soon the directors were hearing the same things from the staff that they themselves had said when they were low-level workers. How had this come to pass?

Like generations of leaders, under pressure they tried to operate by control—holding tight to a sense of what they wanted, leaving no space for other people to have a part of things. The more tightly they held on, the more frustrated they felt. The more they tried to make others do something, the farther they got from their goal. That seems to be the painful reality of many organizations today. Powerlessness runs not just through the lower levels of the organization, but at the top as well. Harvard business school professor Rosabeth Kanter pointed out in *The Change Masters* that many of the controlling and autocratic behaviors in companies are actually expressions of feelings of powerlessness and frustration, rather than the real exercise of power.

LIBERATING THE ENERGY FOR ACTION

The word "power" comes from the Latin "posse," meaning "to be able." Power usually derives from an inner sense of capacity to do what one thinks is important. Getting power and using it seem to be primary human needs. Nowhere are those needs more critical than at work.

Personal power is not getting people to do things or having them behave in a certain way. It is *getting what you want* at work and in your organization, the capacity to meet your needs and move toward your goals and visions. Personal power does not lie outside yourself—in your job title or status. Rather, power is an inner experience of capability.

Burnout, boredom, and frustration arise when you focus on what you cannot do at work, how limited you are. When you begin to shift your attention to what you can do—exploring other ways to get things done, taking risks, implementing your personal goals, and restructuring your job to fit your own personal style—things come alive for you and usually for the people around you. Empowerment by one person liberates organizational energy. It galvanizes others to action. Power involves an attitude that is then joined to *concrete action* for meaningful goals.

The excitement and vitality of work are directly affected by the degree to which you experience personal power. Power does not come attached to a job. Rather, power comes from the general way in which you approach working in that job. While every job, even the highest, has many constraints that limit a person's power within it, you can focus on the other side—the possibilities for making a difference at work. Every job includes a large area of improvisation in which you can increase or diminish your personal power. Every job, no matter where you work, or how rigid the organization, contains much more room for the exercise of personal power than you probably realize.

For example, many people feel assembly line work involves no freedom, no room for any personal expression of power. That is why assembly line work has traditionally been ripe for burnout and worker demoralization.

Yet, working with several assembly lines and factories, we have heard some amazing stories about how people in such jobs have used personal power to make their jobs fit their needs better.

One worker spent many years looking around his plant, thinking up ways to make it run better. That was how he entertained himself. But, since he felt that he had no power to do anything, that nobody would really listen to him, he rarely shared these ideas. Then, he heard some people talking about Japanese management, and about how workers formed quality circles where they proposed better ways to organize things. He spoke one day to a union representative, who told him that management was indeed thinking of starting quality circles. The union representative invited him to become part of a union/management task force to implement the program. While his assembly line work remained the same, he suddenly had an outlet for his creative energy and another way to participate in his job. He became a key member of this team and began to play a greater role in worksite innovation. He felt more valued for his ideas and this made his experience more meaningful and challenging to him. His informal involvement offered a constructive way to get more of what he needed and greatly increased his energy, dedication, and effectiveness at work.

Music promoter Dennis Jones is serving a life sentence in San Quentin, in a five-by-eleven-foot cell. He maintains that he is innocent. Frustrated by his own appeals, he decided to do something. "It took me a while to come out from under the ether. I felt that since I had the ability to do something, I couldn't just sit around," Jones explains. Using mail and his outside network of contacts, he decided that he could help organize prison benefits. He still functions as a concert promoter, organizing benefits for the Freedom Foundation that helps falsely accused prisoners gain new hearings. Jones has learned that empowerment rests in the decisions he makes about where to spend his energy. He could be a bitter victim of the system, or he could create an outlet for his creative energy.

We have yet to find a person or a job with no way to enhance personal power, to make the work better fit the personal needs. The key skill to increase personal power is to find the pathway to make a difference at work, in a way that works for you and helps your company as well. In the rest of this chapter we will show you how to mobilize the key skills that enhance your personal power at work and how they can be applied to the process of *job enhancement*. Enhancement involves expanding or modifying your job so that it provides you with more of what you want, giving you more chance to be effective and powerful.

HEALTH, CONTROL, AND EMPOWERMENT

Personal power also affects what goes on inside the body. Many managers struggle with major chronic and critical illnesses. Health researchers find that people who feel that they have some control over their illness and their future fare better than those who believe they are helpless. A large study of sick days at work due to minor ailments found that people who felt there was something they could do about pain and illness took far fewer days off.

People who survive critical illnesses often see the illness as a lesson, and make major life changes during recovery. Afterwards, they take a more active role in caring for their bodies and focus more consciously on what they want from their lives and how they will get it. Curiously, despite the fact that their bodies in many ways are beginning to fail them, they report a greater sense of personal power after they have recovered from their illnesses. They report things like, "After recovering from a heart attack, everything else I tried to do seemed easy. I got more done at work because I stopped wasting time. I focused on what I wanted, and I went for it. There wasn't time to take things slowly."

A famous long-term study of heart disease in Framingham, Massachusetts, uncovered more support for the concept of personal power. The three work factors most associated with heart disease were suppressed hostility, dealing with an unsupportive boss, and lack of job mobility. People who had more autonomy and control over the work they did were less likely to have chronic medical problems.

We have already mentioned the study of stress-resistant managers by Suzanne Kobasa. She found that a sense of control over what one does at work is the key factor in optimal performance. The more control workers have over their work, the more satisfied, the healthier, and the more effective they will be.

A classic program was developed in the 1960's at a Volvo plant in Sweden. In this experimental factory, each work team was responsible not just for one tiny activity but for a whole part of the finished auto. They met together and decided how they wanted to work, how to divide up the jobs, and when to stop and start the assembly line. As long as they met their quotas, they set their own hours as well. Even years later, this factory has the highest productivity and the lowest number of defects of all other Volvo plants.

In offices, in retail stores, in transportation and service industries, individual control is increasing. While following general procedures and expectations, individual employees have more leeway to decide how to do things. This autonomy is especially important in service industries. Several studies of what a customer wanted from an employee—whether at a ticket counter, reservation desk, shop floor, or telephone—show that customers want the person they talk to to have the authority to help them handle their problem. A British Airways customer survey showed that customers easily tolerate a company's making a mistake, for example, losing a reservation. But when they come for help, they want the person who serves them to be able to work with them to find a way to rectify the situation.

Only an employee who feels empowered to act, to improvise a solution if need be, can be effective on the firing line. When a clerk says, "I'm sorry, there's nothing I can do," or "Well, my supervisor will be here at ten and maybe she can help you," or "Write to our customer service department," the organization loses a customer.

When people feel they have the authority and personal power to do their jobs the best way they can, to improvise and make changes without being second-guessed or punished, everyone benefits. The old image of power was that some people at the top had it and others lower down did not. My power came at your expense. The new vision of personal power does not come at someone else's expense. We have collected thousands of examples of inspired performance at our workshops, and they all have one quality in common. When people recall times when they were working up to their highest capacity, deeply involved and excited at work, they felt empowered and, universally, they reported that the other people in their work groups, including their boss, all felt empowered as well. When one person is empowered in a work group, everyone else feels empowered too. Empowerment can be thought of as team energy, moving through a work group, allowing each individual to contribute the best he or she has to offer.

THE PERSONAL POWER GRID: FOCUSING YOUR ENERGY

Our model for increasing power is the Personal Power Grid. The grid contains four quadrants, representing four styles of response to work situations.

THE PERSONAL POWER GRID — PRELIMINARY VERSION

	CAN CONTROL	CANNOT CONTROL
TAKE ACTION	Mastery	Ceaseless Striving
TAKE NO ACTION	Giving Up	Letting Go

Take a moment, and list the three most stressful situations you face at work. They may involve dealing with difficult people, working under pressure of deadlines, or dealing with an uncertain outcome for an important decision. Usually, these kinds of situations take up a lot of your work energy. They occur over and over again and hence are predictable. They are frustrating, because your attempts to manage or resolve them have not been effective.

Look over your list again. This time, shift your attention from the external situation that triggers the pressure to your own response to it. Many times people find themselves responding the same way over and over again, even though they know that it is ineffective. For example, you may not tell a supervisor certain types of bad news, avoiding a possible negative response. You may continue this pattern even though you know it does not work. This is what we call getting stuck in failed solutions. Much of the energy drain you experience at work comes from repeating responses you know are ineffective. The Personal Power Grid will help you to analyze your response to difficult situations and to create more effective responses.

When you face a frustrating or difficult situation, you may jump into action, feeling that then you are doing something about it. Or, you may hold back and just assume that there is nothing you can do. Look at the most difficult situation you face at work, and begin to think about it differently. Make two additional lists. On one list write down the things that you cannot change about the situation. On the other list write the things that you can change in order to resolve or manage that situation. Take a familiar example: facing the traffic while commuting to work. In San Francisco the Bay Bridge forms a huge bottleneck where thousands of people get stuck every day. What can be done in that recurring difficult situation? First, think about things you cannot change. That includes the speed of traffic. Now, some people think they can change this, by changing lanes, honking their horns, and swearing at other cars. They try to will their cars through traffic. These people end up frazzled, angry, and frustrated an hour later at work, because they have put incredible amounts of energy into trying to change the un-changeable.

Now, what can be changed in this situation? One thing is the time you drive. Many companies are receptive to alternate time arrangements, for example, allowing people to come in at 7:00 and maybe leave by 4:00. This is called flex-time, and many companies and even individual work groups have adopted flex-time strategies. Or you can take public transportation, perhaps taking more time for the trip, but being able to read and relax while you travel.

You can also change the internal environment of your car. Increasingly, commuters are getting sheepskin seat covers, stereo equipment, and even car phones. A car on the way to work can be a comfortable learning or relaxing environment. Time can be used for all sorts of pleasant or enriching activities.

The final aspect of driving to work that can be changed is something we can change in every difficult situation. That is the way we think about commuting. We can see the drive to work as time that is stolen or lost from our productive lives. We can see other drivers as enemies keeping us from our goals. Or, we can see the drive as time to relax, to learn, to relish being alone. How we think about the time determines our feelings about it, what we do, and therefore our sense of personal power.

With this in mind, complete the list of things you have no control over, and the list of things you can change. You will be surprised, when you get started, how many things you discover you can change about a difficult situation. Yet, many people burn out at work because they feel stuck in unchangeable situations. They feel the situations are unchangeable because they are looking at the wrong things. They see their glass as half empty, not as half full.

Now, look at the diagram of the Personal Power Grid—Preliminary Version. On the top of the two columns you will see the headings "Can Control" and "Cannot Control." You will want to place the bulk of your energy into situations that you can control, or at least those aspects that are within your control. The two rows of the Grid are labelled "Take Action" and "Take No Action." The rows refer to whether or not you act directly or expend thought or energy on that situation.

Use this Grid to increase your personal power. If you find yourself taking action primarily in aspects of situations that you can control, you will be in the Mastery quadrant. If you focus on things that lie within your control, you will find that your energy makes a difference, and you will have a feeling of success and achievement; this is mastery.

Now, what if you put a lot of time, energy and activity into trying to affect aspects of difficult situations over which you have no control? As you can see in the next quadrant, you begin to experience what we call Ceaseless Striving. The experience of this quadrant is one of continuing frustration, trying but never succeeding, and draining energy into frustration and resentment. This is what cardiologists Meyer Friedman and Ray Rosenman named Type A behavior. It is connected with heart disease and other serious health risks.

Type A behavior is not, as many people mistakenly think, the behavior of people who work hard and hurry a lot. Many people who do that do not endanger their health or lack personal power. Rather, Ceaseless Striving is a problem because a lot of energy is expended in areas that do not bear fruit. It is a situation not of achievement, but of frustration. The person who operates in this quadrant is always frustrated, angry, and resentful because of never getting what he or she wants.

Now, take a look at the possibility described in the next quadrant. In this case, a person decides to Take No Action in situations he or she Can Control. This is Giving Up, seeing oneself as a helpless victim of circumstances. By Giving Up you do not even try; you assume that you could make no difference. If you are wrong, you never find out. Health researchers have found that chronic Give Up-ers are also at risk for health problems.

The final quadrant is Letting Go. A lot of people get Letting Go confused with Giving Up. Letting Go is releasing yourself from the pressure to take action on things that you cannot control. For example, many times people are concerned about the performance of another member of the work team. Some people find themselves doing Ceaseless Striving, as they frustratingly try to make sure the other person does things just right. They are always looking over that person's shoulder and worrying.

Sometimes, they experience a breakthrough; they physically feel themselves Letting Go of needing that much control. They do not say, "Well, I just wash my hands of the whole thing," which is a form of Giving Up. Rather, they feel themselves let go of their worry and concern, and they trust the other person to do as well as he or she can. Parents, spouses, and others in very close relationships sometimes have a lot to learn about letting go.

You develop your personal power when you focus your energy on areas you can control and let go of things beyond your control. To do this, you need to be clear about what you want to accomplish and set your personal priorities. Then, to apply the Personal Power Grid, you need to look at the question of strategy: the way you apply your energy to achieve your goals. Often this energy analysis is disconcerting. You may find you apply much of your energy along ineffective avenues. The energy drain you feel in your work may stem not from what you want to do but from the way you go about doing it.

Taking your most frustrating situation, in which quadrant do you find yourself when you handle it? Or, you might ask which activities or responses lie in which of the quadrants. You might find yourself largely in Mastery, with some activities in Ceaseless Striving. Or, you might spend some time in Ceaseless Striving and then suddenly flip-flop into Giving Up when the frustration mounts. Finally, you might begin to focus your energy into Mastery, while Letting Go of some other expectations or needs in the situation.

Here is another example. You have waited for Saturday, because you have arranged to play golf with three special friends. You wake up at 6:00, look out the window, and it's pouring. You might keep calling the weather bureau and the golf course, frantically trying to make the rain stop or to find a way to golf in the rain: Ceaseless Striving. Or, you could lapse into Giving Up, and vent your anger and frustration, saying "This always happens to me whenever I try to plan anything." You might, after a few minutes of this, move into Letting Go, saying "Well, I can't golf today, so I'll have to make the best of it." You could then move into Mastery, and think about some things you've been wanting to do at home or make alternate plans with your friends, a trip to the theater perhaps. This model can be applied to any difficult and frustrating situation that limits your power at work.

RISKING AND GROWING

There is another wrinkle to the Personal Power Grid. When people divide their options into lists of things they can and cannot control, there remains a vast gray area in between the two categories. It is not clear whether some responses are under control or not, or whether the response will produce the desired outcome. For example, a branch sales manager of a company had a great new marketing idea. He had a gut sense that it would work, although it was somewhat unorthodox. There was no tradition in his company of branch managers innovating in marketing strategy. So his first assessment was that it was a great idea—for another company. His company did not work that way, so there was nothing he could do. He dropped his idea into the Cannot Control category.

But there were other options. He was not really certain that his idea would not be acceptable. It would represent a departure for his company—but no company can move into the future exactly as it has operated in the past. (Indeed, companies that try to remain the same run into trouble.) However, if he presented his idea to the corporate marketing manager, he would be clearly breaking tradition. This would entail *taking a risk*. A risk is doing something of which the outcome is uncertain. His idea seemed like it would work, but it could also fail, or the marketing manager could feel that he was out of line in even suggesting it. Thus, his risk took the form of seeing whether the idea was workable and whether others would try it. He became an advocate of something new. In fact, and to his pleasant surprise, his idea was welcomed, after he did some hard selling to the marketing manager, who played devil's advocate. Soon, the branch sales manager was asked to join the marketing team.

The gray area between what is clearly under your control and what clearly is not under your control is not clearly defined. *You must discover where the line is for yourself.* The Personal Power Grid—Final Version, on p. 166, illustrates this point. That area in which you test the limits of your powers and even push the line a little is what we call the Risk Zone. People who feel alive, challenged, and growing at work inhabit the risk zone fairly often in their jobs. Only through risking can you increase the limits of your

THE PERSONAL POWER GRID — FINAL VERSION

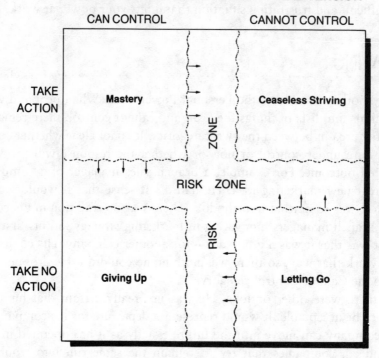

freedom and let your personal contribution shine through to the people who work with you.

Risks are not comfortable for anybody. The fact that something makes you uncomfortable, anxious, or even afraid is not a good enough reason for not doing it. Yet many people operate at work as if doing anything new, controversial, difficult, or unexpected is off limits. "Don't rock the boat," has unfortunately become a basic management principle. But think of what working for years without rocking the boat means: It means you have not found a way to make a difference. Ironically, these same companies are floundering as they find that yesterday's products, marketing, and methods will not continue to work forever. Who will be the source of the new pathways? People who take risks.

Taking risks does not guarantee success. By definition, a risk is something the outcome of which is in doubt. Sure things are not risky. But something that you believe in, or that you feel is worth a try, is worth taking a risk for. There is an old story about IBM's founder, Tom Watson. A young manager had tried out a new idea, very creative, and it had fallen flat. The company lost a lot of money. The young manager was summoned to Watson's office. "Well, Mr. Watson, I guess I'm fired," he said. "Fired?" said Watson. "How could we fire you? We've just spent $5 million educating you." A management climate that respects those who take risks, even when they fail, may be one of the reasons that IBM is consistently the most admired company in America.

Think of your own goals, visions, and dreams—how you might want to make a difference in your job. One way to do that it to think about your company or workplace a few years after you have left. What would you see there that is different because of something that you have done? Now, as you clarify the way you would like to make a difference, think of the risks you will have to take to reach your goals. When you think of risks, remember that some of them will not work out but some of them may be spectacular successes.

Risks do not have to be high-stakes gambles. In personal relationships, in many little ways each day at work, there are places where a risk can make a difference. Think of the areas you feel you cannot control. One of the most common ways people feel powerless is in the behavior of people around them. If somebody does something that is frustrating or annoys you, the risk would be to open up a conversation with that person, taking the initiative and asking what is happening, explaining the effect he or she has on you. Many of the ways people render themselves powerless at work have to do with not taking the personal risks to begin discussions of how things could be different.

Personal power increases as you find new avenues to control by taking risks. Look over your lists of things at work that you can and cannot control. For the Cannot Control list, think about some ways that you can take a risk to determine if the situation is truly beyond your control. People are continually surprised to find that they can control more than they originally believed.

A risk can be a scary thing. Sometimes, you come across something in your organization that you feel is wrong, or ineffective, or leading to trouble. But others do not seem to notice. What happens to managers who take risks by speaking out, who act courageously and go against the grain? The press has sometimes reported on corporate and government whistle blowers whose information was not welcomed and who have been demoted or even fired for their efforts.

Whistle blowers take on their whole organization in public. They do so not because they are reckless, insubordinate or self-destructive. They usually have spent much time trying unsuccessfully to take on an issue within their organization. Then comes a moment, usually agonizing, when they decide something must be done. Ernest Fitzgerald, a Defense Department employee, was disturbed by unnecessary Pentagon cost overruns and finally went to Congress. He was suspended from his job but finally won it back in court. Daniel Ellsberg also worked at the Defense Department and then the Rand Corporation, dealing with papers documenting the history of the Vietnam War. He released them to the press, ending his career. However, Ellsberg has found a new career as a lecturer on peace issues, and he may now have more influence on the peace process from outside government than he could have had from within. Other people have gone to regulatory commissions about unsafe products and corporate negligence. The actual outcome is not the issue, but simply that the people who do these things feel better because they have done the right thing. Often they get other jobs that better fit their values.

Management professor Harvey Hornstein studied smaller-scale courageous acts of scores of executives, with some surprising findings. He found that the majority of courageous risks actually succeeded in getting a fair hearing and creating change. The exception was when the risk involved a negative confrontation, such as trying to get rid of one's boss or attacking the credibility or integrity of other managers. Risks succeed when the risk-taker is an expert in an area, feels that "the facts are on my side," and then develops a strategy to bring the situation to others' attention. Risks can be good business.

Taking a risk is a deeply personal moment of truth. Tony had a deep faith in a new product but was rebuffed several times by management. He felt management was wrong. His risk was not letting it drop. He gathered information and continued talking to colleagues. He asked engineers to bootleg some time to work out specifications, and he worked with marketing people to prepare a case. Finally, he received a new hearing, and his careful work, as well as the support he received from the people he asked to help him, won the day.

Edward, another manager we've worked with, felt that personnel policies of his service company leaned too heavily on getting "the right people," which meant few women or members of minorities. The discrimination was not overt, but it was effective. His response was to keep recruiting minority people and women, justifying their hiring as getting the best person for the job. He ran afoul of his personnel director, who was from the old school. They clashed several times, but Edward held his ground. He was overruled several times. Finally, he decided to leave the company. He did not feel sad or defeated; rather, he felt good about what he had done. Explaining his reasons to other potential employers, who were familiar with the situation, led him quickly to another job with a company with a commitment to affirmative action.

Hornstein found that courageous actions are deeply important to the self-esteem and sense of personal worth of the risker. Managers reported things like, "Self-respect could not be with me if I did otherwise." Another noted, "Behaving that way was self-fulfilling. I felt complete. Once I knew I was right, I went ahead—that's what made me whole, authentic." * After taking a risk, these executives felt a more positive sense of themselves and more competent and worthwhile at work. They felt more connected to their company and to themselves. In a sense, they were acting on their own personal missions and bringing the organization more in line with their inner values. That creates a very powerful tie with one's work.

THE SKILLS OF EMPOWERMENT

Many events in life seem to conspire to tell us that our power is limited. But a setback or misfortune need not signal an ending. Consider an example. Candy Lightner's daughter was killed by one of the thousands of drunk drivers on the road. Out of her personal tragedy, Lightner decided to do something to make a difference to other parents whose children were in danger. She started Mothers Against Drunk Driving, a lobbying organization, with branches now all over the country, that has been responsible for changes in the laws relating to drunk driving, their interpretation, and their enforcement throughout the country. Instead of letting her personal loss become only an occasion for bitterness, or telling herself simply to go on as she had in the past, her loss became the jumping-off point for a new mission. The loss will always hurt her, but she did not allow herself to be paralyzed by it.

There is more to personal power than just having the right attitude.

* Harvey A. Hornstein, *Managerial Courage: Revitalizing Your Company Without Sacrificing Your Job* (New York: John Wiley & Sons, 1986), pp. 35ff.

Specific strategic skills are connected to personal power. Eight skills come into play when a person at work is presented with a challenge. People who are burned out use these skills less frequently than those who maintain their inspiration. The skills are:

- *Clarifying Goals*—having a vision, a set of goals, and a pathway to reach them. Seeing the specific place you want to reach.
- *Setting Priorities*—focusing your time and energy in those areas where they will do the most good. Having the ability to limit distractions and avoid irrelevancies.
- *Being Flexible*—trying several approaches, and not getting stuck in failed solutions. Being able to work smart as well as hard.
- *Taking Responsibility*—not blaming other people or finding fault, but looking to see how to get a job done after a setback.
- *Knowing How Your Company Works*—spending time learning about how things get done in the company, and why they are the way they are.
- *Being Pro-active*—moving directly to confront, resolve, or mediate a troubling or frustrating situation.
- *Working Together*—delegating, sharing, brainstorming, and bringing relevant other people in on a problem or project. Building support.
- *Persevering*—keeping going even if one thing does not work or if things are difficult. Not deciding that the goal was impossible.

These skills will be your allies when you confront a difficulty at work.

Clarifying Goals. People often charge ahead without clearly knowing what they want to accomplish, their specific goals. Or they find themselves working on what they are asked to do, going from task to task without a sense of overall purpose. At any time, you should be able to check in with yourself and ask, "What am I trying to accomplish?" Many times your sense of where you are going can get very murky. The result is never feeling you have gotten anywhere at the end of a day.

There are many ways that the process of clarifying goals can be empowering. For example, in service work, one problem that often leads to burnout is not really knowing what you are trying to accomplish. What end point do you want to reach? How will you know you are helpful? When the client feels good? When a specific service is delivered? Many people find they spend their energy trying to make their supervisor feel good rather than really giving service. So they zig and zag, try to do what the supervisor wants. They never feel sure of what they are accomplishing.

Setting Priorities. The second skill is setting priorities, including time management. Even though everybody has twenty-four hours in each day, some people feel victimized by time, while others feel that their time is a precious resource. You need to organize your time so that you use it doing what is most important and rewarding. There are many courses and programs for time management, as well as a host of organizing tools and books. Structuring your time so that you use it on your work goals is necessary to feeling a sense of personal power. Personal power involves finding ways to make the time you have support your goals and vision.

Being Flexible. The third skill involves flexibility, the ability to experiment with several strategies and focus on the most effective one. As people grow up, they develop thousands of habitual ways of doing things. Habits are valuable. You can think of them, using computer terminology, as software programs that are available to help you move through your usual situations. Because you have habits, you do not have to make things up as you go along. However, a habit is a double-edged sword. Because habits are so easy, you may become overly attached to them. The way you habitually do things becomes the "right way."

The first way you learn to do something is neither necessarily right nor best. If you run into trouble, then you need to be able to shift. How easy to say, and how hard to do. Some people persist in behavior that has not worked for decades.

Persisting in what we label a failed solution is perhaps the primary way that people disempower themselves. People—and organizations—sometimes continue in habitual patterns rather than ask if they really work. People tend to continue to do things the way they are used to, because the process of change is difficult and includes a period of emotional distress.

We find that people need to become comfortable in trying new approaches. When a problem is persistent, stressful, or aggravating, it is time to be flexible. A person we worked with was the senior manager in a small consulting firm. She felt depressed and burned-out because of difficulties between people that she felt powerless to change. She was on the verge of giving up, feeling that the president ought to step in and never did. He actually avoided getting involved, and she felt stymied. Her failed solution was to continue to wait for a person who would not step in and to see herself as incapable of managing the situation.

In talking with her, we discovered that there was an opportunity she was neglecting. There had been talk about a branch office, but, as usual, the boss had not been moving forward on it, even though the office would be furnished without cost by a client organization. She came up with a new strategy, that was empowering to her. Instead of waiting and keeping herself frustrated, she went to the president and asked to negotiate for the branch office herself, and then to be the manager of it. By taking the initiative, she enhanced her personal power. Instead of waiting for something outside of her control, she found something that she could do to further her needs. To her surprise, the boss said it was a great idea, that he really wanted the other office but had not had time to do the work. He appreciated her volunteering; he had not asked her to do it because he felt she was too busy already. So, neither person had been satisfied. She opened the new office in a month, getting herself more working space and taking with her only the two people she worked with directly. She took herself out of the field of conflict.

Taking Responsibility. One of the most common and destructive ways that people at work disempower themselves is by blaming others for difficulties. Sometimes we spend more time searching for a person to blame than we do looking for ways to fix things. When a mistake is made, what is accomplished by blaming someone? When you are the one blamed, the consequences are clear: You feel bad about yourself, angry, defensive, and tend to feel less comfortable and trusting of other people. It rarely spurs you on to greater levels of performance.

Blaming others is a way of keeping yourself helpless. In one organization nobody was willing to do the long-range plan for the division. The division had an interim manager, and each member of the management team said, "It's not my job." But everyone was frustrated by the lack of direction and focus. Finally, one valiant soul decided to take the reins. She called a meeting and announced that she was beginning the planning. While it took up some of her overbooked time, she felt so good about overcoming the frustration that the effort was worth it. She decided the job belonged to everyone. So she took initiative. Her feeling of control and challenge at work skyrocketed.

In a hospital, a system of incident reports was used whenever a mistake was made. The system attempted to assign responsibility for the breakdown.

After a few reports, people just stopped filling them out. Nobody wanted to blame someone else or himself. In fact, most mistakes had several causes. We helped them create an alternate set of assumptions. Instead of assuming an individual was to blame, they decided a mistake was an opportunity to learn about making their system work better. The incident report was changed not to assign individual responsibility but instead to include sections where possible new procedures could be suggested. Everyone shared responsibility for every incident and began to work together to eradicate mistakes. Mistakes were soon cut by two-thirds!

Knowing How Your Company Works. People at work often spend a lot of time in wishful thinking. They think about how their company should be or what they feel would be fair. When things do not meet their expectations, they fall into helplessness. "There's nothing I can do about this." One of the reasons for their helplessness is that they do not know enough about how things are really done in their company. Every company has its formal procedures, policies, and norms. In addition, there is an informal culture, a bunch of influential people at all levels in all divisions, and a lot of informal ways that things really get done.

If you are feeling drained or frustrated with your job, one of the first steps in making changes is to do a full study of how your company really works: Interview people, ask a lot of questions, go to meetings, move around. Like a good detective, you will be surprised at what lies below the surface. You might also find out a lot about why the company does things the way it does, how procedures grew up, and what they mean. Sometimes, you may end up appreciating the company's seeming short-sightedness. Or you may find out how others have made changes, and you may fall upon a strategy for creating change. For example, you may find that your company does not react to informal presentations but is receptive to a carefully researched planning document, with facts and figures, outlining a proposed change. Other companies like you to talk to a lot of people and build informal support before formally proposing something new. They may resent people who seem to be trying to feather their nests with an unsolicited proposal. It is important to know your company before you try to change it or to change your job within it.

Being Pro-active. The burned-out manager just waits for things to get better, for the work climate to improve, or denies difficulties and avoids conflict. The empowered worker sees work as a series of challenges that are often fraught with conflict, differences of opinion, and tasks with no easy solutions. Empowerment means first of all that you deal directly with the problems you face. If there is a conflict with a supervisor, or if a procedure frustrates you, or if your job description needs modification to reflect new realities, you need to face these problems. In the "excellence" books, the slogan "ready, fire, aim" became one of the hallmarks of the excellent manager. The slogan is not intended to suggest shooting from the hip. It means that a person who has personal power is one who begins to resolve an issue when it arises, rather than let it simmer and get worse through avoidance. Taking action can be enlivening even when the first strategy does not work, because the feared result of your risk will usually be less severe than your fantasy. Look at the problem areas in your work life where you might take action, and ask yourself why you avoid them or feel frustrated about making a difference.

Working Together. The biggest sources of stress, and drains on energy and limitations on personal power, come from difficulties and conflicts with supervisors and coworkers. As in a marriage, it always seems to be the other person who makes it tough for us. "If only he would act as I want him to," you may moan to yourself. The key to empowerment is to use energy and creative strategy and to take risks to make your work relationships into working relationships. That does not mean changing other people or making miracles. It does mean that you keep changing and probing and working to improve your relations when there is conflict. If you withdraw and assume you can do nothing, the conflict will not just simmer below the surface. It will become worse and worse.

The most difficult and painful work relationships can improve. There are several ways to work on them. The first is to state your difficulty openly, with clear examples of what bothers you, without blaming the other person. Then, you need to hear out the other person about why he or she acts that way. Then, new expectations or possibilities need to be explored. Often, a third person can be helpful as a mediator or in getting a message across that you are having difficulty communicating clearly. It may take time, and you may have to move in tiny steps, but difficult work relationships do not have to drain your energy and frustrate your attempts to get what you want at work. The next section of this chapter, "Dealing with Work Conflicts," will outline more strategies for changing work and team relationships.

• • •

Persevering. How do you respond to an unexpected setback or obstacle? It is very frustrating to have your hopes dashed, but the empowered person responds by making a midcourse correction, rethinking the strategy, but rarely by giving up the goal. In a world that is continually shifting, people must learn to expect the unexpected. The person who can learn and adapt to obstacles without giving up or assuming that the whole endeavor was wrong from the start will succeed. If you look at the whole stories of people who are successful entrepreneurs or who have innovated within their companies as intrapreneurs, you will usually find they were people who learned from hardship and persevered. When the company president said no to their project, or when the market slumped and cutbacks resulted, they began work on their alternate strategy. They did not give up. They were dogged and uncompromising in their pursuit of their goal, while at the same time being flexible and learning from experience the best means to reach it.

Persevering is like sailing a boat by tacking in the wind. You need to be flexible to respond to new situations but clear about your overall mission and direction. Sport teams must bounce back from devastating defeats, companies must learn from unsuccessful product launches, and litigators and social activists must stick to their goal after frustrating rejections. The 1986 Academy Award for Best Picture went to Oliver Stone, whose movie *Platoon* had been rejected by every major studio and took ten years to make.

Dealing with Work Conflicts

Personal conflicts are the single most draining force at work. Frustration and powerlessness result when you feel that another person is blocking you from doing what you want and you mistakenly assume that it is hopeless to try to change things. First, you must understand that it is nearly impossible to change another person. Are you able to *force* a person to act differently? Probably not. Still, you can change the environment that the other person operates in. For your purposes, the most important part of that person's environment consists of you and your behavior. If you act differently and have different expectations, the other person's response will change as well.

There are many ways that people can be at odds with each other. It is not conflict per se that promotes burnout. In fact, healthy organizations and relationships have a lot of conflict. However, they deal with conflict in two positive ways. First, they are not afraid of it and they do not avoid or hide conflicts. Second, they have a method for working on them, which they practice regularly.

Chronic conflict drains your energy. Others' negative evaluations hurt your self-esteem, and people who are hurt tend to dig in and fight or pull away and withdraw. People have very different ways of doing things, and most people believe there is only one right way: their own. When a supervisor or superior disagrees with you, it can be frightening, as you fight your tendency to fight back.

Most workplaces have a hard time with conflict. Even the new-style organizations often have difficulty with it and want everyone to feel good and to express that feeling overtly. Yet, every day there will be times of conflict. Pressures and challenges can create problems and lead people to blame each other. In addition, conflict produces a rush of adrenaline with the result that the situation that most needs rationality and calmness finds you raging or frightened inside. These feelings are slow to go away; if the conflict is chronic, the feelings wear you down.

Many people handle conflict in one of two self-defeating ways. They may *attack* by blaming someone else for a problem, thus escalating the conflict as each person seeks to protect himself or herself and stops listening to the other. On the other hand, they may *withdraw*, pulling back, even pretending to agree, but being left with boiling feelings that may lead to attempts at subversion, vows to get even, or just self-destructive, gnawing frustration.

Neither of these methods—attack or withdrawal—really works. Why is that? Because each of these responses is primarily aimed at self-protection. People attack so they do not have to listen to the other person and maybe even deal with the criticism. And avoiding or withdrawing leaves all the issues simmering, like underground lava.

With either of these methods the issues that gave rise to the conflict are not addressed, and, even more important, damage is done to the relationship between the two people in conflict. They feel more distant and less understanding of each other, and consequently they have a harder and harder time working together. These submerged or unresolved conflicts are like short-circuits, cutting off the easy exchange and cooperative behavior that keeps organizations flowing and working.

A positive way to deal with conflict is through *confrontation*. Confrontation starts with a different attitude toward the source of the conflict. Sure, the situation may hurt, and your self-esteem may seem to be on the line. But (perhaps after a short or medium time-out to cool down) the empowering response is to stay with the issue. First you need to learn what the other person is really saying. If a colleague begins to disagree with you before you have even finished saying your piece, you immediately know that she is not ready to listen. You should back off until you can create a more open climate.

Confrontation begins not with digging in or standing your ground. It begins with *learning about where the other person is coming from.* About 80 percent of conflicts are easily resolved when two people see that they are dealing with different sources of information or looking at a situation from different perspectives. Instead of arguing, defending, blaming, or withdrawing, all they need to do is clarify what each of them knows.

The next rule of confrontation is to *stick to the issue,* not get off onto the person. Think of the many conflicts where you started talking about a certain work situation and ended up debating a person's intelligence, dedication, or good will. Such debates can never be resolved, because there is no way of measuring inner states to everyone's satisfaction. Try to control your feeling of wanting to hurt the other person, and try to stay on the issue. What needs to be done? How do you and the other person differ?

Confrontation is a method of dealing openly with conflict that preserves the self-esteem of both people involved. Eventually, the merits of the differences can be explored. One person may change position. Or, a person may be left saying, "Well, I don't agree with you, and I don't think it will work, but I have listened to your arguments, and I'm willing to give it a try." Saying that is sometimes risky, but it gives the person who gives in a chance to learn something new or different. And, when issues are explored openly, the energy drain is much less even if the differences are still there.

People drain a lot of their personal energy by not dealing with conflicts. Many people grow up with fears about conflict, or needing to be right and not being able to hear other people. Sometimes it is necessary to bring in a third person as the mediator—perhaps a boss to act as arbitrator.

A company that can deal openly with conflicts and practice a confrontational style is deeply empowering. People feel that they are listened to and that their input is important, even if they do not always get their way. When you feel that the people around you are willing to explore issues, and when you are willing to take the risk to confront differences, a lot of helpful energy is generated.

Confronting conflict in this way is also a learning experience. When you differ with someone, your attitude can be, "What can I learn from this?" not, "How can I win this fight?" Of course, after you listen you may feel that your position still has greater merit. But most often conflicts are not about issues that are clearly right or wrong. There are many ways to do most things, and most conflicts are about two ways to get to the same or similar places.

JOB ENHANCEMENT: PUTTING IT ALL TOGETHER

The particular pressures, aggravations, hassles, and conflicts that you face at work often act as "demotivators," draining your energy and keeping you from getting what you want, and could get, from your work. Now, not all of these can be changed. There are certainly work conditions and situations that are beyond your power. But not as completely as you think. Personal power is not given to you by your job or your organization. It is something that you carve out for yourself, by focusing attention on possibilities and by designing strategies where you can make a difference.

It is time to put all the skills together to create an intervention to increase your sense of personal power by adding something to your job that makes it fit more closely with your own vision and needs. Job enhancement, or job redesign, is taking it upon yourself to change your own job.

Think about the many ways that you might enhance or redesign your work. You might want to change your working conditions or style to fit more closely with your personal needs. You might want to shift some of your duties to someone else or change a reporting relationship. You might feel that you have done something especially well and that you are ready for greater or different responsibilities, or even a promotion. You might face a chronically stressful situation or relationship. You may want to shift jobs or make a lateral move. Or you may think your whole work team might do things differently to be more effective.

There are many times when you might envision a change in your job. You can increase your personal power at work by selecting a specific change and creating an active intervention to make it succeed.

Think about some of the ways that your job does not meet your needs or how you would like it to be different. Let your imagination roam freely for a while, then write down some of the specifics of how you would like your job to look. What would change? Then select a specific goal or change that you would like to make. This will be the focus of your job enhancement exercise.

The first step in redesigning your job is to *assess where you are right now*. The person who is doing well is in the strongest position to ask for a change. So, ask yourself if you are successfully fulfilling the demands of your job and demonstrating your competence. Look at the areas where you need to improve or where you have had difficulty.

The second step is to *document clearly the need for the change*. You may have a hunch that something is needed or that a new arrangement will make things better for you and the company, but you need to check it out. Preparing a careful proposal for your point of view, imagine yourself presenting the information that would sway the most skeptical person at work. What can you say to justify your request or suggestion? How can you make your case? Is there market research or other data that might support your suggestion? Anything you can find might be needed, so build your case carefully.

The third step is to *make your case to the relevant person or people*. It might be your work group, your supervisor, or the president of the company. Make your point clearly, persuasively. Your company might want your proposal in writing or have you make your pitch in a meeting. At your presentation it is important to state the problem or situation, why it might be changed, and then what specific suggestion or suggestions you are making. Be sure to suggest ways that the effects of your proposal could be evaluated.

Next, *listen carefully* and with an open ear to the response. Do not get too frustrated if the first response is defensive, as if people do not really hear or understand what you are asking. Listen clearly to objections, and, if need be, make your suggestion again to clear up misperceptions. Look at reactions as a way to bring potential supporters around to your idea. You might be asked to compromise or to hear a proposed modification to your request that will lead to a key person's support. You may have to modify your original suggestion, and you may even hear ways to do things better than you suggested.

Finally, you will have to *persist and follow up your proposal*. Change often takes more time than you wish, but if you are not persistent and do not follow up you run the risk of being forgotten. At each phase, ask specifically when and how you should follow up. Do not let someone else have the initiative; there is no better way to drain your personal power. Keep going. If one approach does not work and you think you still have not gotten a fair hearing, begin again with another strategy. Remember, the people who have big successes always report that their initial tries met with failure or nonresponse.

When you think of yourself as the major advocate and expert on how you should do your job and begin continually adapting and modifying your job to fit what you see, you will feel more in control of your work process. You will feel less constrained by what cannot be done, and you will continually discover that everyone in a workplace can be a leader and innovator. When it comes to your job, you cannot afford not to be one!

CHAPTER 7

REACHING OUT:
CREATING
CARING
CONNECTIONS

Decide to network
Use every letter you write
Every conversation you have
Every meeting you attend
To express your fundamental
    beliefs and dreams
Affirm to others the vision of the
    world you want
Network through thought
Network through love
Network through the spirit
You are the center of a network
You are the center of the world
You are a free, immensely powerful
    source of life and goodness
Affirm it

Spread it
Radiate it
Think day and night about it
And you will see a miracle happen:
the greatness of your own life.
In a world of big powers, media,
    and monopolies
But of four and a half billion
    individuals
Networking is a new freedom
the new democracy
a new form of happiness.

—ROBERT MULLER, ASST. SECRETARY
GENERAL OF THE UNITED NATIONS,
ENDORSING *NETWORKING*,
BY JESSICA LIPNACK
AND JEFFREY STAMPS

No one goes through life alone. "No man is an island," said John Donne. You live within a web of relationships with family, coworkers, friends, service professionals, and acquaintances who form the fabric from which you gain your strength and resilience. Inspired performance is rarely a solitary event. Even Olympic athletes who perform alone on the playing field have coaches, nutritional advisors, sponsors, family, and cheerers-on behind them who help their star shine. Often, what looks like individual performance is in fact supported by a sense of confidence derived from positive, supportive relationships—connection to the people who are close and important.

THE WORKPLACE AS A COMMUNITY

When people talk about what is valuable and important to them about their work, at the top of most lists is "the people I work with." Your job may not feel that important from time to time, but you continue to feel connected to your coworkers. Because you spend so much time at your job, the workplace becomes more and more like the old neighborhood—a place where people have significant relationships and share their lives with a diversity of others. Some company newsletters look like local newspapers, full of news of achievements, transitions, and community social and business events. The quality of your relationships with people at work is a critical factor, not only in how good your work feels but also in how healthy you remain and how effective you are at your work.

This chapter teaches the skills of connecting to other people and building on the strength of those relationships to reach your work goals. You will learn how to reach out to others—not just when you are in crisis, but in response to any work challenge. Powerful support networks are available to everyone, enabling you to draw upon the freely available resources of other people. Reaching out to others creates a lifeline enabling you to accomplish far more than you could alone.

The development of this book is an example of support systems in action. It was a challenge for us to translate our ideas into a package that could be used outside our workshops. We convened several dinner parties of people we knew who cared about these ideas and were interested in how people created optimal workplaces. They included psychologists, management consultants, writers, and managers. We provided the food and asked them to bring ideas about how people could enhance their connection to work.

When they arrived, there were sheets of paper on the wall with some of our ideas, stories, and possible topics. Everyone shared stories, ideas, techniques, and responses. This book stems from that collective effort. The most exciting part was that people really had a good time and got a lot for themselves. A number of people present adapted some of these ideas for their work. So, it was not just for us but offered something for everybody.

THE STRENGTH IN CONTACT

Your own web of contacts enables you to tackle challenges that might at first seem impossible. Grace was asked to chair the annual company United Way campaign. She had never done anything like that before and felt completely overwhelmed. Her boss suggested she pull together some members of her network to help her out. Many people were helpful, even those she had not expected to be. Her enthusiasm and commitment were contagious. She soon found that when she got bogged down she could go to her group and get a shot in the arm by sharing with others. At each meeting she made a commitment to do something before the next group meeting. She found herself doing more than they ever expected—for her group. And they in response came through and gave her more help than she ever expected.

This is what social support is all about. Problems and difficulties change their shape and strength when they are shared with others. What specifically do other people do that makes such a difference? First, a problem or situation looks different when you tell it to others. It can get you out of going around in circles, getting nowhere. Second, other people reflect back what they see in the situation, which often makes it shift further. Having them ask questions, even the most obvious ones, helps you get a new slant. Also, other people, especially if they are selected well, have relevant information about your problem or things you can do to make a difference. They help you find a new way. Often, what you want offers something to them as well, and you find that you help others when they help you. For example, people who came to Grace's meetings met interesting people and had some good social times together.

Kevin sat and fussed with a program on a computer for several hours. Then, after much aggravation, he called a friend who had the same computer. "Oh," she said, "You need to do this. . . . They don't tell you that, and it gives a lot of people trouble." Bingo—if he had turned to her for help sooner he could have saved hours of frustration.

Why do people wait so long to ask for help? One reason is that many people were taught in school to solve problems on their own. If you asked for help, you were cheating. Early on you got into the habit of working on problems alone. This learning transferred over to work situations where you felt that you had to work alone.

You may have even taken this a step further and felt competitive with others, not wanting them to know you were having trouble. There is a macho tradition of doing it alone, not asking for help, that some people find hard to overcome. Yet, few work problems can be resolved without help. Reflexes learned in school are not a good model for large work challenges. Seeking help and support from others is one of the most effective ways to manage high-stress situations, yet few people really use the help that is available to them.

A support system is a resource pool, which you can draw on selectively to assist you in moving in the direction of your choice. The people closest to you also validate your sense of competence and self-worth. In times of challenge they can pitch in and offer information and other resources. They also offer emotional support and caring. They can help you undertake new challenges and attain your objectives.

HEALTH, BURNOUT, AND SOCIAL SUPPORT

It is easy to spot people who are burning out. The surest sign is when they pull back from others. Instead of letting you in on their struggles or difficulties, all you get is a sarcastic remark, or a brush-off. The message is, "I don't care about myself or you." Of course, inside the opposite is true—these people care, or have cared, too much. Then, they have just given up. The cycle of burnout gets worse and worse, as they cut off from the potential caring, help, and exchange of other people.

How do networks and support systems help overcome burnout and promote inspired performance? Networks form the veins, arteries, and connective tissue for efforts that fire-up work. Burnout is a self-defeating response to pressure, demands, and challenges. Burned-out people pull back, feeling that others will not help and that the problem cannot be solved. They retreat into helplessness and hopelessness. They become stuck and isolated. Burnout continues because there are no open channels to others.

Personal relationships make a difference in how you feel at work, and how effective you are. The quality and quantity of help you receive are the major determining factors in how well you cope with stressful situations. The amount of social support you receive also affects your health. University of California researchers Breslow, Belloc, Syme, and Berkman found that the quality and size of our social networks influence our physical and mental health.

Connection to others even helps you live longer: Married people, especially husbands, live longer than single people. Even people who have a pet have a better chance of survival after a heart attack than non–pet owners. Many people are known to have gotten sick or died soon after suffering the loss of a loved one. They die of a broken heart. Another mental health study found that the more extensive a network of contacts and friendships people have, the greater their emotional health. This finding prompted a recent California Department of Mental Health campaign entitled "Friends can be good medicine."

You might think that the way to help yourself is to go out and get lots of friends and keep them on tap for when you need them. But it is not necessarily the number of friends but the amount of closeness you feel to them that makes the difference. Just one confidant, one person you communicate deeply with, provides a "social inoculation" against stress. Just having a network is not enough, because it does not work unless you use it.

MAJOR SUPPORT SOURCES

Think of all the people you know—not just friends, but also people you have met briefly and know a little bit about, other people who work in your department and in branches of the business far-removed from you, distant relatives, school chums, people who live in you community. Estimate how many there are: probably hundreds. These people are your support net— the people you can call on for help. An insurance broker friend refers to this as using her "thick Rolodex" approach to problem solving. When she is faced with a problem, she calls people in her support net. Your network even includes people you do not know, because each person in your network has another gigantic network, which becomes available to you when you ask. It is often said that you are no more than five people away from finding the answer or resource you need to make a difference in any situation you face.

There are four major kinds of support networks. The first one most people think of is the family. Traditionally, family members lived near one another and functioned as ongoing sources of support generation after generation. With today's more mobile lifestyles many people do not have family close by. To take up the slack, many people develop a familylike network of close friends who fill in. A number of churches, for example, connect young families with older couples to promote intergenerational sharing. They sponsor events people attend in their new family groupings. People are pleasantly surprised that they can have the feeling of family with others who are not actually blood relatives. It is a sense that you belong to others, that they accept you not for what you do but for who you are.

The need for family feeling runs deep. Family feeling provides a deep connectedness and stability that helps people through many transitions. Family support allows you to keep in touch with your personal history through many changes. Your family remembers who you are in times of transition and helps you remember your accomplishments when you have forgotten them.

The second kind of network is made up of friends and community. These are the people you come to know in your everyday life: people you turn to to find a plumber or babysitter and to go to parties with. They help you with information and keep you posted on community affairs. They are part of your everyday activities. You see them at the bus stop or at the market. They are supportive in that they are familiar and helpful. Some of these acquaintanceships are transient, until you move away, while others deepen into friendships and continue over long distance and time.

The third is your work network. These are the people you work with and call on for work-related support, advice, and information. Some of these people could be thought of as mentors, people who take a special interest in your career development and growth. This network often extends beyond your immediate work world, including former professors and prior job contacts.

The last kind of support is your service and professional network, helpers outside your usual pathways, people you contact for a specific reason. They may be counselors, clergy, home repair specialists, physicians, or consultants. You usually have rather formalized relationships with them for a specific problem. They can be paid helpers. One advantage of this network is that you can use whom you need for the time you need, and you can change them if they do not satisfy you. This network becomes more vital as people lead more complex lives. Assistance in one professional form or another allows people to be more responsive to new demands and challenges.

ASSESSING YOUR SUPPORT NET

One of the keys to keeping yourself renewed and vital both at work and home is cultivating thick support networks. Take a moment now to reflect on the quality of your connection to other people. Imagine your networks as a series of rings around you, acting as cushions to lessen the effect of any stress that occurs. In the inner circle are people closest to you, the people you can count on through thick and thin. In the second ring are people who

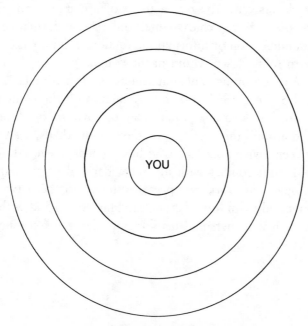

YOU

NETWORK MAP

are emotionally significant to you. The third ring contains people who have been helpful to you. The fourth ring contains distant relationships, people helpful on special occasions, or whom you call on in a professional-client relationship. Take some time and fill out your network map on p. 187. Remember all the people in your life who in one way or another give you encouragement: verbal support, nonverbal looks, or even just knowing that they are on your side. Include family, friends, neighbors, pets, coworkers, and professional resources.

Some people move from one ring to another depending on the kind of support you get from them. This map changes at different times in your life. As you grow, some support grows in importance and other support fades. Some people may be central during a particular challenge and change their importance when the crisis passes. To build on your support map, look now at the interlocking connections between people in your map. Draw lines between people on your map that know each other. The more interconnecting lines you have the thicker your web is, and the more help you will receive when you need it.

Network mapping is also a way to take the pulse of a company. Netmap International, a San Francisco company, assesses companies using this same form of network analysis. The real activity of a company often does not show up in its organization chart, which only shows formal connections, not lateral communication or informal interaction. Netmap asks everybody in a company to write down whom in the company he or she has regular contact with, and how important that contact is. If a contact is confirmed (by being listed by both parties) then it is entered on the company's map. Netmaps are circular diagrams, where connections among different work groups (arrayed around the circle), and among individuals, are shown. The difference between a vice president who has a finger in everything and one who is isolated from contact with all but a handful of assistants will be graphic. A company or work group is healthy when the network map is richly interconnected, with lots of cross-hatching across and within groups. It is the same with your personal network profile: A healthy network has many connections.

MANY FACETS OF SUPPORT

Another way to look at your support map is to think of the different functions different people fill. Think of the one or two most important people whom you turn to in these situations:

For close friendship
To share problems
To play with
For expert advice
To energize you
As teachers
As helpers
As mentors
For acceptance and approval
To help you discover and try new things
For professional contacts and access
When you are hurting
When you need advice with a personal problem
When you want to be with someone who knows you well

You may find that you included the same people several times. Some people provide many kinds of support. However, there is a down-side to relying on one person too heavily. The responsibility of being "everything" can be overwhelming. Some people feel a tremendous burden when they believe they are the only person in a support net. Others become uncomfortable when they put all their eggs in one basket—this person may leave. You may find your net thins as you grow older; you lose people and do not put the effort into rebuilding the broken connections. Sometimes the people you lose are so important that you cannot imagine anyone ever taking their place. Losing people and not taking steps to reweave your net puts you at risk in challenging times.

You may not have anyone available to you in some areas of support. This is fairly common. People often do not think of whom they would turn to until they get stuck. This inventory is a good way to assess how thick your net is before you need it. Use it as a guide for where you need to develop more support.

DIFFERENCES BETWEEN MEN AND WOMEN

When we do this exercise in workshops invariably we notice a difference between the support nets of men and women. Women list more people in more categories. Men tend to list fewer people and to have more categories completely blank. They also tend to list the same person, often a woman, over and over. In discussions about this, men talk about how difficult it is to create friendships, especially with other men, and how they often feel isolated from contact outside their families.

This fits Lillian Rubin's research. Her book *Intimate Strangers* examines differences in the meaning and composition of friendships between men and women. She found some startling answers. When she asked men to name their friends they listed one or two people, often friends from school or military service, relationships developed in early years. When she asked women to name their friends they often produced lengthy lists of both men and women whom they considered friends. Women spend more time developing and participating in friendships. Rubin found men did not have as much experience initiating, sustaining, and cultivating friendships. Men have less experience using what she calls the "language of intimacy," a language of feelings and sharing that creates connectedness from which friendship grows.

Men think they create friendships when they talk about sports or business, but they often find it difficult to talk with those friends in difficult times. We are struck by a pattern we see among executives. When we ask, "Whom do you talk to," almost invariably, they say, "No one." This may be part of the "lone wolf" syndrome, whereby, as they go higher up the ladder, they feel that no one else can understand them. There is also a tendency in various professions to think that anyone outside the profession cannot understand someone in it. Police, doctors, and lawyers often have this belief, which leads them into dangerous isolation.

Some men, because of their inexperience with the language of intimacy, let the women in their lives tend the friendship garden and participate only at harvest time. This has important implications when it comes to nurturing supportive relationships. If for some reason they do not have a person fluent in the language of intimacy around, they feel cut off from their emotional experience. This makes men particularly vulnerable in times of divorce or at the death of their translator.

James Lynch, in *The Broken Heart: The Medical Consequences of Loneliness,* notes that the incidence of premature death from heart disease is significantly higher among the loneliness-prone: the widowed, divorced, and separated, people living alone, and children from broken homes. Drawing from his own work with patients in coronary care and shock trauma units, he demonstrates that even the most simple forms of human contact—such as holding a nurse's hand—have dramatic effects on the body and especially on the heart. He concludes that in a time of family fragmentation, weakening social bonds, and lonely children, physical survival may be threatened. He encourages people to learn to reach out to others as if their health depends on it, because it very well may.

Other researchers have found that if you have even one confidant, a person you can speak to about your deepest feelings, then you have a powerful buffer during difficult times. If you have not been watering your garden of friendship all along, it will not be there when you need it. Support and connection are not instant; they grow from attention and care. If you find your support net a little thin, perhaps it is because you are leaving the job of gardening to someone else.

BALANCED SUPPORT

Another question to ask about your support net is whether it is balanced. Support works both ways—you need to give as well as receive. There are some people who act like pillars of support, always a source of help to others. But they claim they do not need any help for themselves. One person we knew was ignoring her own needs and neglecting herself. Her need was expressed by stress-related illnesses, one after another. Her body said to her, "Hey, I need some support too." Sometimes the most supportive people are doing for others what they most need to do for themselves. If you find yourself being "the rock" for others, ask yourself what you need also. Relationships should not flow all one-way. Two-way exchange—helping and being helped—keeps the "heart" muscles flexed.

Remember that you have to give to receive. Support nets function on the principles of exchange. Help moves back and forth between the members of the net. Everyone pays into the system and receives help when needed. In the most effective nets nobody really keeps score of what goes back and forth. But if serious imbalances occur, they lead to further imbalance and bad feelings all around. When people sense imbalance in their net they often react by having less time to help because others have not been helpful to them. It is important at that point to talk with the key members of your net and find out what the imbalance is and correct it. Not everyone can be on call all the time. Occasionally you can put your friends "on alert," notifying them that you will be especially busy for the next week and will not be as responsive as usual. This provides a cushion so that they will not feel neglected and left out. Maintaining your support net is an important activity, not to be put off for times when you are definitely in need.

SUPPORT GROUPS

In the 1960's when women were consciously changing their roles, a special type of support group emerged to help in the transition process. These were consciousness-raising groups. They included women who were all in similar situations. In meetings, they would share their experiments, feelings, and struggles. A sense of comradeship grew up, and people felt freer to try sometimes very risky experiments. This is one form of self-help group, one of the most powerful means for mobilizing support and for making personal change.

Self-help groups have grown up in response to the need for people to feel supported and empowered. They are voluntary small groups designed for mutual aid, usually formed by peers who come together for mutual assistance in satisfying a common need, overcoming a common handicap or life-disrupting problem, or bringing about a desired social or personal change. Support groups always involve face-to-face interactions, and encourage participants to involve themselves in the support process.

There are over half a million different self-help groups in the U.S. today. Self-help groups exist for victims of every major disease. Other self-help groups focus on personal change and growth for gamblers, alcoholics, schizophrenics, parents of battered children, ex-prisoners, widows, and single parents—all focused around critical issues in the participants' lives.

Support groups are very important in the work world, too. Some chief executives seek them out. It is lonely at the top, and the pressure can be immense. Yet, CEO's often cannot share their burdens with anyone in their company. That is why executive networks have become so important. One of the largest network organizations is The Executive Committee, or TEC, based in San Diego. TEC organizes support groups of from ten to fifteen company presidents of small and medium-sized companies. There are hundreds of TEC groups meeting in different areas. The members have a leader, who might be an experienced businessman or a management consultant. The groups meet for one full day a month and several weekends during the year.

In the mornings, a speaker or presenter at a TEC meeting works informally with members on some business area. Lunch and afternoons are taken up with members' sharing their current challenges, struggles, and achievements. In TEC groups, there is no line between the personal and the business. In one group we worked with, a member was going through a divorce, in conflict with his grown children, and facing serious financial pressures. The members shared information about their own similar struggles. The TEC meetings include deep and personal discussions. For many of the members, few of whom are women, it is their first experience of letting their hair down and talking openly and honestly in a safe atmosphere. Loyalty to these groups is high, and members see their meetings as one of their most important activities.

Dennis runs a support group for heirs of family businesses. These sons and daughters who are inheriting businesses and moving into management face extraordinary pressures to perform, to learn quickly. Like their CEO or entrepreneur parent, they can find few peers within the business, and it may be difficult or awkward to share everything with Dad or Mom. Cynthia convenes a support group for health professionals (dentists, physicians, etc.) with the goal of creating healthy practices. They find that their busy careers have left them little time to develop personal and professional leadership skills. Members see this group as a personal malpractice buffer.

Support groups have become very important in the creation of meaningful work. Numerous self-help groups assist people in developing new career goals, gaining information, and networking with others in their fields. Many universities, colleges, YMCA's, and religious organizations offer career counseling and support groups for career exploration. These are different from the traditional placement services offered by national firms. These self-help organizations look far beyond resume writing and job hunting; people become personally involved in each other's lives. In addition, support groups do not contain professional leaders and hence are usually free.

Working with one of these self-help career planning groups involves three phases. The first includes extensive self-assessment, not only of your skills but of your values and interests. In the new work ethic why you work is often just as important as what you do. These assessments often show people that they have underestimated their abilities or work in areas where they have no interest. The second phase involves exploring and gathering information about career areas beyond your current experience. As new careers and jobs develop, you may not know of their existence. Many new jobs are in fields that did not exist a decade ago.

The final phase involves designing a specific, targeted job search strategy in the new area. This involves using networking in the marketplace to discover "hidden" jobs, constructing effective networks with present contacts, and increasing your visibility in the job search. It also involves learning how to take risks, gain support in the decision making process and be assertive in getting what you want. All through this process you are supported by peers. No one knows the ropes as well as other people involved in this process. Because this job change process takes time, it is vital to have a group to bounce ideas off of and learn from.

This is especially important for people in a midlife crisis. People in their forties become conscious that the hopes, dreams, and aspirations of their youth may not be fulfilled. Some people find they are in careers not suited to them, perhaps because a counselor or family member thought it was a good idea. By midlife many people find themselves burned-out and feeling empty about the future. They often need a careful self-assessment, a period of exploring, information gathering, developing, and following through with a strategy that will lead in a new direction.

Support groups provide a number of important functions. People in your network may be role models, showing you what is possible, what works in certain situations, and alternative approaches that you would not necessarily have thought to try. They are often strong motivators, cheering you on and reminding you of your strengths and talents. Their close contact increases your hardiness and capability. Your group provides specific help in times of crisis and strain, and encouragement and mentoring in times of change. They encourage you to respect your skills and see new ways for you to use them. They connect you with resources and knowledge that can be invaluable in getting through tough situations. Your network also provides a source of challenge, pushing you to take on new responsibilities, make needed changes, and stretch yourself beyond your present limits.

NETWORKING ON THE JOB

In the past, "network" was only a noun, not a verb. How did the term become a verb, a term of action? It happened when people started concentrating on informal means of gathering information and support. "Networking" refers to a process of informal exchange, of creating channels to gather information, build support, and get things done. Networks contrast with formal channels and organizational pathways. For example, a request for budget information from one's department head, sent directly to the financial planning group, is the formal way to gather information. That is not networking. Networking, the active process, would be remembering that you met a person from the planning department a few weeks ago at the company health club. You and he had a nice talk, and you even learned some interesting things about how the planning group actually works. So, you pick up the phone and give him a call. You talk, he remembers you, and he tells you what you need to know. You also agree to meet next week for lunch.

First, you got the information you needed much more easily and quickly, at less cost to everyone, by networking. But something much more important is at work here. You created a bond between people in two different parts of the company, a potential working relationship. This contact will never appear on an organizational chart, yet such connections are the lifeblood of any organization. They move information and they get things done. If there is a job available, if help is needed, when a task force is formed, when a person gets promoted and needs new staff, he or she turns to personal networks, inside and outside the company.

People are often part of professional groups, allowing them to keep in touch with their counterparts in other organizations. This makes it easier to call up someone in another company and ask, "How do you deal with this sort of problem?" and to hear some creative ideas. That is how networks help you get information quickly and get your job done more easily.

Networks are not part of formal organizations, yet they seem necessary to keep any organization moving. While organizations are finite and limited, networks are infinite and unlimited. They extend out in all directions.

Networks are patterns of relationships between people. Increasingly, they are self-created groups of people that share a need or an interest. For example a computer network allows people to share information on-line with other members. Often, people who use these networks will never meet each other face to face, but they become important friends through electronic means. These networks are democratic in that they are not limited to people of a certain background and social status. All that is needed is access to equipment and an interest in communicating with others.

Exchanging information is important no matter what the challenge: writing a proposal, working with a difficult client, or trying to find a way to change things at your workplace. Take a few moments and think about one part of your personal vision or one particular challenge you face at work. Get a clear picture of what you want to accomplish. Now, generate a list of people at work who would have something helpful to say about your idea or who control resources that would help you reach your goal. For each person, plan a presentation where you explain your vision or project, and then solicit that person's help. You might imagine both ends of a conversation with the person. Think of things from his or her perspective—how would he or she react, what does this person need in order to support you.

Do this with each person who might be helpful. Then, continue your list with people outside the organization who might also be helpful. Many people put their spouse or closest friend on the top of the list. Those people can always be counted on for support and, in the best relationships, warnings and honest feedback. Finally, imagine that you have taken the time to speak with each of the people on your list. How do you imagine your vision will change as a result of those contacts? While the essence of what you want to achieve remains, you will probably have made some very important modifications in the pathway to achieving it. You will not be selling out your idea, but rather improving and enhancing it to make it more effective.

To expand your networking capability, you may be able to take advantage of one of the executive networks, or roundtables that are becoming common. For example, the Southern California Technology Executives Network gathers key executives from over 100 new companies. While many of them compete with each other, they find that they have much in common. Similarly, in many towns and cities, networking clubs meet regularly. People meet after work, armed with business cards, circulating among tables of material about business opportunities. Often there is a time when members can stand up and say what they want or what they do. These networks are far more than social clubs. People report finding jobs, meeting new clients, and generally making their work more effective through these gatherings.

THE ART OF BUILDING SUPPORT

As much as anything, work burnout stems from wanting to achieve something important but feeling reality frustrate that grand dream. Yet, when we look at the actual situation of people on the edge of burnout, we often see that their frustration stems from difficulty mobilizing the energy resources of their workplace to support their vision. They need to build support for their dream.

Many dreamers adopt a kind of purity about what they want to accomplish. In their pristine world, they have a vision and everyone acts together to make it happen. Then they look at their actual work world, and they see many people with different ideas of how things should be, as well as a vast majority of people who just do what they are told. People complain that "company politics" prevents them from bringing their visions to reality.

The organization's politics—the intricate web of exchange, negotiations, connections, and tradeoffs that exists within all groups—can stand in the way of realizing your vision. But politics can also become the resource to make it happen.

Chuck House at Hewlett-Packard was working on a new video technology, which he had a strong hunch would lead to an important product. However, very few marketing people agreed with him. He had almost no budget to work with. Slowly, he convinced person after person that the idea would work. Each individual contributed some of his or her group's resources—materials, consulting, space—to the new project. House persisted even though the head of the company personally told him to stop working on it. He felt he was right. But he did not make a secret of his ideas and become embittered at the company. Instead, he began a process that Harvard Business School Professor Rosabeth Kanter calls "tin-cupping," which she found was common in successful corporate innovations. Like a street panhandler, House went from group to group, selling his ideas and asking for a contribution. Then, by the time the innovation was ready to fly, enough people had bought into the project to insure that the whole company could become committed to its success. At Hewlett-Packard, House's innovation was highly successful, and everyone shared in the rewards.

Building support is the guts of innovation and of making a job work for you. When you enter a job, you enter a community. Just as you do with any new community, you need to make yourself known. You cannot expect people to know what you have to offer by reading your resume or by hearing of your sterling reputation. In each new community you enter, you need to let people know who you are. The first thing to do in a new job is get to know people. You need to let people know about you—what excites you, what you would like to contribute, and the kind of person you are generally.

Why do this? First of all, you want to become part of their networks, and to do this they need to know all that you have to offer, not just what it says in your job description, which has nothing to do with you. Second, in order for anything to be possible for you, you need to know who the others are, not just their formal jobs, but what their special roles, skills, and positions are within the company. How does the company *really* work? Then, like House, you will be able to know whom to approach informally when you need information or want support.

Building support is not just a way to make others do what you want. Kanter points out that another aspect of tin-cupping is that in the process of getting others on board for a new idea, the idea becomes much improved. For example, say you are a designer with an idea for a new product. You have a sense that it has a market and that it will work. First, you go to engineers for support. They contribute to your idea, but they also help you see that it needs something more to make it work well, and they give you some other information on costs and practical necessities. By the time they have bought in, you have a better product. Then you go to marketing people. They have reservations, which you counter with your own enthusiasm, and they are won over. But, in the process, you learn about some new concerns, and you make further changes. By the time a project is completed, many people have helped to improve it, and it is really ready for the test of the market.

MENTORS

The most important support people in a company are those who have been there a long time, and have amassed vast amounts of wisdom, large networks, and great credibility. These are the elders of the community. Most people who are successful in organizations find a special person who is one or several levels above them and who becomes their mentor. A mentor is someone with whom you have a special relationship, not a friendship exactly, but more like a teacher/student connection. This person teaches you about the organization, helps you with problems, and sponsors you for special projects or responsibilities or looks for opportunities that fit your special gifts. In return for mentoring, you become a person that your mentor can count on for energy for his or her special projects, to put in extra time getting something done, and for fresh ideas.

Being in a mentoring relationship can be deeply gratifying. People who have risen to the top of large companies speak of their very powerful relationships with mentors. Protégés can count on moving on in their own careers and becoming mentors to a new generation. In politics, for example, many staff assistants for political figures move on, with their sponsor's help, to their own political careers.

When you enter a new job or start a career, even if you have been to technical or professional school, the real learning begins. In one family business, the older brother, Ed, entered the business and was taken under the wing of Bill, his father's key associate. Privately, Bill told Ed that he had a lot to learn and he would spend time with him. He also assured Ed that he would not be talking to Dad about it. Ed grew up under Bill's tutoring, as he moved into greater responsibility. In contrast, his younger brother, Kevin, was not so fortunate. He entered the business and rotated through several jobs, but he never really was able to learn them. He was afraid to admit mistakes, and, when he made them, others covered them up. He finally quit because he felt he just was not able to do what was needed.

Although having a mentor can be helpful, relying on a single relationship can create some difficulties. Putting all your eggs in one basket makes you vulnerable in time of change. It is common to feel very indebted to your mentor and develop this relationship as a strong resource. Sometimes individuals think that they would not be where they are except for the help of that one key person. When this person is removed from the picture they think they cannot function. This kind of a mentoring relationship leaves one person in control and the other feeling powerless. You will feel more in control of your work environment when you create a multiple set of mentors, weaving them into your larger support net.

ACTIVATING YOUR WORK NETWORK

You have been reading about networking in general. Now see how to apply it specifically to making your job work for you. You are about to learn a specific process designed to give you information about your work setting that you may have partially known but never made explicit. Your Informal Work Net (IWN) consists of a group of people who pass information to you that helps you keep on top of your organization's plans, decisions, actions, and benefits. You already have such a network, but you are probably not making the best use of it.

Start by making a formal organization chart of your company. You may want to get one from the Personnel Department, to make sure that you understand it in the way that others in the company do. Do not expect it to be completely up to date if there have been a lot of changes recently. Now that you have the formal diagram, draw the organizational form as you understand it. Who really reports to whom? How do the lines of communication work? You may find many more dotted-line relationships than shown on the formal chart. Who is bypassed in the reporting structure? Who are the people who are "retired on the job"? This helps you discover the "real" organization.

To increase your understanding of your work environment, make a list of four or five key people with whom you interact often. Describe their styles of management, their personalities, their strengths, interests, weaknesses, and pet peeves. The more you know about the people you work with the better you can involve them in your network. Your goal is to have an understanding of the climate which surrounds your work. Because people often see what others do not, it is important to check your perceptions about these key people with members of your IWN.

Your IWN is a net of resources that you can pull when you need help. You want only productive, successful, and emotionally positive people in your net. You may find yourself nominating a few people who are not really supporters. They are there because they "should be" and not because they are good resources. The network is for giving and asking for information and resources. Because your net is broader than your immediate workplace it will allow you to harvest information and resources from a wide area. Staying in touch with friends inside and outside your work setting may be especially helpful in times of change.

This information network functions in an elastic manner, with people giving and taking on both sides. When you are a good source of information then others will be the same for you. Your value in the network increases as you become a "fat Rolodex" of information, inspiration, and support to others in your net.

Often people wait for information to be offered through formal organizational channels. Formal channels are fine when they work, but they rarely do. The kind of information most useful to you, like when an opening occurs or when a merger or acquisition is going to take place, will move too slowly through formal channels. Information is power. Knowing what is happening will give you the most options in times of change. It will help you be poised for needs and opportunities as they arise. People who are connected to an active IWN will be ahead both personally and professionally.

IWNs work outside your company as well. You probably found your last house or aparment through a friend who let you know about a good deal. Keeping your eyes and ears open will connect you to community opportunities. This is especially important to remember when you move. Getting established in a new place is disorienting and often takes a lot of energy in the middle of an already difficult time. Using your work IWN you can often shorten the time it takes you to get established. Use this net to find out where the best Chinese resturant is, who to call for plumbing, and where to find a babysitter. Reconnecting yourself in a new community takes time and energy; let your network help you.

Here are some steps to keep in mind as you build your network:

1. Make a list of people in key positions in your company that you feel comfortable talking with. This means more than just a hello. At first this may be a short list. That is all right; it is a beginning.
2. Now add the names of people you know only a little bit but whom it would be helpful to expand your relationship with.
3. Now list people (and other resources) who are important to you, but whom you do not have a relationship with. This group may be in decision making positions or they could be lateral or subordinate. They are connected to sources of information that will be important to making your job work for you. Include in this listing people outside your company that are important to know. Include people in professional organizations, people with your position in other companies, and even resources like trade publications, newsletters and professional meetings.

To begin to grow your network, start with the people in the first grouping. Check in with them every day, even if only briefly. Keep the focus on business and what you know and are interested in. Use this method to add new members to your network. Pick out several new members at a time and make opportunities to have conversations with them. Talk about the company business and the strengths and interests of the person you are talking to. Once you get started you will find it easy to add people to your IWN. As the momentum increases, you will be sought out for other people's networks.

As you find yourself becoming close to people in your network, resist the temptation to use your IWN to spread rumors or negative information. When you are under stress it is natural to want to turn to members of your IWN for support and a sounding board. This is precisely the time *not* to talk to them. Talk instead to a close friend or counselor not in your work network. We are not suggesting that you keep your troubles to yourself, only that you keep your personal distress outside of your IWN. People may seem interested at first, but if you say negative things about someone else, sooner or later they will begin to wonder if you say similar things about them. This kind of communication will crumble your network faster than anything. There is great benefit in being known as trustworthy, discreet, and constructive.

MAGNIFYING YOUR VISION

Staying connected to work involves not just having a job where you can do what you want or feeling free to pursue your personal vision. Rather, it comes about when you take your vision, what you want to do, and share and build it with the help of other people. Your creation is that much stronger when it benefits from all the special ideas of those around you. Second, you feel better—more a part of things, more cared for, and more energized when you have a bunch of others on your side. While the process of creating support nets can be difficult and complex, it is necessary to effective and inspired achievement at work.

The basic skills and attitudes that build positive connection between people encourage individuals within a company to become inspired performers. Keeping the channels between people open encourages a team to be supportive of each other's work. This feeling produces a high-energy climate where people react in responsible, caring ways toward their work. It is hard to remain disconnected, frustrated or burned-out when you work in a company that respects you and invites you to participate. A caring work environment is like a healthy body—it makes it difficult for serious illness to set in, and when there is an illness it makes a full and quick recovery likely. A healthy organizational body keeps its individual organs—the people who work there—healthy and vibrant.

HUMAN RELATIONSHIPS

The relationships in your network are not really friendships, even though many of the people are your friends. You can have a supportive work relationship with a person you do not know personally. Building support is not the same as having a lot of friends. Some people have a lot of friends who have very little ability to help them get what they want at work. Friendships are not necessarily used to share visions or to create support for a project or achievement.

At the core of networking relationships and work support is a willingness to learn. Both people involved in the sharing will learn and grow from their encounter. The give-and-take of discussion makes each person a teacher as well as a learner. Sharing ideas and reactions is not simply giving a yes or no. The person who is selling an idea must be open to learning new possibilities. Nothing kills support for a vision more than saying, in effect, "Here is my idea, but I don't want to hear yours."

BUILDING SUPPORTIVE TEAMS

There is a new understanding of how people can connect and help each other. In the 1950's people spoke of the organization man, the gray-suited conformist connected to the group by becoming the same as everyone else. Today, the work group is the means by which many people enhance their creativity. Achievements, success, and inspired performance are rarely, if ever, lone actions. The loner is less likely to be a creative genius and more likely to be a burnt-out case.

Burnout at work results when teams feel disconnected. A poor work team is like a machine in which the parts are not lubricated. They press against each other but they do not flow easily together. People do their work and interact, but they do not operate out of a sense of connectedness and unity. The things that help groups work well together have nothing to do with the specific tasks or responsibilities of the team. Rather, they are the styles people use to relate to each other.

When people recall times of inspired performance, when they felt most alive and excited, they report that everyone in their work team felt a sense of personal power. Personal power in the new workplace does not come at the expense of others. In fact, the opposite is true. If the other people on your work team do not feel empowered, then your own sense of personal power will be limited, and you will end up feeling angry and frustrated. When people talk about work situations where burnout was endemic, they always mention their coworkers as frustrating and limiting them. In fact, one of the common symptoms of burnout is negative views of coworkers, clients, or customers. Burned-out managers talk about other people in the most hostile and cynical terms, as if to say, "Those bad people have made me this way."

DEMORALIZING COWORKERS

The major obstacle to achieving your goals and feeling charged-up at work is often other people. You do not feel that you can get others to do what you want. Managers go to seminars on Building Motivation, Negotiating, and Making the Sale. These all involve ways to persuade others. Yet, many companies expect people to frustrate each other. A time management study in one organization found that half managers' time was spent checking up on other employees. People find it very difficult to create an environment where people trust each other.

In an empowered work climate workers feel respected as people. Caring is more than just being helpful or doing favors; it involves a basic respect for the needs and desires of others. This is an attitude, not just a type of behavior. Respect involves communicating with others in a way that enhances their self-esteem. In many organizations, people unthinkingly reduce self-esteem by ridiculing, blaming, belittling—acting as if the other person has nothing to offer. When things are not going well, it is easy to blame someone else. We have all heard people saying, "This group is crazy," or "They don't know what they are doing." Such defensive behavior disclaims responsibility and passes problems off without making things different.

A person can feel let down or angered by someone he or she respects. If the feelings are communicated directly, then the problem is shared. For example, coming up to Joan and saying, "I'm really upset at the way you responded to my proposal. You gave a bunch of general comments, and I'm not sure you even read it. That isn't helpful to me. I really value what you have to say, and I would like the benefit of your analysis." Such a statement might lead to a positive response, whereas just saying to yourself that Joan just does not care about the company or is out to get you would simply create distance and frustration.

Sadly, in the daily interaction of work teams at scores of companies, we see people relating to others in offensive ways. Each negative contact, while intended to get something important done, actually has the opposite effect. It diminishes the interconnection among people and makes it harder for them to work together.

As we report common demoralizing ways that people try to get other people to do things at work, do not imagine yourself using them with other people, even though, if you are like most people, you will have used them frequently. Rather, imagine or remember when someone you worked with acted this way with you. To really understand the negative effect of these techniques, it is important to experience those effects.

Here are the most common ways that teams diminish their support for each other. First, people often demand or request that something be done. Period. Take a moment now and imagine that happening to you. What is your response? The first thing that usually happens is you ask yourself, "Why?" or "What is this for?" You want to understand how the things you are asked to do fit into the whole scheme of things, and sometimes you will want to add something or suggest something else that might work better. There is nothing wrong with simple demands, except that they tend to diminish motivation. People want their work to be meaningful, and for it to be so they need to know how what they are doing fits into the whole. Before you are expected to do something, you want to agree to do it and share your own ideas.

Some managers smirk when they hear consultants make suggestions like this. They think this means there will be a long discussion before asking a secretary to type a letter. Our response is that such exchanges are only infrequently necessary. After a while, a brief explanation is all that is needed, and employees know their input is expected. When exchange is expected in a workplace, the manager has extra confidence that the task will be done as he or she expects.

The second demoralizer is coercion. When people are threatened or verbally abused, they may appear to be motivated. But threats generate intense negative emotional responses and make people pull back from the threatener. They feel that such a person does not care about them. For example, in one organization the senior manager called a lunch when sales figures fell below expectations. Beside each plate was a small coffin. The message was clear: Those who do not perform are dead in the organization. The discussion at lunch was full of generalities, vague proposals, and not much specific exchange. People were intimidated, not inspired. Coercion makes the threatened person distrustful and want to withhold information. In most cases, threats are signals of frustration and powerlessness in the person who makes them. While intended to get things moving, they actually act as turn-offs, short-circuiting the critical support that could create a charged-up team to resolve the difficulty.

A third common method of demotivation is blaming people, trying to assign responsibility for past events. That is different from being held accountable for one's behavior. A company that tries to blame a particular person for any failure soon develops a CYA, cover your anatomy, approach to management. In such a climate, people try not to make decisions, take risks, or exhibit any initiative.

In contrast, in a bank that just had a tremendous write-off of bad loans, which clearly involved a lot of people, the CEO called a meeting. He let everyone know that he was not trying to lay blame. Everyone was involved, or should have been. What he wanted to do was explore how the loans had been made, what procedures were involved, and how mistakes could be prevented in the future. Everyone there felt connected to the failures, but with this announcement, they began a constructive rethinking of basic systems and relationships. Participation in a disaster led the whole bank's management to come together in a more empowering and more effective way. Blame and recrimination would have made this recovery impossible.

TRUST

Trust is more than just a feeling. It is a whole working climate that says people can depend on each other, that they can be open. One image of trust is a series of houses in a community where no doors are locked, the open space between houses does not contain fences, there are many common community spaces, and there is a lot of interaction among people helping each other. A contrasting image is an urban fortress neighborhood, where people avoid each other, and every house has three deadbolt locks. You can imagine how it would feel to live in each community. Similar contrasts exist among organizations.

Several qualities of people generate trust. In a study of hundreds of supervisors, management professor Jim Kouzes asked, "What traits do you look for in a supervisor?" With incredible consistency, respondents used the same four terms: honest, competent, forward-looking, and inspiring. These four qualities define credibility in a leader, a person who can be trusted. At the top of the list is honesty, a feeling that the person has a character that you can depend on. But good intentions and morals are not enough to inspire trust. The trustworthy person must also be able to come through and, in the case of the leader, know where he or she is going and communicate that to others.

Trust is difficult to build up and easy to destroy. For example, after years of building trust between unions and management, including wage concessions in hard times, an auto company voted its executives large bonuses without including the union members. Anger and frustration followed. In contrast, another situation arose when several tainted bottles of Tylenol were found on the market. Knowing that public trust was its deepest asset, Johnson and Johnson immediately took the product off the market and modified its packaging to be tamper-proof. Its quick action at huge cost allowed it to win back its market and maintain its corporate credibility. Any lesser response might have endangered the public's trust in this company. The effort paid off. Two years later, when there was a similar poisoning episode, the company again acted swiftly and surely. The public trusted the response, and sales did not suffer.

In many large and small ways, work groups see the trust level fluctuate. When a leader does something that the rest of the team disagrees with, or which violates basic values or good sense, if there is no outlet for review, trust can plunge and is hard to recover. One company evolved a curious tool —everyone was given a supply of colored tokens. Green ones signify increasing trust, and red ones indicate diminished trust. Supervisors or employees who get a lot of red tokens left at their work station need to look at their recent behavior. Such a system is needed sometimes, because it is precisely when trust is plunging that people have the greatest difficulty in communicating about it.

Jack Gibb, who has designed many organizational interventions to increase trust, defines two types of behavior: communications that increase defensiveness and those that are supportive. Defensiveness is behavior that does not further the organization or help people, but only protects an individual. Defensive behavior includes making global judgments about people's character, trying to control others' behavior, indifference, a sense of superiority, unwillingness to hear new information, and acting distant.

The opposite behaviors are more supportive: giving people specific descriptive information about things that bother you, trying to solve problems rather than control behavior, allowing new information to help create a joint strategy, empathizing with another's feelings and situation, and helping and sharing. Each of the above styles is contagious. If a person is treated in a certain way, he or she tends to mirror it. And, just as bad money drives out the good, distrustful behavior tends to spread, especially if it is modeled by the supervisor or key manager. People tend to copy each other's behavior in organizations, so the example of the leader is especially important.

JOB REDESIGN: YOU CREATE YOUR WORKPLACE

We hope that this book has guided you on a journey resulting in a new, more fluid sense of what it is to have a job. A job is something that exists in your own mind and in your actions and relationships with the others at work. It is based on who you are, on what you want and need, and also on what is or may be possible in your company. We hope the examples, exercises, and questions in each chapter have led you to redesign your own job and your style of working.

The major obstacle to fulfillment, well-being, and excitement at work is not a "bad" company. Rather, your work is what you make of it. You must not take your work for granted or assume you are stuck with it; rather, think of it as an evolving interaction with yourself and others that is probably the most important relationship in your life. In a deep sense, you are your work. If you accept less than what you are capable of, or give up before exploring and becoming active in remaking your job, you are becoming less of yourself.

We do not try to teach you to make do in an unfair world or to trick others into giving you what you want. Rather, our sense of job redesign grows out of a vision of what workplaces can become and out of a sense that every individual can work today to help create the new workplaces. Everyone can be a corporate innovator, a creative activist, who can play an important role in the current shift of values and workstyles.

SELF-ASSESSMENT
WHAT IS YOUR LEVEL OF HEART WORK?

During our workshops, we ask participants to fill out an assessment to find out what amount of Heart Work^{sm} *exists in their jobs. A simplified version of this tool is printed below. It is divided into six areas, corresponding to the chapters in this book.*

As you fill it out, think about your work and how you feel and act at work. Check the choice that is closest to how you think you are in your work. Since this is a self-assessment, answer each question.

If you would like a more in-depth analysis of your response to this assessment, you can send your test to us, with $5.00 for processing and mailing, with your name and address and a short description of your job and company. We will respond with a personalized interpretation of your Heart Work^{sm} *style. Mail them to Jaffe/Scott, 764 Ashbury St., San Francisco, CA 94117.*

(so we can return your questionnaire)

Name: _____

Address: _____

_____ (zip) _____

Part I: How effectively do you utilize the support and help of the people around you?

	VERY MUCH LIKE ME	SOME-WHAT LIKE ME	NOT SURE	SOME-WHAT UN-LIKE ME	NO AT ALL LIKE ME
1. I ask for help from others.	☐	☐	☐	☐	☐
2. I know who to ask when I need something.	☐	☐	☐	☐	☐
3. I have a close person I regularly confide in.	☐	☐	☐	☐	☐
4. I seek out other people to find out what is happening at work.	☐	☐	☐	☐	☐
5. I learn a lot from the people I work with.	☐	☐	☐	☐	☐
6. My ideas change when I talk to others about them.	☐	☐	☐	☐	☐
7. I know informal ways to get things done at work.	☐	☐	☐	☐	☐
8. I trust the other people at work to care for my welfare.	☐	☐	☐	☐	☐

Part II: Do you experience a sense of empowerment in your work?

1. I am able to accomplish what I want to at work.	☐	☐	☐	☐	☐
2. I find myself taking risks when I feel things are important.	☐	☐	☐	☐	☐
3. I know what my priorities are at all times.	☐	☐	☐	☐	☐
4. I let go of things when I get overloaded.	☐	☐	☐	☐	☐
5. I listen to both sides of an issue.	☐	☐	☐	☐	☐
6. I know how to say "no" to people.	☐	☐	☐	☐	☐
7. There is enough time for me to accomplish what I want at work.	☐	☐	☐	☐	☐
8. There is usually a way to solve a problem.	☐	☐	☐	☐	☐

Part III: Do you draw on your inner resources to make your work effective and satisfying?

1. I always think about what can be done in a situation.	☐	☐	☐	☐	☐
2. I feel that I am competent and effective in my work.	☐	☐	☐	☐	☐
3. I encourage myself to try new things.	☐	☐	☐	☐	☐
4. I see the positive side of things.	☐	☐	☐	☐	☐
5. I know what I feel about something.	☐	☐	☐	☐	☐
6. I am able to say what I feel to others.	☐	☐	☐	☐	☐
7. I don't let negative feelings build up until I explode.	☐	☐	☐	☐	☐
8. I listen to my hunches.	☐	☐	☐	☐	☐

Part IV: Are you an effective master of the changes taking place around you?

	VERY MUCH LIKE ME	SOME-WHAT LIKE ME	NOT SURE	SOME-WHAT UN-LIKE ME	NOT AT ALL LIKE ME
1. I enjoy doing new things.	☐	☐	☐	☐	☐
2. When I find myself upset about a change, I can change my feelings.	☐	☐	☐	☐	☐
3. I look for what I can do about something.	☐	☐	☐	☐	☐
4. I'm not likely to blame other people for problems.	☐	☐	☐	☐	☐
5. I feel the future is likely to be better than the past.	☐	☐	☐	☐	☐
6. When I experience a lot of change, I take time off to get my bearings.	☐	☐	☐	☐	☐
7. When something doesn't work, I look for another strategy.	☐	☐	☐	☐	☐
8. There's always a better way to do things, and I try to find it.	☐	☐	☐	☐	☐

Part V: Do you have a clear sense of your personal mission, meaning, purpose, and goals at work?

1. I know what I stand for.	☐	☐	☐	☐	☐
2. I am willing to take a stand for my basic values.	☐	☐	☐	☐	☐
3. My workplace shares the same basic values that I have.	☐	☐	☐	☐	☐
4. I have a vision of where I want to be going.	☐	☐	☐	☐	☐
5. My work feels meaningful and important.	☐	☐	☐	☐	☐
6. I like what my company stands for.	☐	☐	☐	☐	☐
7. I feel that my life is organized around some basic goals.	☐	☐	☐	☐	☐
8. I believe there is some higher order or purpose in the universe.	☐	☐	☐	☐	☐

Part VI: How much does your workplace or company encourage you to use your fullest capacities, stay healthy, and grow?

1. My workplace or company has a clear and consistent set of values.	☐	☐	☐	☐	☐
2. I am included in decisions that affect me at work.	☐	☐	☐	☐	☐
3. I feel that my supervisors and superiors have my best interests at heart.	☐	☐	☐	☐	☐
4. I am expected to help the company improve and do a better job.	☐	☐	☐	☐	☐
5. I am learning new things in my job.	☐	☐	☐	☐	☐

6. My workplace is concerned about my health, and encourages me to pursue healthy behavior.
7. My company regularly changes in response to new information.
8. People's feelings and needs are respected at my workplace.

Please answer the following questions so we may compare you with people in work like yours:

Type of work:
Manufacturing _____ (what kind?) _____

Sales _____ (what kind?) _____

Service _____ (what kind?) _____

Managerial _____ (how many people do you supervise/manage?) _____

Professional _____ (what kind?) _____

Clerical _____ (what kind?) _____

Research _____ (what kind?) _____

Marketing _____ (what kind?) _____

Maintenance _____ (what kind?) _____

Other _____

_____

How many people work in your company? _____

How many years have you been there? _____

Your age _____ Your sex _____

Ackoff, Russell L., *Creating the Corporate Future: Plan or Be Planned For.* New York: John Wiley & Sons, 1981.

Adams, John D., *Transforming Work.* Alexandria, VA: Miles River, 1984.

————, ed., *Transforming Leadership.* Alexandria, VA: Miles River, 1986.

Agor, Weston H., *Intuitive Management: Integrating Left & Right Brain Management Skills.* Englewood Cliffs, NJ: Prentice-Hall, 1984.

Bennis, Warren, and Bert Nanus, *Leaders: The Strategies for Taking Charge.* New York: Harper and Row, 1985.

Blanchard, Kenneth, and Spencer Johnson, *The One Minute Manager.* New York: Morrow, 1982.

Bridges, William, *Transitions: Making Sense of Life's Changes.* Reading, MA: Addison-Wesley, 1980.

Burns, James M., *Leadership.* New York: Harper and Row, 1979.

Cherniss, Cary, *Staff Burnout: Job Stress in the Human Services.* Beverly Hills, CA: Sage, 1980.

Cognos Assoc., *High Tech Layoffs.* Los Altos, CA: Cognos, 1986.

Csikszentmihalyi, Mihaly: *Beyond Boredom and Anxiety: The Experience of Play in Work and Games.* San Francisco: Jossey-Bass, 1975.

Dass, Ram, and Paul Gorman, *How Can I Help?* New York: Knopf, 1985.

Friedman, Meyer, and Diane Ulmer, *Treating Type A Behavior: And Your Heart.* New York: Fawcett Crest, 1984.

Fritz, Robert, *The Path of Least Resistance: Principles for Creating What You Want To Create.* Salem, MA: DMA Press, 1984.

Gardner, John W., *Self-Renewal,* Rev. Ed. New York: Norton, 1981.

Gibb, Jack R., *Trust: A New View of Personal & Organizational Development.* San Diego: Omicron Press, 1978.

Golembiewski, Robert T., et al., *Stress in Organizations: Toward a Phase Model of Burnout.* New York: Praeger, 1986.

Grossman, Richard, *Choosing and Changing.* New York: Dutton, 1978.

Harman, Willis, and Howard Rheingold, *Higher Creativity*. Los Angeles: Jeremy P. Tarcher, 1984.

Hornstein, Harvey A., *Managerial Courage: Revitalizing Your Company Without Sacrificing Your Job*. New York: John Wiley & Sons, 1986.

Illich, Ivan, *Medical Nemesis*. New York: Pantheon, 1976.

Jaffe, Dennis T., *Healing from Within*. New York: Fireside, 1986.

—— and Cynthia D. Scott, *From Burnout to Balance: A Workbook for Peak Performance and Self-Renewal*. New York: McGraw-Hill, 1984.

—— and Cynthia D. Scott, "Training for peak performance." *Vision Action*, December 1984.

—— Cynthia D. Scott, and E. Orioli, "Visionary Leadership." In *Transforming Leadership*, edited by J. Adams. Alexandria, VA: Miles River, 1986.

Kanter, Rosabeth M.: *The Change Masters: Innovation for Productivity in the American Corporation*. New York: Simon and Schuster, 1985.

Kidder, Tracy, *The Soul of a New Machine*. Boston: Little, Brown, 1981.

LaBier, Douglas, *Modern Madness*. Reading, MA: Addison-Wesley, 1986.

Lipnack, Jessica, and Jeffrey Stamps, *The Networking Book: People Connecting with People*. New York: Methuen, 1986.

Lynch, James J., *The Broken Heart: The Medical Consequences of Loneliness*. New York: Basic Books, 1979.

Maddi, Salvatore R., and Suzanne C. Kobasa, *The Hardy Executive: Health Under Stress*. Homewood, IL: Dow Jones-Irwin, 1984.

Maslach, Christina, *Burnout: The Cost of Caring*. Englewood Cliffs, NJ: Prentice-Hall, 1982.

Maslow, Abraham, *Eupsychian Management*. Homewood, IL: Dorsey/Irwin, 1965.

Michael, Donald N., *On Learning to Plan and Planning to Learn: The Social Psychology of Changing Toward Future-Responsive Societal Learning*. San Francisco: Jossey-Bass, 1973.

Mitchell, Arnold, *The Nine American Lifestyles: Who We Are and Where We Are Going*. New York: Macmillan, 1983.

Naisbitt, John, *Megatrends: Ten New Directions for Transforming Our Lives*. New York: Warner Books, 1984.

—— and Patricia Aburdene, *Re-Inventing the Corporation*. New York: Warner Books, 1985.

Neustadt, Richard E.: *Presidential Power: The Politics of Power from FDR to Carter*. New York: Macmillan, 1980.

Ouchi, William, *Theory Z: How American Business Can Meet the Japanese Challenge*. Reading, MA: Addison-Wesley, 1981.

Pascale, Richard T., and Anthony G. Athos, *The Art of Japanese Management: Applications for American Executives*. New York: Warner Books, 1982.

Phillips, Michael, and Salli Raspberry, *Honest Business*. Englewood Cliffs, NJ: Prentice-Hall, 1981.

Rubin, Lillian, *Intimate Strangers*. New York: Harper and Row, 1983.

Scott, Cynthia D., and Dennis T. Jaffe, "How to survive and thrive in times of change." *Vision Action,* Fall 1987.

Toffler, Alvin, *The Third Wave*. New York: Morrow, 1980.

—— *The Adaptive Corporation*. New York: McGraw-Hill, 1984.

Terkel, Studs, *Working*. New York: Avon, 1972.

Welch, Mary Scott: *Networking*. New York: Warner Books, 1981.

Yankelovich, Daniel: *New Rules*. New York: Bantam, 1982.

About the Authors

Dennis T. Jaffe is an organization consultant, psychologist, and keynote speaker. He is a Professor of Organizational Management at Saybrook Institute and past president of the Association for Humanistic Psychology. His column, "New Management," appears in the *San Francisco Business Times*.

Cynthia D. Scott is also an organization consultant, psychologist, and keynote speaker. She is currently conducting research on malpractice and professional impairment prevention at the University of California, San Francisco. She specializes in managing organizational change and health-promotion programs.

For the past ten years, Dr. Scott and Dr. Jaffe have created programs for corporations, business leaders, health-care settings, and professional education that help people develop their personal capacity to contribute to their workplaces.

Books and Materials

Order Form

	Quantity
Heart Work A program for changing your work without changing your job (3 tapes)	☐ $25.00
StressMap: Personal Diary Edition A learning tool assessing stress/ performance level; Scoring Grid, Workbook	☐ $15.00
Managing & Mastering Change A program for surviving and thriving in turbulent times (3 tapes)	☐ $25.00
Coping Skills Package Complete trainers package. Includes masters for workbook (44 pgs.) and step-by-step Facilitators Guide (118 pgs.) and sample StressMap	☐ $250.00
From Burnout to Balance: A Workbook for Peak Performance and Self-Renewal by Jaffe & Scott. McGraw-Hill, 1985. Winner, Medical Self-Care Book Award. Self-management worksheets and exercises for learning to overcome personal burnout	☐ $9.00
Heal Thyself: The Health of Health Professionals by Scott & Hawk. Brunner-Mazel, 1986. An encyclopedia for impairment prevention (306 pgs.)	☐ $35.00
Healing from Within by Dennis T. Jaffe. Simon & Schuster, 1985. Winner, Medical Self-Care Book Award. "How to become your own best health advocate"	☐ $8.00

☐ Please send information
on seminars & keynote
presentations

Postage/handling $1.50 per item $ _____
(Cal. residents add 6% tax) $ _____

TOTAL ENCLOSED $ _____
Make checks payable to **Jaffe/Scott**

Name

Organization/Title

Address

City   State   Zip

Phone (   )   -

Mail to: DENNIS JAFFE & CYNTHIA SCOTT
764 Ashbury St.
San Francisco, CA 94117